JEFFERSON PARISH

Rich Heritage, Promising Future

by Paul F. Stahls Jr.

Commissioned by the Jefferson Chamber of Commerce

Historical Publishing Network
A division of Lammert Incorporated
San Antonio, Texas

To Glenn Hayes, my friend,
to the mighty Galatas
Chargers—especially those
two bad 44s of the 1980s—and
to the "citizen historians"
of Jefferson Parish

PHOTO BY ERIC LINCOLN.

First Edition

Copyright © 2009 Historical Publishing Network

ISBN: 9781893619975

Library of Congress Card Catalog Number: 2009923837

Jefferson Parish: Rich Heritage, Promising Future

author:	Paul F. Stahls Jr.
cover photographer:	Eric Lincoln
contributing writer for "Sharing the Heritage":	Elizabeth Branley

Historical Publishing Network

president:	Ron Lammert
project manager:	Curtis Courtney
administration:	Donna M. Mata
	Melissa Quinn
	Evelyn Hart
book sales:	Dee Steidle
production:	Colin Hart
	Craig Mitchell
	Glenda Tarazon Krouse
	Roy Arellano
	Charles A. Newton, III

Contents

Sculptor Donald De Lue's statue of Thomas Jefferson at the Jefferson Parish Courthouse in Gretna.

PHOTO BY THE AUTHOR.

JEFFERSON: THE PLACE AND ITS PEOPLE

INTRODUCTION

Jefferson Parish begins in the shallow waters of Lake Pontchartrain, wades ashore in Kenner and Metairie and stretches sixty miles south, across the Mississippi River, through a borderland of bayou-laced swampland and then over miles of marsh and coastal bays to two barrier islands for some surf-casting in the Gulf of Mexico. It is Louisiana's largest parish and also, despite that enviable stretch of wetland wilderness, the state's most populous. Any story of the place, therefore, must necessarily describe the works of its people as well as its gifts of nature.

Lake Pontchartrain, for instance, is certainly a work of nature—specifically the handiwork of the Mississippi River—but those remarkable Pontchartrain Causeway bridges, the longest (northbound) and second-longest (southbound) in the world, required the vision and skills of man.

The Mississippi River—not the longest or deepest or widest but unquestionably the dad-gummedest river on earth—is a natural attribute of Jefferson's setting, but the sprawling shipyards beside it and the great-and-now-greater Huey P. Long Bridge above it are the doings of man.

Man did not dig Bayou Barataria, but it was human engineers who conceived and created America's great Gulf Intracoastal Waterway and incorporated the old bayou as one of its vital links.

We did not create the flat delta acres that flank the river as it flows through Jefferson, but it was as a key ingredient of man's urban development that a swathe of it was set aside and transformed into Louisiana's great international airport.

Finally, speaking of the achievements of man, perhaps the single most significant accomplishment of an American president has been Thomas Jefferson's doubling of this nation's size by the acquisition of the Louisiana Purchase Territory, the choicest morsel of which retains the name. It was, in the words of Jefferson's foreign minister Robert Livingston, "the greatest work of our lives," and when Orleans was divided in 1825 and the opportunity thus arose to name a new parish, it was a fitting tribute to the man and an honor to the place that the name bestowed on it was Jefferson Parish.

Great works by learned historians (to be acknowledged in due time for knowledge gleaned from them) have been published about the parish and its cities through the years, but this review of its past and its prospects, a project of the Jefferson Chamber of Commerce, comes at an opportune moment. The "tincture of time" and an incredible dose of individual and community effort have largely healed the wounds of Hurricanes Katrina and Rita, and within these covers can be found our first opportunity to combine the stories of our founding, our original development, our recent and ongoing recuperation, and our vision of the future.

JEFFERSON PARISH

CHAPTER I

IN THE BEGINNING...

The Lord did not get much rest. On the eighth day He began Louisiana.

Geologists say, in fact, that there was a time when the continent's southern coast was the Ouachita Mountain Range of Arkansas, higher than the Rockies, now eroded to the status of major hills. What became of the runoff? Well, it became the eighteenth state on April 30, 1812, along with silt deposits provided by the southernmost stretch of the Mississippi River over the past 5,000 to maybe 7,500 years, part of which became Jefferson Parish on February 11, 1825.

Practically every major topographic feature of the parish can be credited to the beds, basins and natural levees of the river's frequently shifting channels, including one early route to the Gulf of Mexico that began with Bayou Manchac, below Baton Rouge, and gave us Lake Maurepas, Pass Manchac, Lake Pontchartrain, and Lake Borgne.

Another prehistoric "meander" of the river created Metairie Bayou, already practically dry when discovered by eighteenth-century settlers, but its gift to the newcomers was a natural levee formation that became known as Metairie Ridge, complete with a mile-wide deposit of rich alluvial soil and seven feet of bonus elevation for flood protection. Although cross-cut by Bayou St. John in very recent centuries, the Metairie meander had originally flowed through today's Gentilly and New Orleans East, leaving segments that eventually acquired the names of Bayou Gentilly and Bayou Sauvage.

The Westbank's major distributaries and meanders include Bayou Segnette, Bayou des Familles and, of course, Bayou Barataria, which today departs the river below Algiers and winds past Crown Point, Jean Lafitte and the village of Barataria to the marshlands. In fact, the marsh itself is nothing less than the final phase of that old river-delta system's life, the natural deterioration of the system once the Mississippi, satisfied with Jefferson, had drifted east to improve Plaquemines and St. Bernard.

Geoscientists call lower Jefferson the "Barataria hydrological unit" of the Des Allemands-Barataria Basin, which, as the last item on the punchlist of creation, arrived too late to

▲

▲

accommodate the Mississippi Valley's earliest human arrivals during the so-called Paleo-Indian and Archaic periods. The earliest archaeological sites discovered in the parish, around the rim of Lake Pontchartrain and along Bayou des Familles and other major bayous, were occupied by people of the Tchefuncte culture (500 B.C. to 100 A.D.) and Marksville culture (100 B.C. to 500 A.D.), beginning at a time when heavy delta deposits and major distributaries reached practically to the Grand Isle area. By the end of that era, however, the des Familles had lost its status as a major distributary, thus beginning its inevitable phases of subsidence and erosion, and many of the earliest gathering places of humanity were already being overtaken by the northward march of the marsh.

The years of 700 to 1200 A.D. saw the coming of the Coles Creek culture, a regional branch of the larger Mississippian culture, noted for its midden deposits and its great temple and platform mounds, especially along upper Bayou des Familles and at key points along Bayou Barataria. The traditions and craftsmanship of the Coles Creek people helped shape the local Plaquemine culture that appeared about 1200 A.D., and the dominant Mississippian culture also contributed such influences as larger mound groupings and shell-tempered pottery. The Jefferson citizens of that age lived and worked in at least thirty-two surviving sites

that have been discovered, thus far, around the parish.

Chitimacha Indians made their first appearance in the early 1700s, coinciding with the arrival of our first Canadian and European settlers, and one can easily imagine them gleefully elbowing their Choctaw neighbors and other contemporaries and saying, as they saw French scribes scribbling notes about them, "Hey, we're not prehistoric anymore. We're historic!"

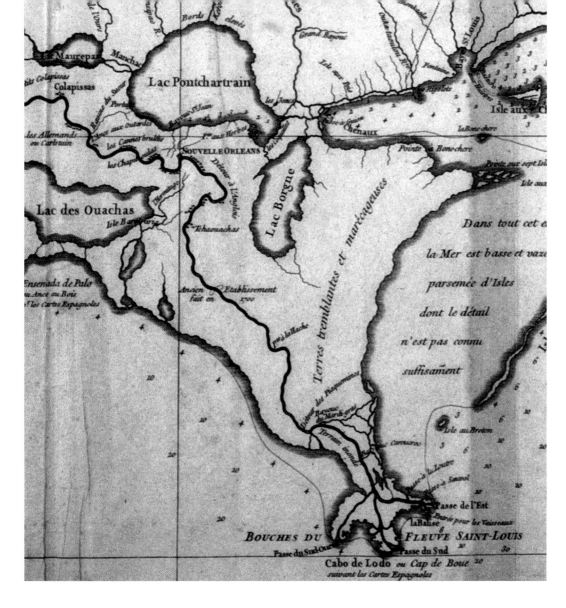

CHAPTER II

EXPLORATION & SETTLEMENT

In 1682, Robert Cavalier, Sieur de LaSalle, with 22 French soldiers, Recollect missionary Father Zenobius Membre and a notaire (official documenter and journalist), departed Canada and canoed down the Illinois River to its junction with a larger stream that would be known and charted for years to come as the St. Louis River. On April 3, far down the big river in the vicinity of a small distributary that decades later would be named Bayou Metairie, the party sighted Indians on the "left bank" and paddled over for a palaver—an event commemorated in that vicinity today by a plaque and wooden sculpture at LaSalle's Landing Park in Kenner's Rivertown district.

When the natives fled in their pirogues, LaSalle sent two soldiers and two Indian scouts to scatter and search for them beyond the reed-covered marsh, but when the scouts drew near the natives' village and were greeted only by flying arrows, the party reported back to LaSalle (in some haste) and the explorers departed. Six days and perhaps 90 miles downriver, LaSalle performed his famous ceremony of possessing and naming Louisiana for King Louis XIV.

On his second expedition two years later, attempting to return to Louisiana by way of the Gulf of Mexico, LaSalle overshot the river passes by many miles and, wandering hopelessly lost in Texas, was killed by his own men near little Navasota where there stands today a handsome bronze statue of the man who named our state.

Those who were listening in their very first history classes will remember, if nothing else, that when Iberville sailed along the Gulf Coast in search of LaSalle's Louisiana in 1699, he succeeded in locating

▲

The Cannes Brulees, Chapitoulas, and "trembling lands" of the marsh appear in this detail from the Carte de la Louisiane by "Royal Geographer" Jean Bourguinon d'Anville, drawn in 1732 and published in France in 1752.

COURTESY OF THE HISTORIC NEW ORLEANS COLLECTION, ACCESSION NO. 1957.261,II.

the natives kept clear, for unclear reasons, by routinely burning off the vegetation.

"Two leagues" downstream, centering on the river's "second crescent," lived a group of hunting and fishing natives who inspired the second name. Because they were too shy or suspicious to meet with the French newcomers, and because they eventually vanished without proper introduction, the journals and correspondence of the explorers simply referred to them by the local Indian word *chapitoulas*, meaning "people who live by the water." With the help of a capital "C" the same word became a placename on maps of that era, indicating that mysterious tribe's old campgrounds and erstwhile hunting territory. With the vagaries of spellings and pronunciations that naturally occur over time, the name survives today, more often than not, as Tchoupitoulas.

Bienville's own Eastbank land grant extended from today's Bienville Street in the French Quarter to the Anse des Chapitoulas ("Riverbend of the Chapitoulas," roughly at Nine Mile Point), with a grant just upriver from Bienville's being made in 1719 to Claude Dubreuil and, above him, large riverfront grants to three Chauvin brothers and a Chauvin nephew named Jacques Bellair.

Just as we now usually refer to the LeMoynes of Canada—Jean-Baptiste LeMoyne, Sieur de Bienville, and his brother Pierre LeMoyne, Sieur d'Iberville—by their "descriptive surnames" of Bienville and Iberville, so were their Canadian friends, the Chauvin brothers of the Chapitoulas, destined to be remembered by their various "descriptive" names. Thus we know Joseph Chauvin de Lery as Delery and Louis Chauvin de Beaulieu as Beaulieu and Nicholas Chauvin de la Freniere as Lafreniere (his son Nicholas the Younger destined to be executed with other leaders of "America's first colonial revolution"—their defiance of the 1768 arrival of Spanish governor Ulloa—after Louisiana's unceremonious cession to Spanish rule in 1762).

By the time Father Charlesvoix, a Jesuit scientist and chronicler, stopped at the Chapitoulas and visited the landowners during his sightseeing tour of 1722, the clearing and cultivation of every property was well under way, producing admirable

and ascending the river. In his company was Father Anastase Douay who, believe it or not, had actually accompanied LaSalle fifteen years before but had survived the mutiny as well as a miraculous overland trek back to Canada.

Iberville and his men celebrated Mardi Gras and named Bayou Mardi Gras (site of the future Fort St. Philip) in Plaquemines Parish on March 3, then ascended the River of St. Louis (which also bore many Indian names, of course, our favorite being Michi Sepe) to explore, map, fortify and settle the place once and for all.

In 1718, at a site where Bayou St. John would provide access to Lake Pontchartrain, and thus a shortcut via the Rigolets to the sea, Iberville's brother Bienville supervised the laying out of a little grid of streets that we now call the French Quarter. Even as the first trees began falling in Nouvelle Orleans, holders of land grants began clearing and cultivating their own properties along the east and west banks of today's Jefferson Parish.

EASTBANK

The first placenames along the Eastbank, dating to the earliest days of the eighteenth century, were Cannes Brulees and Chapitoulas, the first arising because official journal keepers and other river travelers inevitably mentioned passing an area of *cannes brulees* or "burned canes" (essentially where today's upriver parish line meets the Eastbank levee), which

When Indian attacks began occurring along the river in the 1740s, Debreuil built his own fort, complete with cannon, again not only for his own security but for the entire colony's. The main building was a two-story structure, 22 feet in height, surrounded by, as Debreuil himself described it, "a good palisade with bastions" and "a big tower high enough to post a sentry."

Soon after those first riverfront grants came former "counsellor to the King" Pierre Chartier de Baulne, to cultivate a land grant along Metairie Bayou and serve as the "King's Attorney" (essentially an attorney general) of the colony, and the Rev. Monsignor Henry Bezou (historian and author of *Metairie, a Tongue of Land to Pasture*) credits him with being "probably the first colonist whose main buildings were located on or near the Metairie Road we know today."

In 1720 Count Joseph Montespuiou d'Artagnan and former Naval officer Jean Baptiste Martin d'Artaguiette (who had served since 1708 as advisor to the king on the conditions and needs of Louisiana) both received generous grants at Cannes Brulees. In the Harahan area, under the directorship of Pierre Ceard, land-clearing began in 1723 on the Sainte-Reyne concession (land grant), followed by other grants throughout the 1720s for riverfront parcels that lay between the Chapitoulas and Cannes Brulees.

As the Chauvins and other planters began to enjoy enough prosperity to establish share/lease arrangements for the operation of their lands by others, Monsignor Bezou believes the word "metairie" first entered the local vernacular, a word used in France since feudal times (originally "moitoierie" from "moitie," meaning "halves") referring to a land-rental system where the rent is paid with agricultural produce rather than cash. Thus that historian believes it was the Chauvin estates that first became known as "the metairie," with the old Chemin des Chapitoulas eventually becoming known as "the Metairie Road."

WESTBANK

Upon commencing the clearing and construction of New Orleans in 1718, Bienville

quantities of rice, beans, potatoes and indigo, as well as vitally important cypress beams and boards from the Chapitoulas swamps (to be followed in due time by kilns for baking bricks and roof tiles) for building the new colony.

From the beginning the sine qua non of the entire enterprise was the shiploads of slaves arriving at the New Orleans riverfront on a regular basis—labor to clear the land and till the fields, cut the trees and mill the timbers. Thousands were doomed to lives of grueling labor and servitude, while others were soon numbered among the largest landowners of the parish, having earned or inherited their freedom, their lands and, in some cases, slaves of their own.

Dubreuil soon made history by building levees along his riverfront and other strategic points, protecting not only his own lands (where Ochsner Hospital stands today) but diverting the previously routine Mississippi overflows from much of the Eastbank. Dubreuil was, in fact, Louisiana's first levee-builder, and he and the Chauvin brothers also devised the beginnings of the canal-grid drainage system that we know so well today.

secured for himself not only a sprawling Eastbank concession but a 112-arpent-long and three-mile-deep land grant comprising much of the Algiers and upriver frontage of the Westbank. Like most of the huge original concessions, that acreage was eventually parcelled out, by lease or sale, for development by many settlers, with the prime location—directly across from the Vieux Carre—passing through the hands of planters like the Chevalier Jean de Pradel, whose home and lands would eventually be purchased and occupied by the great John McDonogh.

MCDONOGHVILLE/ MECHANIKHAM

John McDonogh was born in Baltimore in 1779 and visited New Orleans as a young businessman in 1800, or perhaps even earlier. Soon he returned to stay and, despite his youth and limited experience, invested so widely and wisely in properties that by 1806 he was able to retire from regular employment to manage his own affairs.

In 1815 he faced the British army as a member of Beale's Rifles, on Andrew Jackson's defensive line at Chalmette, and in 1817, at age thirty-eight, acquired Jean de Pradel's colonial home, called Monplaisir, and de Pradel's portion of the old Bienville concession that soon would be known as McDonoghville. There he occupied himself with attending to the properties and investments that would finance the endless philanthropies for which he is now remembered, and with devising a systematic procedure for freeing his slaves.

DESTREHAN'S DITCH

Drainage ditches were the rule, not the exception, on early West Jefferson estates of any size. The first landowners, in fact, had a common agenda, and their priorities—outranked only by the need for suitable shelter—were to drain their lands and create cashflow by getting at least a few arpents of properties into production quickly. That explains why vast expanses remained in their primordial wooded or watery condition for years, virtually unpopulated, and the scant population explains, in turn, why unbridged

canals could stretch for miles across a man's land grant without being a public nuisance. Only two of the many, however—Harvey's and Westwego's—were of such significance that the birth and prosperity of cities were directly tied to the humble enterprise of ditch-digging.

And so we come to the story of the Harvey Canal and that stretch of Westbank riverfront comprised by Harvey, Gretna and the early village of Mechanikham, which would become, like McDonoghville, part of incorporated Gretna.

The *Dictionary of Louisiana Biography*, virtual bible of the achievements of individual Louisianians, tells us that Jean-Baptiste Destrehan de Beaupre, whose name survives at his son's great eastbank plantation in St. Charles Parish, came to the colony as Treasurer of the Marine in 1722 and (before taking on new duties as comptroller of the colony in 1746) completed the first manifestation of the Harvey Canal in 1739.

By 1825, Jean-Baptiste's grandson Nicholas Noel Destrehan had purchased lands surrounding the canal from his daughter and son-in-law, who had acquired it around 1821, and it was Nicholas who surveyed part of that land to create Mechanikham in 1836, other portions of Gretna shortly thereafter, and was in the process of creating Cosmopolite City along the canal at the time of his death. Jefferson historian and author Betsy Swanson tells us in *Historic Jefferson Parish from Shore to Shore*, however, that these activities of Nicholas marked the first time and place that any Destrehan actually owned Westbank property, and here is where a line is drawn between two factions of history-minded Jeffersonians—a line as stark and stubborn as the ditch itself.

Tradition and lore, dear to the hearts of Faction 1, has it that Jean-Baptiste Destrehan owned the property and hired newly arrived German immigrants to dig a drainage canal in the 1720s and to enlarge it soon thereafter (conceivably the 1739 date mentioned in the dictionary of biographies), paying them with small homesites within a portion of the plantation near the river that would become Mechanikham. Faction 2 points out that Mechanikham was not subdivided till 1836 and that neither ditch nor canal appeared on any Westbank maps before 1845.

Both sides agree that the Harvey family had a hand in the expansions of the canal, and true enough, when Nicholas Destrehan died in 1848, his daughter Louisa and her husband, former sea captain Joseph Hale Harvey, bought the lands and canal from the estate and, shortly before Joseph died in 1882, gave the canal its final "civilian" widening, providing at the same time the long-awaited locks that allowed direct access to the river.

Could it be that both versions contain elements of truth, and that seeming contradictions could be explained away? Where there's smoke there's fire, and where there's lore, no matter how charred and buried in ash, there once was kindling.

Thus inspired, run this up the flagpole—if only as a flag of truce to both factions—and see how it flies:

If Jean-Baptiste Destrehan had dug a drainage ditch and even enlarged it somewhat in the early 1700s, it might have been insignificant enough in size to escape the notice of cartographers and, in terms of timing, would certainly have coincided with an influx of impecunious German immigrants who would happily have traded labor for a homeplace. After all, the genealogy of Mechanikham/Gretna bears overwhelming evidence of German settlement predating official incorporation of any village or town. On the other hand, it is also possible that Jean-Baptiste could have masterminded and/or personally supervised the land drainage for a client or friend, or perhaps have held a minor ownership position that escaped permanent documentation. Then a century later, as we know to be true, the owner is his grandson Nicholas, whose daughter and Harvey son-in-law would bring the long-long story of the Harvey Canal to within one chapter of its happily-ever-after.

Farfetched? Perhaps, but this much is certain: that ditch-turned-canal not only drained a quagmire to create a monumental percentage of today's urban Westbank, but provided a century or so of improved lives as a short, navigable route for the fishermen, oystermen, shrimpers and trappers of the Gulf coast and wetlands to the bank of the big river, where distributors waited with wagons to transport the bounty of Barataria to the markets of Jefferson and Orleans. And the story of that canal was far from over.

UP THE RIVER

Along the river from McDonoghville through the neighboring land grant of the Ursuline nuns (future site of Mechanikham/Gretna) and on to the St. Charles Parish line above Avondale, a sightseer would have found little diversity in scenery through the eighteenth and much of the nineteenth centuries: mile after mile, field after field, of sugar cane, pastures, an occasional cotton crop, a bit of rice and sizable stretches of timberlands. Even after the Civil War most of the large plantations would remained intact until the practice of subdividing land for truck farming came into vogue around 1900.

Agriculture was, however, just a steppingstone to other things, and at the future site of Westwego, just as in Harvey, the story begins with a canal.

The stretch of Westbank riverfront around Nine Mile Point was known from the earliest times as Petit Desert or "Little Wilderness," a swampy and uninhabited morass that richly deserved its name. It was first granted by John Law's Company of the Indies to the French Minister of State, Monseigneur Claude LeBlanc and his associates, who arranged in 1719 for a contingent of troops under French military engineer Captain Ignace Francois Broutin (future engineer-in-chief of the colony and

▲

A portrait of Jean Baptiste Destrehan, believed by many to be father of the Westbank's canal-digging tradition.

destined to design many of its public buildings) to oversee the clearing of a riverfront site and erecting of a trading post. Thus, as recorded in *Lost Plantation, the Rise and Fall of Seven Oaks* by a young historian and descendant of that plantation, Marc R. Matrana, M.D., the Little Wilderness was established as the staging area for shuttling slaves and materials upriver to other concessions and arranging shipment of colonists' crops and other exports.

By the 1760s, LeBlanc's original grant had passed via successions and sales to Claude Joseph Villars Debreuil, Jr., and was a thriving plantation. Its greatest asset, for the moment and for the future, was one of the Westbank's first canals actually meant to connect to navigable waterways, a small but strategic one dug by Debreuil connecting the property via Bayou Segnette to his landholdings in Barataria (the same incentive that had prompted his father, in about 1730, to dig the Gardere Canal that still exists in Harvey, below and roughly parallel to the Harvey Canal).

In 1794 or shortly before, the Little Wilderness estate was purchased by members of the Zeringue family who soon would build the famous Seven Oaks manorhouse, marking the birth of the Westbank's era of lavish antebellum plantations, to include Derbigny, Magnolia Lane, Avondale and the rest.

BAYOUS & BAYS

Like the Canadian "woods runners," the *coureurs-de-bois* who pursued lives of nomadic trapping and trading throughout this wilderness continent in the eighteenth century, the first European inhabitants of Jefferson Parish's seacoast and wetland interior were no doubt self-sustaining loners who quickly learned to live off the fish, fowl and fur-bearing critters that nature provided. Soon enough, however, as land grants brought agriculture to the high grounds and the growth of colonial towns created the necessity for more systematic marketing of fish and seafoods, placenames began appearing at strategic points like the village of Barataria at the mouth of Bayou Barataria and Crown Point a few miles farther up.

Meanwhile, far to the south at the two fragile barrier islands that separate Barataria Bay from the Gulf of Mexico, newcomers were beginning to take an interest in those lonely strips of sand with their little groves of oddly leeward-bending trees. That was two centuries and many hurricanes ago, when Grand Isle and Grand Terre Island were hundreds of acres larger than they are today, and in the 1780s and '90s, Louisiana's Spanish Governors Galvez and Miro issued land grants for agricultural purposes on both—four on Grand Isle, to Francois Rigaud, Francois Aufrey, Joseph Caillet and Charles Dufresne, and one, encompassing the whole of Grand Terre, to Joseph Andoeza.

Grand Terre was purchased almost immediately by Francois Mayronne, who first used it to some extent, it appears, for ranching activities, but soon—in consideration of payments, some form of partnership arrangement or perhaps simply helplessness— he allowed it to become a harbor and haven for pirates. No later than 1809 a young sea captain named Jean Laffite arrived in Louisiana to join his brother Pierre, who had come around 1803, and while Pierre stayed in New Orleans to create a smuggling network within the business community, Jean made his debut in the "society" of Grand Terre and somehow managed to assume a leadership role almost immediately. A stage was definitely being set…but for what?

Jefferson's other Gulf Coast settlement was almost an island but not quite. One word learned quickly when we go exploring our coastal wetlands is "cheniere" (from *chene*, the French word for "oak"), meaning a marshland or swampland ridge rising high enough above water to sustain the growth of oak trees, and one of the best known of these (a fame born of tragedy) is Cheniere Caminada. The little oak ridge whose name honors an early settler, Francisco Caminada, actually begins at the southeastern tip of Lafourche Parish but protrudes as a peninsula into Jefferson Parish waters.

Like its neighboring islands it first became a sugar plantation, but the little peninsula soon boasted, besides its landowners, a village of fishermen and trappers who would quickly establish cultural and economic ties with a far-off settlement on the Mississippi, then known as "Little Wilderness" but known today as Westwego.

CHAPTER III

TOWNS TAKE SHAPE

The agricultural empires that awaited Jefferson's pioneer planters were the gift of our fertile delta soil and that soil was the gift of the Mississippi, but it was also the river that dictated a short life for the era of the great plantations. The "Isle of Orleans" was destined by geography to become a major world seaport and, inevitably, a sprawling metropolis—with bustling population centers lining Jefferson's Eastbank, Westbank and lakefront, and with modern highways and lifestyles extending to the remotest points of our wetlands—but the legacy of adventurers who could abandon the comforts of civilization to brave a wilderness, who could look upon tangled swamplands and envision verdant fields, will always be the "once upon a time" that begins our story.

THE EASTBANK

Kenner

William Kenner was only about twenty-four when he arrived in New Orleans from Virginia at the dawn of the nineteenth century, and he quickly wooed and won Mary Minor, the pretty fourteen-year-old daughter of a family prominent in the military and political history of Natchez. He made his presence known not only as a successful businessman in New Orleans and a wildly successful sugar planter upriver (today's Ascension Parish), but also by serving on the Legislative Council after the Louisiana Purchase and, during the War of 1812, helping to organize and prepare the local militia

▲

Harvey Canal and Locks.
PHOTO BY ERIC LINCOLN.

Gretna City Hall, built in 1907 as Jefferson Parish's fourth courthouse.

PHOTO BY ERIC LINCOLN.

prior to the Battle of New Orleans. When Mary died in 1814 followed by William in 1823, they left seven young children who would grow to maturity and leave a Kenner family legacy that would be remembered for shaping today's Jefferson Parish Eastbank.

William's son, George Kenner, sought his fortune in Texas and young Duncan Kenner took the reins of their father's Ascension plantation (commissioning the famed architect James Gallier, Sr., to build Ashland, a Greek Revival manorhouse that still stands, alternately known as Belle Helene), but brothers Minor and William Butler Kenner set

their sights on acquiring the already historic Cannes Brulees territory in its entirety. Starting with Minor's Belle Grove Plantation (site of today's Rivertown Historic District) and William's Oakland Plantation just upriver, their holdings soon spread upstream to the St. Charles Parish line with the purchase of the Trudeau family plantation, and downriver by the piecemeal acquisition of a huge tract called Pasture Plantation.

William and his twelve-year-old son died in the yellow fever epidemic of 1853, but Minor Kenner carried on. Observing the annual migration of Orleanians fleeing their muddy, open-sewered city during fever season—coinciding with a national boom in the extension of railroad lines—he conceived a plan to create a new, clean, well-drained city in the healthy "country" air, with rail service provided by a line then being built from New Orleans to Jackson, Mississippi, that would connect with Chicago's new Illinois Central. He hired surveyor W. T. Thompson to measure and map his vast Cannes Brulees empire and chart a plan for laying out his model city, and Thompson's survey and street plan, completed and signed on March 2, 1855, could be considered the birth certificate of today's city of Kenner.

Thanks, however, to the railroad, which provided an easy means of distributing food crops to the markets of New Orleans and the region, the first residents of "Kennerville" were not yellow fever refugees but vegetable farmers, mostly Irish immigrants who had fled the potato famine in their homeland, laid the tracks and dug the canals of their new land, and now were anxious to get their hands into Jefferson Parish's almost magical alluvial soil.

Minor died in 1862, leaving his own wife and the widow of his brother William to cope with the conditions of war and Reconstruction. The final blow to the family's Cannes Brulees cane farming was dealt by the viral, leaf-withering plant epidemic called mosaic disease that swept through Louisiana's cane country in too many successive years, so the course was clear for Kennerville: with assists from the railroad for the shipping and several new box and barrel manufacturers for the packing, it was Kenner's destiny to become the small-crop capital—the vegetable center—of all Southeast Louisiana.

By then the Irishmen had been joined by waves of Germans, Italians and freed blacks, and "truck farm" parcels covered the landscape. The Italians and freedmen dominated in edible crop production, and, according to *Kenner, an Historical Sketch* by the late television personality Mel Leavitt (distributed in 1980 by Merchants Trust & Savings Bank), many of the Germans planted fields of flowers and ornamental shrubberies for the florists of New Orleans.

With the coming of refrigerated rail cars came interstate commerce, with the Illinois Central (which had absorbed the old Jackson Line) putting Kenner tomatoes on dining tables in Chicago and east-west lines filling the larders of housewives on the Eastern Seaboard. Kenner would reign through World War II, in fact, as the largest produce center in the South.

Lafayette & Carrollton

Just as the development of East Jefferson was moving downriver from Kenner, it was also, prompted by new transportation links, moving upriver into the parish from New Orleans. Today the entire seven-mile route of a St. Charles Avenue streetcar, from Canal Street up St. Charles and Carrollton Avenues on "America's oldest continuously operating streetcar line," takes place within the incorporated city of New Orleans. In 1835, however, when the line was born and christened the New Orleans & Carrollton Railroad, the downriver border of ten-year-old Jefferson Parish was Felicity Street and fully half of that streetcar ride would have been a tour of Jefferson Parish towns.

The first town up the line was Lafayette, Jefferson's first parish seat, which caused no confusion because Louisiana's city of Lafayette on the Vermilion River was still named Vermilionville in those days. According to *Jefferson Parish Courthouses* by Mary Grace Curry, Ph.D. (member of parish and city historical societies and chair of the parish's Historical Commission), the first Jefferson Courthouse, on Jackson Avenue at Rousseau Street, was built about 1834. Just around the corner at 2229 Rousseau, a jail was built in 1836 that would become, after an 1843 Egyptian Revival facelift by architect James Gallier Sr., the parish's second (and oldest surviving) courthouse.

Next up the streetcar line came Jefferson City and finally the City of Carrollton, and by 1840 Carrollton had a second streetcar line, this one following Levee Street and the new Seventeenth Street Canal to Lake Pontchartrain at East End/ Bucktown. Carrollton became the parish seat when Lafayette was absorbed by New Orleans in 1852, and the great landmark memorializing that era is the third Jefferson Parish Courthouse, a Greek Revival beauty designed by the great Henry Howard in 1854, which still stands at 719 South Carrollton Avenue near the corner of St. Charles.

With each expansion of New Orleans the parish line moved farther up St. Charles, until 1870 when Lowerline Street, marking the "lower line" of the town of Carrollton, became the lower line of Jefferson Parish as well. In 1874 Carrollton itself was annexed, the old courthouse becoming, and to this day remaining, an Orleans Parish public school.

Upriver from New Orleans, the old footpath and carriage trail called the Chemin des Chapitoulas and later Metairie Road (called City Park Avenue on the Orleans side of the Seventeenth Street Canal) became the primary landmark for mapping of real estate divisions and transactions in this quadrant of Jefferson Parish. Just below Metairie Road and west of the canal lies Old Metairie, traversed by historic Upperline Street, where shady avenues pass pre-World War II residences and lead to the old Metairie Country Club.

In tracing the progression of Metairie from swamp to thriving residential community, and the evolution of this interesting placename, the Reverend Monsignor Henry C. Bezou's *Metairie, a Tongue of Land to Pasture* tells us that a land division north of Bayou Metairie and east of today's Papworth Street, called Metairieville, was surveyed in 1837 (briefly there was even a Metairieburgh on the Orleans side of the Seventeenth Street Canal), and that the lands lying west of Papworth were first plotted out in 1839 for towns to be named Bath 1 and Bath 2 (namesakes of that English city on the Avon). The two Baths did not materialize but that district would, soon enough, be crisscrossed by Metairie streets like Shrewsbury, Severn, Causeway and Bonnabel.

Thanks to streetcar lines, the Pontchartrain lakeshore became an entertainment center by the mid-1800s, with the Seventeenth Street Canal serving as boundary between the West End of Orleans and Jefferson's East End, lined with men's clubs, hotels, restaurants and dancing pavilions. That northeast corner of Jefferson is still widely known by its early nickname of Bucktown, bestowed, according to Henry J. Theode's *History of Jefferson Parish and Its People*, in honor of a popular boat-rental proprietor named Oliver "Buck" Wooley, and the last of its original homes was the ancestral home of the Bruning family just across the canal from venerable Bruning Restaurant. It survived long enough to serve as location for a Cajun dance party in the 1987 film *Big Easy* before succumbing to Hurricane Georges in 1998.

Meantime, much of East Jefferson continued for decades to serve as sugar cane fields for such landowners as the Labarre family and Henri Bonnabel, and serious residential development would have to await the digging of reliable drainage canals and a transitional phase that virtually gridded today's Metairie with a landscape of truck farms and modest farmhouses.

As the nineteenth century gave way to the twentieth, the river villages above New Orleans, previously connected to the Crescent City by a single railroad and a few dirt roads, suddenly outgrew their isolation. Jefferson vets came home from the first World War to find streets being paved and the O-K streetcar line (Orleans-Kenner) taking Mom shopping on Canal Street or the entire family to a good melodrama at one of the new silent-screen movie palaces.

Small industries were popping up here and there between the farmyards, and the old plantation lands upriver from Carrollton were becoming fledgling population centers with names like Southport, Jefferson Heights and River Ridge. The word "suburb" (replacing "faubourg") came to town with a group of Canadian investors who developed their "Suburban Acres" on the streetcar line for, presumably, Jeff Parish's first commuters.

McDonoghville & Mechanikham

Although John McDonogh was a young man when he made the move across the river from New Orleans to the former de Pradel manor, he lived out his days in McDonoghville totally preoccupied with amassing enough profits from his many landholdings to finance the missions he had set for himself in life: caring for his slaves and preparing for the great philanthropies that would benefit Louisiana and his homestate of Maryland.

McDonogh allowed his slaves to work for profit one half-day per week, plus extra hours on regular days, to earn the wherewithal for purchasing their freedom, and he provided education and technical training to prepare them for that event. When he died in 1850 many were already free, well established in a colony in Liberia, and his famous will benefitted his current and former slaves as well as endowing public schools in Baltimore and Orleans/Jefferson for the free education of children of every caste and class. Three of the schools were erected in McDonoghville itself, one of which, McDonogh No. 26, remains operational (although in a more modern structure) and, in fact, still performs the simple McDonogh Day flower-laying ceremonies at his tomb each year (on the first Friday in May) as the old philanthropist had humbly requested. The tomb still stands as a memorial in McDonoghville Cemetery, although his remains were moved after a time, as he had directed, to share the burial place of his family in Greenmount Cemetery, Owings Mills, Maryland.

The subdividing of McDonoghville and sale of homeplaces therein, begun in John McDonogh's lifetime, accelerated in the decades following his death. Even when Jefferson Parish was carved out of Orleans in 1825, leaving in Orleans a portion of McDonoghville now called Algiers, the large numbers of German immigrants and railroaders provided a McDonoghville population in Jefferson that was adequate, when merged with the villages of Mechanikham and Gretna, to meet the census

requirements necessary for Gretna (already the parish seat) to qualify for incorporation as a city in 1913.

So large was the railroad faction, in fact, that a section of McDonoghville had come to be known briefly in the 1880s as Gouldsboro, by virtue of "robber baron" Jay Gould's ownership of the local Texas & Pacific Railroad. The volunteer firehouse there still bears the name of Gould Steam Fire Company No. 2 and now, in fact, occupies the site of the original McDonogh No. 26 schoolhouse.

Gretna

Growth of the young cheek-by-jowl communities of Mechanikham and Gretna, with homesites first surveyed and sold in 1836 and 1839, was boosted by the establishment of the St. Mary's Market Steam Ferry Company in 1838 and, in 1853, the New Orleans, Opelousas & Great Western Railroad. The rails, of course, brought not only increased population but also additions to the community's roster of manufacturing concerns and other employers, a roster that had already included a large foundry and other enterprises on one side of the levee and ship-building activities on the other.

Although it was named the parish seat of Jefferson in 1884, Gretna would not be incorporated until 1913, delayed somewhat by a power struggle between Westbank citizens and Jefferson officials over—bottom line—taxing authority. When Governor Luther Hall granted the incorporation on August 20, 1913, it was based on a qualifying headcount that was met by combining four villages to form the new city— old McDonoghville, Mechanikham, Gretna and a separate parcel called New Gretna. The first meetingplace of city government officials was the already historic David Crockett Volunteer Fire Hall on Lafayette Street.

Despite its river frontage and burgeoning business climate, the area retained aspects of a rural community in many ways, not the least of which was the forest that formed its southern border. The writings of early history buff Henry J. Theode tell us, in fact, that the woods began just beyond Fourteenth Street, a convenience for the intrepid members of the Woolomooloo, Sprauer, Ehret and Independent hunting clubs. The young nineteenth century held promise for the development of a full-fledged urban center, however, and any who doubted it needed only notice the horsedrawn streetcars giving way to electric railcars and the early appearance of fireplugs and streetlights.

Harvey

The 1840s saw the old Destrehan/Harvey-family plantation prospering. Besides the sugar cane operation, Nicholas Destrehan was selling lots in Mechanikham/Gretna and the family's canal to Barataria was enjoying a steady stream of toll-payers.

Whether built by Nicholas shortly before his death, or by his son-in-law and daughter, Joseph and Louisa Harvey, is uncertain, but in the late 1840s a family manorhouse that would attain legendary status was built alongside the canal, facing the river. The so-called Harvey's Castle retained the traditional shape of Louisiana

▲

Young John McDonogh, from the cover of author Harnett Kane's biographical novel, Pathway to the Stars.

plantation homes, complete with long upper and lower galleries, but it was thoroughly castellated—its eaves and flanking turrets ringed with battlements—a product of that era's Gothic Revival fad epitomized by architect James Dakin's new State Capitol in Baton Rouge.

Joseph and Louisa occupied their castle through the Civil War years, finally extending the canal the two hundred yards necessary for actual connection to the river in 1881. Harvey died the following year and, when the new locks were condemned for technical reasons, Louisa in 1898 undertook the daunting project of installing new and larger locks. She died in 1903, before completion, but her canal survived to become a link of the Intracoastal Canal. Harvey's Castle, leased for a time to serve as the Jefferson Parish courthouse, stood until it was removed for the 1923 widening of the canal by the Corps of Engineers.

The canal was finally bridged, at the locks, in 1911, whereupon the Parish upgraded Gretna's historic Fourth Street to gravel-road status and extended it upriver to the Barataria Road (today's Barataria Boulevard) in Marrero (known in those days as Ames Plantation or Amesville), where it jogs a bit to the south before continuing upriver to Westwego. Paved by the State in 1932, Fourth Street acquired an alter ego, officially becoming the downriver terminus of Louisiana Highway 18, the beloved River Road that hugs the west bank of the Mississippi all the way to Donaldsonville.

Amesville/Marrero

The old Millaudon Plantation upriver from the Harvey Canal, encompassing much of the land area of today's Marrero, was purchased after the Civil War by A. B. Merrill, a ten-thousand-acre empire stretching from the river to Bayou Barataria. At the hands of Chinese and newly freed black laborers his acres flourished, described in the press as an Eden of lush fields, banana trees and orange orchards.

The Merrill plantation was purchased in 1873 by Oakes Ames, member of a Boston-based family of railroad investors, and it was Daniel Alario, Sr., and William Reeves, in their 1996 history of Westwego, who connected the dots regarding that family's mission on the Westbank: Oakes had come with a fellow agent, Robert Merrill, to scout and buy likely sites for future depots and trainyards. As Oliver and Frank Ames were acquiring and managing lands that lay below the Harvey Canal, other agents of the group were establishing Texas & Pacific railyards above the Company Canal in Westwego and, in between, Oakes was enlarging his Millaudon property from a one-mile to two-mile frontage thus stretching all the way to Westwego.

It was the Ames acquisitions that led to the T&P's dominance of Westbank railroading, and by the 1890s the settlement of Amesville was appearing on maps, near the river in the area north of today's Archbishop Shaw High School.

Before the century was out, a former Confederate colonel named Louis H. Marrero was operating a mercantile establishment in Amesville, according to Henry Theode's *History of Jefferson Parish and Its People*, when he began buying acreage within today's corporate limits of Marrero, subdividing it for truck-farming purposes. The venture was so successful that by 1904 the population required ferry service from Louisiana Avenue on the Eastbank to Barataria Road, by 1914 the Marrero name had replaced Amesville on the map, and by the dawn of the Roaring Twenties the sale of residential and industrial lots was in full swing under the auspices of the Marrero Land and Improvement Corporation.

Colonel Marrero had a knack for attracting industry, and in the political arena he held the all-powerful position of Jefferson Parish sheriff from 1896 to 1920 and such other offices as Police Jury president and state senator, sometimes simultaneously. By the time of the death of the paterfamilias in 1921, his family had become by anyone's definition a real estate and political dynasty, with Louis Jr. serving for a time as Jefferson District Attorney while heading his own four-parish law practice, and his brother Leo heading the Marrero Land and Improvement Company while serving as their father's chief deputy sheriff.

Salaville/Westwego

The role of the original concession called Petit Desert—Little Wilderness—serving as a

trading post and shipping-receiving point for all manner of colonial commodoties, ended when those lands came into the hands of the Zeringue family around 1794, but commerce and transportation would forever be key themes in the development of today's Westwego.

When the Barataria and Lafourche Canal Company was chartered in 1829 by Judge Charles Derbigny, Camille Zeringue, and other planters to create a canal large enough for steamboat traffic to the interior, Zeringue persuaded the group to do so by enlarging the existing canal on his property, dug by Claude Joseph Villars Debreuil, Jr., on his Little Wilderness land grant in the 1760s. According to Dr. Marc Matrana's *Lost Plantation, the Rise and Fall of Seven Oaks*, the company allotted Zeringue forty shares of stock for the old canal (a one-arpent right of way), as well as right of way along a length of Bayou Segnette that wound through the Zeringue property.

And so it was, with his enormous plantation producing bumper crops of cane and the first navigable canal of the steamboat era being dredged across his property, that Camille Zeringue built famous, almost mythic Seven Oaks, with the glowing plaster of its twenty-six soaring columns and broad galleries surrounding, by Dr. Matrana's

description, about eighteen rooms. At the peak of the roof, rising above the tall dormers, was a balustraded lookout point (called "widow's-walks" in seagoing regions) that would later be enclosed as a large, many-windowed cupola where family and guests could observe traffic on the river and activities on the plantation.

After taking a loan from the State in 1850 to finance the construction of locks at Bayou Lafourche and the river, various delays and competition from those newfangled locomotives led to default and the forced sale of the Barataria and Lafourche Canal Company to a group of investors in the Lafourche-Terrebonne region, headed by Robert Ruffin Barrow, a descendant of that large West Feliciana-based family of Louisiana planters. The efforts of Barrow and his partners were countermatched by history, namely the Civil War, and when Robert died in 1875 with his Barataria and Lafourche Canal still unfinished, it remained for Robert Jr. to take up the task and complete the ambitious project that had been the dream of so many for so long.

By 1890 an observer in the cupola of Seven Oaks would have witnessed heavy traffic entering and leaving the Mississippi from the Barataria and Lafourche Canal—the first

Westbank canal with locks to provide direct river access from the wetlands and for paddle-wheelers steaming to and fro with passengers and merchandise bound for Barataria, the lower Lafourche and finally, by 1910, Morgan City.

Meanwhile Camille Zeringue in 1852 had sold a narrow right of way across the plantation to the New Orleans, Opelousas & Great Western Railroad, with the stipulation that no station would be placed on his property, and it was that seemingly wise and innocuous act that began the downfall of his empire. That right of way was purchased after the war by the railroad development consortium headed by the Ames family of Boston, which soon reorganized to create the Texas & Pacific Railroad and attempted to buy a vast swathe of Seven Oaks property for its terminal—which is to say, acres of railyards, dozens of buildings and massive transfer wharves at the river for crossing railcars by barge. Old Camille declined, of course, but with expropriation powers granted by the State of Louisiana, the railroad sued for ownership and won.

Camille died in 1872 and the remaining parcels of the old plantation were mortgaged and sold, one by one, until 1891 when its remains were lost to foreclosure. Camille's widow, Magdeleine Roman Zeringue, died 1892, leaving her beloved Seven Oaks doomed to a long and painful death.

Later that year an elderly developer named Pablo Sala bought the homeplace and fragments of the plantation lands at auction, quickly establishing a nightclub called Columbia Gardens and Pleasure Resort at Seven Oaks while subdividing the downriver side of the old Company Canal for a small residential and commercial development called Salaville. The lots sold slowly—mostly as homesites for business owners in the area's tiny cluster of taverns and stores, and with two lots purchased by former Zeringue slaves for their new True Vine Baptist Church—but the old canal and the ruthless hand of fate would soon deliver Salaville something of a population explosion.

For years the Company Canal/Bayou Segnette connection to the village of Cheniere Caminada, at the farthest southern extremity of Jefferson Parish, had created a bond between the two communities as the shrimpers and oystermen routinely traveled the little waterway to market their catch at the riverfront. When Caminada was obliterated by the infamous hurricane of 1893, with perhaps half its 1,300 residents killed and virtually all of its 1,200 structures swept away, Salaville became home for many of the survivors, with their faithful canal serving as their escape route and, for generations to come, their commute to continue working their traditional fishing and trapping areas.

With its railyard acreage above the Company Canal handed over by courtesy of the court decree and the subsequent collapse of a once-proud plantation empire, the Texas & Pacific was suddenly in a position to center the commerce of half a nation on this bend of the river, and then to provide a name for the place when, according to who's telling the tale, its engineers or its conductors or its passengers or its railcar-ferry captains would give the jolly cry of "West we go" at every departure.

To that riverbank came barges of grains from the upper Mississippi to fill the T&P's elevators and steamships from around the world to fill and empty its giant merchandise warehouses. Its own rails stretched across Louisiana to fetch cotton from Red River Valley plantations like Lake End and Caspiana and, from hill-country rail-stops like Pleasant Hill and Provencal, to haul pulpwood to the paper mills of Louisiana and crossties for building its ever-expanding network of rails that reached as far west as El Paso.

From a local standpoint, however, more important than a mogul's dream of interstate railroading empires, the steel rails and wheezing engines meant, for the first time since the fall of the plantation South, that the Westbank stood unified by a common destiny: a solid civic and economic future that would reach through every West Jefferson city up to and including the little Avondale Plantation village of Waggaman, whose future significance was as yet unimagined.

TOWARD THE GULF

The gigantic antebellum plantation called Millaudon that once covered today's Marrero, purchased in about 1873 by Oakes Ames, by 1900 had grown from an estimated 10,000 to 13,000 acres with its southernmost acreage, known as Estelle Plantation, still owned and operated by Oakes, Oliver and Frank Ames. Encircled on its west side by a great bend of Bayou des Familles, the Estelle name survives to this day, borne by the community that lies between the Barataria Boulevard route to Lafitte National Park and the Lafitte Parkway route to the town of Jean Lafitte on Bayou Barataria.

Despite its long history as gateway to the commercial fishing, fur-trapping, Spanish-moss picking (to be cured for stuffing upholstery), shrimping and oyster dredging occupations of the wetlands, Bayou Barataria was also the point where Jefferson's swampland and marshland heritage overlapped with its plantation tradition. Historian Betsy Swanson has written, in fact, that at least fourteen plantations existed even as late as 1880 in the region of Estelle, Crown Point, the village of Barataria and town of Jean Lafitte. The Mavis Grove home in Jean Lafitte, much altered through the years and now unoccupied, still stands in sight of the town's famous Berthoud/Fleming Cemetery, nestled in a bend of Bayou Barataria atop its prehistoric Indian midden mound.

And so it is that Crown Point at the confluence of Bayou des Familles and Bayou Barataria, and the communities of Barataria and Jean Lafitte along Bayou Barataria (with its outlets to Lake Salvador), have been not only important fishing villages in their own right since the 1700s but doubly important as our link between the separate worlds of upper and lower Jefferson, with that legendary bayou serving not only as the physical border but as an unmistakable symbol of the change that occurs there.

Bayou Barataria, for three centuries the waterway of pioneers, pirates and pleasure-boaters—deep, broad and robust enough to carry the shipping of the Intracoastal Waterway from the Mississippi River to the town of Jean Lafitte—parts company with the Intracoastal in sight of the old Berthoud/Fleming Cemetery, then flows on southward through the town and thereupon, its mission complete, disappears into the marsh.

GRAND ISLE

Below Bayou Barataria, beyond nearly forty miles of marshland, lakes and Barataria Bay, the Gulf of Mexico laps at the shores of Grand Isle, where many leisure-time fishing families keep high-stilted, funny-named camphouses and where other weekenders come to divide their time between fishing and enjoying the beach at Grand Isle State Park.

The original Spanish grants continued as thriving sugar plantations, with but few changes in ownership, until the Civil War, but from the early 1800s the farming operations had begun edging over a bit to make room for the tourist trade. It began with miscellaneous plantation buildings being suited up as guest

▲

Shrimp boats in port at the town of Jean Lafitte.

PHOTO BY ERIC LINCOLN.

houses, but soon there were small hotels and rows of new guest cottages to accommodate vacationers (like the characters of the famous Kate Chopin novel, *The Awakening*), who arrived daily on the little steamers that plied the Westbank canals. By the 1870s the cane farms were gone, giving way to small-plot vegetable farms and homesites for men who worked the waters.

Hurricanes, tornadoes and time have virtually cleared the island of historic landmarks, one of the last lost and most missed being the home of Jean Laffite's faithful Louis Chighizola—nicknamed Nez Coupé or "No-Nose" in reference to his none-too-subtle battle scar. The cottage stood, albeit in failing health, well into the twentieth century, a favorite subject of visiting photographers and an endless source of history and lore to be shared by Nez Coupé's direct descendant— famous storyteller and souvenir shop proprietor, the late Nat Chighizola.

Grand Isle has also been an embarcadero for offshore fishing charters since the 1940s, when a young flier named Charles Sebastian came home from World War II and, from the air, picked the little barrier island as the obvious place to start a charter service. The island's protected bay-side waters are also home base for Coast Guard patrols and, ever since Humble struck offshore oil in 1947, for rig personnel and rig-service fleets.

GRAND TERRE

The deed to Grand Isle's neighboring island, forever famous as Jean Laffite's stronghold and his gateway to Barataria, was actually held throughout those rowdy years by absentee- owner Francois Mayronne, who had purchased Grand Terre from its original land-grant holder, Joseph Andoeza. Mayronne sold it soon after the departure of Laffite and his pirate/ privateers (saved by their role at the Battle of New Orleans but quickly fallen from grace), and by 1821 the new owner, Jean-Baptiste Moussier, had established a sugar plantation there that prospered until his death in 1831. Thereafter the island was parcelled into smaller plantations, with a commercial shrimp cannery established on one site in 1867, Louisiana's first. The U.S. Army acquired the strategic western point for the construction of Fort Livingston, and the last active sugar cane planter on Grand Terre was, according to historian Betsy Swanson, the famed New Orleans fencing instructor and duellist, Jose "Pepe" Llulla, who had retired to the quiet life of a planter and died there in 1888.

Fort Livingston was decommissioned in 1872 and, after the State of Louisiana acquired the island in 1923, the Wildlife and Fisheries Department established an experimental and monitoring facitity there which is still in operation.

▲

The Coast Guard Station on Grand Isle in the 1930s.

Coast Guard Station, Grand Isle, La.

CHAPTER IV

JEFFERSON AT WAR

In the Year of Our Lord 1814 and of our Independence the 38th, Louisiana, eighteenth state of the Union, was two years old. It was not a good year. The very existence of the United States, in the midst of the War of 1812, hung in the balance, and if the British won this one, there would be no "best two out of three."

Probably the most famous—certainly the most infamous—citizen of the lands and waters that now form Jefferson Parish was the "Boss" of Barataria, apparently named for Don Quixote's fictional island of Barataria (meaning, depending on the translator, a deceptive place, an inexpensive place, or possibly even skullduggery at sea). Louisiana's Barataria is a world of twisting bayous and vast marshlands that give way to large lakes and finally the immense Barataria Bay, which is set apart from the Gulf of Mexico primarily by two barrier islands, Grand Isle and Grand Terre.

Jefferson's World War I memorial on Huey P. Long Avenue in Gretna.

PHOTO BY ERIC LINCOLN.

The pirate/privateer/corsair/"buccaneer" Jean Laffite built his home, wharves and warehouses—virtually a fortress—at the western end of Grand Terre, facing the eastern tip of Grand Isle from across Barataria Pass, and from locals he learned a zigzag route that led from the bay all the way up to Bayou Rigolets and Bayou Barataria, from which a choice of routes led to different points on the Westbank: Bayou Segnette toward today's Westwego, Bayou des Familles into the area of today's Marrero or—nearest of all to the riverside and the city—an old plantation channel known as the Gardere Canal, parts of which can still be found just east of the Harvey Canal.

That maze of waterways made a convenient smuggling route for Laffite, but if ever discovered by an enemy of Louisiana, it would become a dangerous backdoor approach to New Orleans and the river—a threat taken so seriously that it would be guarded by artillery placements in two wars and later by one of America's key coastal forts.

If only poor Jean and his brother Pierre (who conducted their dealings in New Orleans) could have visited one of our tourist welcome centers and found a map showing L-a-f-i-t-t-e National Park and the town of Jean L-a-f-i-t-t-e, they would have realized immediately that they and their L-a-f-f-i-t-e ancestors in France had been misspelling their own name for generations. Embarassing!

More important to them than their name on maps, however, was their name on "letters of marque"—documents issued by warring governments which essentially licensed the capture and plunder of their enemy's ships.

The Caribbean and Gulf of Mexico were ringed with ports like Campeche, Havana, San Domingue, Guadaloupe and Cartagena where letters of marque could be had for the asking, and Spanish ships were the targets of choice during the years of Laffite's "privateering" activities. Suddenly the capture and looting of Spanish vessels was a legitimate (and profitable) act of war, meaning that with proper flags and credentials, the former pirates could now enjoy safe access to American ports and, if apprehended at sea, would not be hanged.

That left only two problems in the brothers' quest for the perfect loot-smuggling operation: greed, which tempted some of the captains of the loose Grand Terre alliance to ignore the nationality of their prey, and the tiresome necessity of evading U.S. Customs. Customs officers in New Orleans, who inspired the enthusiasm of plain-clothes agents by paying them on a generous percentage basis, were eager to impose import duties on the plunder and confiscate any illegal cargo, which usually meant human contraband—slaves—whose importation had been banned as of January 1, 1808. Thus began a longlasting game of cat and mouse, with the Laffites establishing agents of their own to handle smuggling operations in and around ports like Pensacola, Bayou Lafourche,

Berwick Bay and Lake Charles. The lion's share of their "prizes," however, followed that tricky pole-and-paddle route through Barataria, with an ancient Indian midden-mound/cheniere about halfway up, at the eastern end of Lake Salvador, becoming their most famous site for wholesaling to dealers or auctioning ill-gotten goods to private citizens. Called the Temple (or sometimes "Little Temple," in deference to the "Grand Temple" mound near the western shore of the lake), Laffite's mound was a sizable patch of clamshell-covered earth abruptly rising fifty feet above water, offering fairly easy access to Laffite's customers and also, because of its naturally protected position in the fork of Bayou Rigolets and Bayou Perot, a dandy defensive spot for guarding those bayous against interlopers should the need ever arise.

It did.

Toward the end of the War of 1812, after their famous "Star Spangled Banner" attack on Fort McHenry and burning of the U.S. Capitol, British warships began massing in the Gulf of Mexico intent on wresting control of the Mississippi River valley. Realizing the value of securing an alliance with the Baratarians, who held that "back door" key for at least one potential prong of the attack, a British contingent visited Jean Laffite on September 3, 1814, to make an offer: a tempting sum of bribe money, a captain's commission in the Royal Navy and positions of appropriate rank for his officers and men, all in exchange for his assistance with the coming invasion.

It happens that the British visit to Grand Terre coincided with a crescendo of animosity in New Orleans against the Laffite brothers, by merchants who resented the competition from the smuggled goods, by ship captains and investors who were filling court dockets with lawsuits over lost ships and cargoes, and by civil and military officials over what amounted to a non-American navy controlling that vulnerable segment of the Gulf Coast. An attack on Grand Terre by the U.S. Navy, in fact, had been planned for some time. All in all, then, when Jean Laffite hurriedly reported the British offer to his contacts in New Orleans and requested a meeting with Governor William C. C. Claiborne to offer his services, it comes as no surprise that Claiborne distrusted his intentions and did not exert his influence to dissuade the Navy. Commodore Daniel Patterson led the assault on September 16, burning warehouses and confiscating or burning 27 ships as upwards of 400 of Laffite's captains, seamen, and "guests" escaped into the Baratarian interior in an almost comical armada of skedaddling pirogues.

House of Nez Coupe, Jean Lafitte's Lieutenant, Grand Isle, La.

▲

A 1930s postcard view of the old Grand Isle home of Baratarian Louis "Nez Coupé" Chighizola.

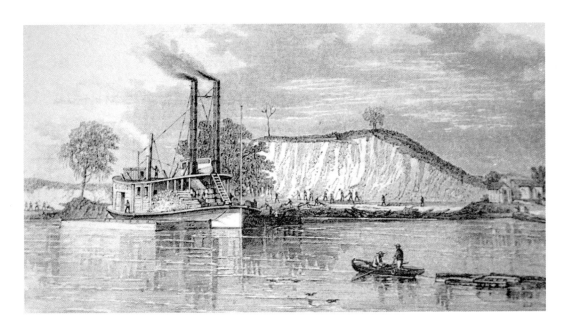

Finally confident that the British invasion would begin in Louisiana rather than Mobile, as he had first suspected, Gen. Andrew Jackson arrived in New Orleans on December 1 and established headquarters on Royal Street. It was there, and on personal reconnoiters along the river and lakefront, that he studied the playing field for the contest to come, and it was there that he made his very politick selections of Louisianians who would aid him in leadership roles—a roster of locals representing (and therefore sealing the cooperation of) every special-interest faction of local society, commerce and government.

As for the meetingplace of the general and Jean Laffite, we all love our historic buildings and sacred legends, but alas, neither the famous claim of the Old Absinthe House nor of Lafitte's Blacksmith Shop—both on infamous Bourbon Street where most anything is possible—is possible. The (alleged) former blacksmith shop now houses a not-old-enough but righteous-old piano bar, so a claim that Laffite met Jimmy Driftwood there to discuss that folksongster's lyrics for Johnny Horton's future hit, "Battle of New Orleans," would be no more farfetched than the notion of Gen. Jackson meeting the "Buccaneer" in a smithy to plan the defense of America.

It is not even true, despite those famous Fredric March and Yul Brynner movies, that Jean Laffite was on the line at Chalmette with Pierre, Dominique Youx, "Nez Coupé" Chighizola, Beluche, Gambi and the other privateers-turned-patriots from Barataria. The truth is that Jean served in today's Jefferson Parish.

Somewhere along the line Old Hickory had become aware of the indispensible role the Baratarians could play in the battle to come, and it was at his Royal Street headquarters on December 22 that he met with Jean and Pierre Laffite, assigning Pierre to a unit that ultimately faced the main enemy assault. At the general's request, however, Jean would assist with placement of defenses at various points along the Westbank river road and then lead Major Michael Reynolds with three fieldpieces and fifty regulars to fortify the Temple, to prevent that long-feared end run by the Redcoats.

With orders and safe-conduct papers in hand (since until that moment he had been a wanted man), Jean left immediately to complete those Westbank and Temple Mound preparations, although when it became clear on December 23 that the British had chosen the river approach for their attack, the Temple's guns and troops were withdrawn and reassigned to the makeshift defenses he had helped establish along the river.

After the smoke cleared at the Chalmette and Westbank battlesites on January 8, 1815, the Laffite brothers enjoyed a brief period of citizenship and hero worship before they dropped out of sight. Jean departed for Galveston, later for parts unknown, and thus, in the oft-quoted words of *The Corsair* by Lord Byron, "left a corsair's name for other times, marked by a single virtue and a thousand crimes."

Jackson's experience in coastal Louisiana inspired a plan that he would later, as President, set in motion: construction of a chain of masonry forts at key points around the Atlantic and Gulf coasts to thwart future naval attacks by foreign powers. Within five years those stolid and handsome forts began appearing in Louisiana, beginning with Forts Pike and Macomb at the Rigolets and Chef Menteur passes into Lake Pontchartrain, followed by Forts St. Philip and Jackson, facing each other from the east and west banks of the river in Plaquemines Parish, and Fort Proctor, guarding Lake Borgne from Shell Beach in St. Bernard.

Jefferson Parish's souvenir of that era is wonderful old Fort Livingston, which has guarded Barataria Bay since 1841. Named for Edward Livingston, President Jackson's secretary of state, it stands at the most strategic spot on Grand Terre, the very site instinctively chosen for the stronghold of Jean Laffite.

WAR BETWEEN THE STATES

In January 1861, three months before Gen. P.G.T. Beauregard ordered the artillery barrage on Fort Sumter that would begin the "Recent Unpleasantness," Fort Livingston was seized by the Louisiana Militia. The Confederate Army soon relieved the militiamen and held the fort with 15 pieces of artillery and a force of 300 until the fall of New Orleans in 1862, and, though reoccupied by Union troops for the duration, it saw no further action.

Although abandoned by the Army in 1892, Fort Livingston still guards its bay, a lonely sentinel battered by storms and baked by the sun. Despite its midden-mound foundation and brawny mortar (a mix that incorporated shells and even pottery shards from the Indian midden), the venerable landmark is slowly sinking and portions of the walls have separated and fallen.

With binoculars, visitors to Grand Isle State Park can see the still substantial ruins from the park's observation tower, and some take the short boatride to Grand Terre, now site of a Wildlife & Fisheries experimental station, to walk the old ramparts and discover

▲

The ruins of old Fort Livingston on Grand Terre, sketched in 1933 by artist George Izevolsky.

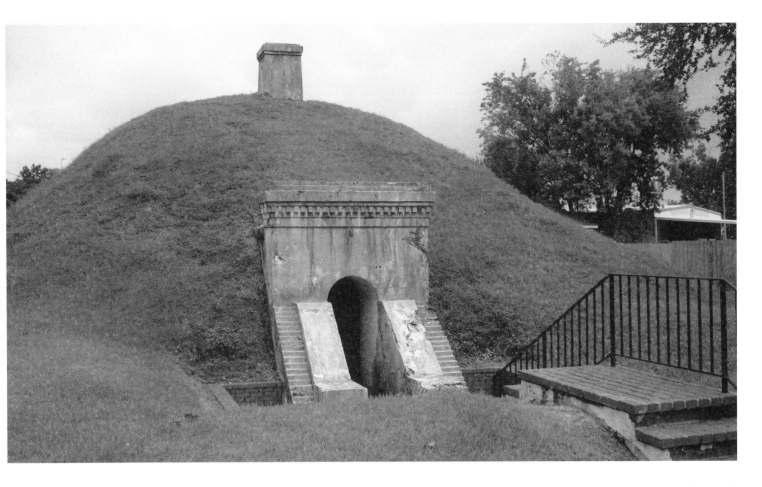

such architectural details as the interior brickwork of the corridors. The granite blocks shipped around from New England quarries to serve as treads for stairways, and as lintels for the many doorways that open from the corridors into the fort's interior compound, are almost all still in place.

Before Admiral David Farragut's Union fleet had blasted past Forts St. Philip and Jackson below New Orleans, in the five-day artillery battle that allowed the capture of the city in April 1862, the theory had been that invasion of the region would come from inland: gunboats approaching from upriver and troops delivered by rail or riverboat. With Jefferson Parish thus considered the first line of defense, the Jefferson Police Jury appropriated funds to mount artillery at the Temple as Laffite had done in 1814 (although the small fort they planned for the historic mound was never completed and perhaps never begun), and artillery outposts were positioned at Pass Manchac and North Pass to protect the rail line that circled into Jefferson, as it does today, from around the Maurepas side of Lake Pontchartrain.

In October 1861 Major General David Twigg, who served briefly as Confederate commander of the region, ordered two sets of fortifications to be constructed on both sides of the river above New Orleans. The first pair consisted of an apparently unnamed redoubt on the west side near Nine Mile Point, later named for U.S. General Nathaniel Banks after the Union occupation, and an east-side defense built on Roman's Plantation and so nicknamed Camp Roman. Its official Confederate designation was Fort Morgan, in honor of a popular Confederate raider from Kentucky, General John Morgan, and its sole remaining landmark—one surviving powder magazine of its original three—is still known and loved by its Yankee name, Camp Parapet.

A Union vessel headed downstream would have been met in Jefferson Parish by a withering crossfire from the artillery of those two installations, and, somehow surviving that greeting, it would have been rewarded with another crossfire from the second brace of riverfront batteries, positioned at Carrollton and Westwego.

Beneath its overcovering of earth—just downriver from the terminus of Causeway Boulevard and two blocks back from the river at the deadend of little Arlington Street— Camp Parapet's old brick powder magazine still crouches low and tough. Maintained by Jefferson Parish Parks & Recreation, the magazine is occasionally open for a day by the Jefferson Parish Historical Commission to allow Jeffersonians and visiting history buffs to mount the little manmade hill and enter the structure. Partway up the mound a low brick retaining wall surrounds a small terrace, from which a classic dentil-ornamented portal and a narrow arching tunnel of plastered brick lead to the final iron-barred gateway that opens into the austere storage chamber—hard to see from the river; if seen, hard to hit; if hit, hard to rattle.

As a defense against infantry attack and protection for the entry points of local rail lines, long earthen breastworks were shovelled up on both sides of the river. The Eastbank line stretched from Camp Parapet's river position all the way to the lakeside swamp, protected by a small moat in front and gun emplacements here and there along the way. From the artillery position at Westwego, the Westbank's mile-long breastwork stretched along the Company Canal (which later would mark the upriver boundary of the future town of Salaville) from river to swamp.

According to a tally by author Codman Parkerson's for his *New Orleans, America's Most Fortified City* (1990, a masterful survey of the region's defenses since the earliest days of colonization), the forts, defensive lines and artillery batteries of Jefferson, Orleans, St. Bernard and Plaquemine were manned by 3,500 Confederate troops and supported by 6,000 local militiamen in units like the Kenner Guards, commanded by Captain John Humphreys, brother-in-law of Kennerville founder Minor Kenner.

But then the invasion of the bluecoats, like that of the redcoats a half-century before, came not through Jefferson but upriver from the Gulf. It took five days of blasting by Admiral David Farragut's U.S. gunships, but in the end he was able to get his operable vessels past Forts Jackson and St. Philip, which marked not only the end of the Confederacy's hold on the region but, in fact,

▲

World War II's "7th Ward Honor Roll," on the Eastbank River Road.

PHOTO BY THE AUTHOR.

the end of the age of handsome brick forts as an effective defense against modern weaponry. All war-support industry, like cannonball manufacturing at Kennerville's Coleman Iron Foundry, came to an abrupt halt, shipyards were abandoned (leaving only Shreveport to continue Louisiana's Confederate ship-building effort), and Union occupation of the Isle of Orleans began.

Ben Franklin quipped that company, like fish, smells after three days; it was for three years of remaining warfare that Jefferson and the entire New Orleans area endured the privations and indignity of hostile military rule, and then for dessert came a dozen devisive years of Reconstruction.

THE TWENTIETH CENTURY

By the time Jefferson's post-Reconstruction generation of children grew up, America would be at war again, but blessedly, this time, not in their own front yards and town squares. Hundreds of local lads signed on as doughboys and sailors to face the Hun from the trenches and battleships of the

World War, and, a quarter-century later, their children would join the rest of the "best generation" to smash the Axis Powers and retake Europe and the Pacific in World War II. And Jefferson remembers.

Perhaps our grandest war memorial, thanks not only to its size and design but also to its dramatic location, facing the Greek-columned pediment of Gretna City Hall from the median of Huey P. Long Avenue, is the Jefferson Veterans Memorial Arch. The classic *arch du triomphe* was erected in 1918 by the efforts of a Gretna ferry captain named Jacob Huber and the energetic members of his Jefferson Memorial Organization.

On the Eastbank at the American Legion's Jefferson Post 267, the "Seventh Ward Honor Roll," smaller but equally inspiring, consists of a giant granite book and pedestal with the names of those who served in World War II engraved around its base and the names of non-survivors appearing on the pages of the open book. A vintage howitzer in the tiny memorial park guards the monument, which faces River Road at the ground-level terminus of Causeway Boulevard.

JEFFERSON COMES OF AGE

CHAPTER V

ROADS TO PROSPERITY

Economic development and the evolution of transportation in Jefferson Parish have always gone hand in hand, the cornerstone of both being the Mississippi River. The first trails were defined by their relationship to the river, following it or leading to it, with the River Roads creeping gradually upriver past the *Cote des Allemands* and *Cote des Acadiens* as other plantations and communities appeared.

The first designated roadway on the Eastbank was probably the fifty-foot right of way established by the Territorial Legislature along the old Chemin des Chapitoulas, high atop Metairie Ridge from Bayou St. John to the Cannes Brulees, later to be called Metairie Road and numbered Louisiana Highway 611-9.

On the Westbank, even after the concessions there began to be opened for settlement, it was decades before the bridging of the Harvey Canal gave those communities their first through street, Fourth Street (quickly dubbed Louisiana Highway 18), and the bayou settlements of Barataria had to be content with their north-south canals until a right of way could be established through the plantation lands of today's Marrero.

GRAND ISLE

Gov. Huey Long's two-cent gas tax of 1930 gave rise to State Highway projects that improved key urban pass-throughs as well as rural routes, including the granddaddy of our State highway

▲

Westbank Expressway crosses the Harvey Canal.

PHOTO BY ERIC LINCOLN.

A rail ferry docks at Avondale with a train and its passengers.

This first train crossing of the Huey P. Long Bridge, on Dec. 16, 1935, ended the era of "rail-ferry" crossings.

system, Louisiana 1, which crosses Louisiana diagonally from the far northwest corner to end on Jefferson Parish sand. When a few daring engineers extended Lafourche Parish's bayou road downstream from Leeville in 1931, betting that the old hurricane-wrecked Cheniere Caminada peninsula could support a highway and launch an auto bridge, their success allowed that new stretch of road to span Caminada Pass and become Grand Isle's first and only link to the mainland. That new stretch of road was first tagged 620 but, sometime between the printings of the official 1954 and 1955 Louisiana highway maps, it became one of ten State routes renumbered to form today's Louisiana 1.

A whole new world of commercial and residential possibilities was born along a very special corridor through the Jefferson after 1915, when one Eastbank street became a critical link for both of the major national highway projects of that era. That was the year planning began for converting the Florida-to-California "Old Spanish Trail" of Colonial times into a modern highway, good old U.S. 90, and also the year of a kick-off meeting of the Jefferson Highway Association in New Orleans, attended by delegates from every Louisiana Purchase state and Winnepeg, Canada. U.S. 90 would be a business and tourist route from St. Augustine to San Diego, and the new Jefferson Highway would honor President Jefferson and his Louisiana Purchase by linking the major attractions of the original Louisiana Territory states and Winnepeg.

A marble obelisk at St. Charles and Common Street in New Orleans still marks the starting point of the thirteen-year north-south project which provided dandy upgrades for existing streets along the way, like the East Jefferson stretch along the old Orleans-Kenner Streetcar route to Williams Boulevard, a street that still proudly bears the Jefferson Highway name. Meantime the east-west U.S. 90 project, arriving westbound through New Orleans, junctioned with Jefferson Highway before hopping a ferry to the Westbank and following the levee from Westwego to Luling before striking out cross-country toward the sunset.

Inspired by the importance of the Old Spanish Trail, Governor Long chipped in $7 million to the Highway 90 kitty for construction of a Mississippi River bridge to replace that route's ferry ride. The bridge, bearing his name, was dedicated in December 1935, three months after his assassination. The cantilevered through-truss bridge, which originally carried two rairoad tracks plus auto traffic at an over-water height of 135 feet, is still the longest rail bridge in the United States and still brawny enough to support its dramatic widening, begun in 2006, from two nine-foot traffic lanes in each direction, with no shoulders, to three eleven-foot lanes each way with ample shoulders.

The Huey P. Long Bridge,
Connecting New Orleans, La, with the Great West and First Train to Cross the Bridge

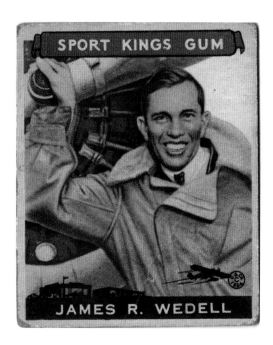

SPORT KINGS GUM

JAMES R. WEDELL

The unincorporated community of Jefferson and incorporated village of Harahan came into their own during the rise of the Jefferson Highway corridor, with paving, lighting, cozy residential areas and shopping spots along the street and, for Jefferson, a bright future that would eventually include the establishment of the Ochsner Foundation Hospital and Clinic.

Named for James T. Harahan, president of the Illinois Central Railroad from 1906 to 1911, Harahan grew to "town" status in the 1920s. It built its future on a well-rounded industrial base that included the Freiberg Mahogany Company, Kieckhefer Container Corporation and Atlas Lubricant Corporation, but it will forever be remembered as the child of, or perhaps parent of, the age of modern transportation in Jefferson, from its great railyards of the nineteenth century to its Huey P. Long Bridge in the twentieth. Along the way the town also hosted and witnessed an incredible chapter of aviation history when the metro area's first commercial airfield occupied ninety acres between Jeff Highway and the river, thus able to accommodate seaplanes as well as conventional aircraft.

Owned and operated by the Wedell-Williams Air Service, founded in 1929 in the Bayou Teche town of Patterson where Harry P. Williams was running the world's largest cypress lumber company, the Harahan field was home base for the service's original Baton Rouge-Alexandria-Shreveport network in Louisiana, its sportsman's-special amphibian flights to Grand Isle and its Jackson-Memphis-St. Louis interstate network.

Besides its passenger and mail-carrier business, Wedell-Williams provided aircraft

▲

Wedell-Williams gave Jefferson its first commercial airfield, and Jimmie Wedell designed racers that made him famous.

"PIECE OF DYNAMITE"

44

WEDELL-WILLIAMS AIR SERVICE CORP.
PATTERSON, LOUISIANA

Above: *"Tourist courts" like the Sugar Bowl lined the Airline.*

Below: *Construction of Moisant Air Field, not even halted during World War II, was completed in 1946.*

and Eastern President Eddie Rickenbacher. The design of Jimmie's famous 44 racer, modified for "dogfighting" and painted with toothy tiger-shark snarls, became the P-40s of General Claire Chennault's legendary Flying Tigers (defending Chinese airways from the Japanese during and even before America's official involvement in World War II). Today a marble-eagle monument honors Wedell at the head of Canal Boulevard, a branch of the State Museum in Patterson preserves memories of the Williams family's cypress empire and history of aviation in Louisiana, and the lavish St. Charles Avenue home of flier and entrepreneur Harry Williams and his screen-star bride Marguerite Clark is preserved as New Orleans' Latter Library.

Kenner and Metairie were still small-farm and plantation lands, to a large extent, when planning began in the mid-1920s for a thoroughfare that would be called the Airline Highway. By 1937 that streamlined highway was completed as far into East Jefferson as Shrewsbury—an amazing 41.5 miles shorter than the winding Jefferson Highway route to Baton Rouge—and completed through the parish to Tulane Avenue by 1940.

repair services, offered flight instructions for its own students and headquartered the Delgado Aviation Trade School at the Harahan field, yet it was during those busy years that Jimmie Wedell found time to create some of his most advanced aircraft designs and began collecting trophies from the big air races that would make him a national sports figure.

The company moved its operations to the new Shushan (Lakeside) Airport when it opened in 1934, and today only a historic streetside plaque remains in Harahan to mark its chapter in the story of pioneer aviation. Heirs of the two partners eventually sold Wedell-Williams, during the formation of Eastern Airlines, to World War I flying ace

Besides the spurt of business/industrial development along the highway and along its flanking railroad tracks, Airline Highway transformed its Kenner corridor and southern boundary of Metairie into a world of art deco diners, bowling alleys, skating rinks, "tourist courts," and finally, in 1946, a landmark development that would reshape Kenner, introduce a new world of transportation for the entire metro area and, incidentally, justify Airline's name: Moisant Airport.

In the midst of it all, as its newest enterprise called Trans/Match began cranking out over half the matches sold in America each year, Kenner was promoted to "city" status in 1952.

Four-laning of the Airline was complete by 1955, and now, a half-century later, the new millennium has bestowed upon the well-worn road a gentrified name change: "Airline Drive."

The selection of Minor Kenner's old canefields for the new airport immediately

Moisant International Airport

boosted employment and land values, setting off a building boom that tripled Kenner's population during the 1940s and '50s. Dedicated on January 12, 1946, it was first named for John Bovins Moisant, a popular exhibition flier from Chicago who had crashed to his death near Marrero in 1910 (an all-around bad trip for him, having just flown and lost a race at City Park with a Packard), and today its name honors New Orleans' favorite son, America's musical ambassador and perfecter if not creator of the eight-bar break, Louis "Satchmo" Armstrong.

The worst manmade disaster in Jefferson history occurred at the airport on July 9, 1982, when infamous Pan American Flight 752 crashed on takeoff, killing 145 on the plane and nine on the ground as it smashed through five blocks of the Roosevelt subdivision. That tragedy focused new attention and study on the forces of "wind shear" and inspired the wind-shear detection systems now employed at airports around the world.

Veterans Memorial Boulevard forged through Metairie and Kenner in the early 1950s, followed by the momentous completion of the first Causeway Bridge span in 1956, creating the Vets-Causeway intersection which practically begged for the development of Lakeside Shopping Center. The second span, completed in 1969 and dedicated to northbound traffic, is the longest bridge in the world at 23.87 miles, while a southbound drive on the older span, 20 meters shorter, holds second-place honors. The surprising stability of the bridges and immense need for that crossing before and after Hurricane Katrina has refocused attention on the need for a third span, which many predict will exist by the end of the 2010s. Will it fall in beside other two and become one of the world's three longest? An irresistible notion.

Continued population growth in the 1960s and '70s required more drainage canals and the paving and extension of West Metairie, West Napoleon, Veterans and West Esplanade, and Interstate 10 made its first baby steps into East Jefferson—with exits at Williams, Clearview Parkway and Causeway Boulevard—in 1962.

WESTBANK

At first Gretna was as much an island from the rest of Jefferson as Grand Isle, with the river at its face, Bayou Barataria at its back, the Harvey Canal on its left hand and Orleans Parish (Algiers) on its right. So, the river was its only doorway, but the city was an energetic self-promoter and soon had commerce and industry knocking on that door between the 1870s and turn of the century, including Stumpf Insecticides, the giant Southern Cotton Oil Company and other large oil mills, the N. K. Fairbank Company (maker of the product called Cottolene), the Union Stone Company and other enterprises, producing everything from lumber and stone products to bricks and barrels.

The Westwego, Gardere and Harvey Canals remained vital links for decades, but the strategic widening of the Harvey Canal gave the city of Harvey great appeal to industry and

▲

The spans of the Lake Pontchartrain Causeway: the two longest highway bridges on earth.

PHOTO BY ERIC LINCOLN.

transport corporations. Its giant Louisiana Cypress Lumber Company of the nineteenth century was soon joined by the likes of Swift & Company, the Stern Shell Fish Company and, following the Texas Company's and California Company's oil strikes around Bayou Barataria in 1935 and '39, endless oil-related enterprises along the canal and riverfront.

Those successes coupled with the early commercial boosterism of Gretna, the canal/railroad/river-centered commerce of Westwego and the Marrero family's residential and business development of the old Millaudon/Ames plantation lands soon had the Westbank firmly established with active industrial base, feverish home-building and long-awaited street improvements.

It was the evolution of Barataria Road from a plantation trail to State Highway status, Highway 45, that really brought the communities of Crown Point, Barataria and Jean Lafitte, with their fisheries, fur trade and shrimp canneries, into the mainstream of Jefferson life. The catalyst was Louis Marrero, with his early creation of small-farm parcels and Mississippi ferry crossing at Barataria Road, followed by sales of residential and industrial sites centering around that vital north-south link in the 1920s.

The road's status as heart and backbone of Marrero was affirmed by the establishment of the city's greatest architectural landmarks, the ornate Spanish Colonial Revival and Mission Revival structures of Hope Haven and Madonna Manor, on Highway 45 near its intersection with the Westbank Expressway. Conceived by Monsignor Peter Wynhoven as havens for the shelter and training of orphans of all faiths, Hope Haven for boys was built in 1925 and Madonna Manor, for girls and younger boys, followed in 1932. The facilities now house various categories of adult care, administered by Catholic Charities.

Later in the '30s came such solid corporate citizens as Continental Can and Johns-Manville, followed by the giant Celotex Corporation of Chicago in 1947 which created insulated building board from the sugarcane-grinding residue called bagasse.

In Westwego small shipyards established along the old Company Canal did well,

building luggers, conventional shrimpboats and the distinctive one-man shrimpboats called Laffite skiffs (its likely designer identified by Reeves and Alario's *Westwego from Cheniere to Canal* as Shiro Perez, whose family like some others had boat-building operations in Lafitte as well as Westwego). Early oil and gas explorations in the wetlands created a market for small wooden supply boats and crewboats, and by World War II the demand had skyrocketed and the families had incorporated steel hulls into their designs.

Meantime the Westwego riverfront had seen the arrival of enterprises like the Hercules Power Company and American Distilling, and, thanks to the Westbank's heavy train traffic (and several odd "train ferries" that continuously shuttled passenger and freight cars over from the Eastbank), a good hand could count on employment at the Westwego railyards.

A century earlier and one river-bend upriver, U.S. Senator and Federal Judge George A. Waggaman had built a manorhouse called Avondale on his plantation of that name, and, even though a duel and shifting river had quickly dispatched the man and his mansion, the names of the village of Waggaman and unincorporated Avondale lived on, destined to produce a legacy of railroading and shipbuilding equalled by very few places on earth.

▲

Opposite: Once a plantation lane, by the early twentieth century Barataria Boulevard led from the Mississippi to Bayou Barataria, passing Marrero's handsome Hope Haven complex along the way.

PHOTO BY THE AUTHOR.

Above: Rails and new roads meant that canneries on the river, bayous and barrier islands could provide Louisiana seafoods to the nation.

COURTESY OF THE LOUISIANA FISHERIES MUSEUM

▲

Northrop Grumman's Avondale Shipyards.

That story began in 1935 with the growth of Avondale railyards that occurred once the Huey P. Long Bridge had replaced the barge-ferrying method of railroad river crossings (not to mention the Huey's fortuitous westerly-curving descent that sent every westbound train right into the lap of the place), and with the birth in 1938 of a small barge-repair company called Avondale Marine Ways.

With U.S. 90 and the River Road at its front and back doors, and with the broad river for delivering the ships that it would build or modernize, Avondale Shipyards surged into the future as a world-famous shipbuilder and one of the largest employers in the region, still thriving as part of Northrop Grumman's national shipbuilding network and employing, by the end of 2007, more than five thousand employees.

Joining river and rails as the final great connection for most West Jefferson cities, construction began in the 1950s on the Westbank Expressway in anticipation of the 1959 completion of the first span of today's Crescent City Connection. By commandeering the three-years-older Harvey Tunnel, created for a State highway that was absorbed by the larger project, the new ground-level highway was able to move West Jefferson traffic steadily,

if sometimes slowly, until the 1977 groundbreaking for today's six-lane elevated highway. On takeoff today's "Business 90" carries traffic an impressive twenty-three feet above the General DeGaulle exit, then quickly soars to its dizzying hundred-foot clearance over the Harvey Canal and remains elevated until the Barataria exit marks the start of its gradual descent for a soft landing in Marrero.

Many of Jefferson's top-fifty employers are manufacturers, distributors and service companies that simply could not exist here without the Mississippi River and Jefferson's incredible manmade transportation assets: companies like Northrop-Grumman/Avondale, Acme Truck Line, WalMart Stores East, Universal Sodexho (offshore caterers), Coca-Cola Enterprises, Sysco Food Services and Cytec chemical manufacturers. Continued prosperity depends on the continued upgrading of those assets—such as the future triple-spanning of Lake Pontchartrain and the forthcoming absorption of the Westbank Expressway by Interstate 49, which will certainly involve a limited-access extension westward from Marrero to Avondale/Marrero and, along the way, an upgraded northward fork to connect the six-lane Huey P. Long Bridge.

CHAPTER VI

LEGACY OF LAWMEN

They can talk about their Bat Mastersons and Wyatt Earps, but no Dodge or Tombstone ever arrayed a more colorful cast of lawmen than Jefferson and its municipalities, from sheriffs to small-town police chiefs like Clarence "Uncle Pat" Matherne back in the 1990s.

The *New York Times* called Uncle Pat "the law in Jean Lafitte...also its conscience," because despite having the wherewithal to handle bad situations with bullets or brawn, he instead combined "familial kindness and no-nonsense authority," or, in his own Cajun-accented words, "It's like this: I feel that if I just talk to the boys—and they're not bad boys—it's better than just banging them against the wall." And sure enough, after a chat with Uncle Pat, "perpetrators" not only showed up at the station voluntarily but routinely came in carrying the stolen property.

In Gretna, law enforcement became a family affair in the late 1800s when Captain Beauregard Gustavus Miller strode the dusty streets (not unlike Dodge City's) as Police Captain until his death in 1911. His son Beauregard H. Miller was only eleven at the time, but fifteen years later he ran for the election that began his 53-year career as marshall/police chief, during which time Gretna law enforcement grew from a force of one to a department of 34. Upon his death in 1979, his son B.H. Junior ended a 21-year stint on the Police Jury/Parish Counsel to succeed his father, completing the final months of that term by appointment. He won the office in the election of October 1979 and served until 2005.

▲

The new Kenner Police headquarters.

PHOTO BY THE AUTHOR.

Old Southport Club, Jefferson Parish, Louisiana

▲

Above: The Southport Club.

Below: Sheriff Louis H. Marrero.

Early-day lawmen like Gustavus Miller would be stunned to witness a typical day at any law enforcement agency of twenty-first-century Jefferson, where large forces with incredible diversity of duties is a surprisingly recent phenomenon. The office of Sheriff, for instance, although it has existed since the birth of the Parish in 1825, remained essentially a one-man show in the almost totally rural parish until the widespread incorporation and population growth of the twentieth century.

Law enforcement was largely a military affair once Confederate New Orleans fell in 1862, a situation that did not end in 1865 after Appomatox. Military occupation by the U.S. Army continued through the Reconstruction era until 1877, a twelve year span that saw seven sheriffs come and go without much opportunity to create a noticeable personal legacy or public institution. The next six sheriffs enjoyed a total of only nineteen years in office (including Oliver V. Waggner, 1883-1890, the last Republican sheriff until the election of 2007), but that was about to change. Following Sheriff Bill Langridge's four-year term that ended in 1896, only eight Sheriffs held office in Jefferson Parish through 2007, three of whom accounted for 79 of those 112 years.

At the inception of Louisiana's unique "Police Jury" system, central power in a parish was held by a judge who was assisted by a "jury" permanently named for that purpose. The office of Sheriff came along in 1810, replacing many and eventually all of the executive powers of the judge, after which, until the new Louisiana Constitution of 1974, a Louisiana sheriff, especially in a parish enjoying growing population, tax base and works projects, found himself in a position of real political power.

The first of Jefferson's three longterm sheriffs, with or without the title, was a creator of dynasties. The Confederate Army was not enlisting minors as early as 1862, so we can imagine that Louis H. Marrero was not altogether straightforward about his age when he signed up at age fifteen. Before war's end he had been wounded and suffered the privations of a Union prison camp, but he survived it all to return home and become, among other things, president of the Jefferson Parish Police Jury, president of the Jefferson Commercial and Savings Bank and, from 1896 to 1920, Sheriff of Jefferson Parish.

At the same time, Sheriff Marrero was working with his son Leo A. Marrero and other family members to create the Marrero Land & Improvement Association, which can be credited with establishing much of the Westbank, particularly Marrero and Harvey, as we know it today.

Then, after two four-year terms by Sheriff John Dauenhauer, there came a character, one of the most colorful in Jefferson history, who to this day holds the record for the longest reign as sheriff, Frank J. Clancy, who was to hold that office for a quarter-century, May 21, 1928, to May 17, 1956. He took office on the eve of the Great Depression, the Prohibition era and, in Louisiana, the Huey Long era, an age when it was routine and even expected for powerful politicians to distribute patronage with a benevolent hand while ruling with an iron hand.

Father John Clancy had set the stage for his son by establishing leadership of the vegetable farmers of the parish and serving as head of the parish School Board while Frank, a lifelong lover of New Orleans Dixieland jazz, was attending Tulane Law School and supplementing his pocket money by playing in local bands. He began his own political career by serving as clerk of court and alderman before settling into his twenty-eight-year rule as Sheriff, meting out justice and favors which included arranging scholarships for musically gifted Jefferson kids, while also attending to his great preoccupation, running his sprawling Jefferson Parish ranch.

Casinos were already thriving on the Westbank and, conceding to the demand by Eastbankers for entertainment centers of their own, he allowed the Beverly Country Club (later Beverly Dinner Theatre) to open in 1945, with a one-eighth interest owned by an ambitious businessman named Carlos Marcello. He later allowed Marcello to run three other gambling operations—including the lavish Old Southport Club—along with parishwide distribution of slot machines and establishment of "racing wire" services.

By 1950, with the nationwide spread of racketeering, U.S. Senator Estes Kefauver's Special Committee to Investigate Organized Crime in Interstate Commerce also turned its attention to the growing suspicion of governmental collusion with criminal elements. In New Orleans the testimony given by Kefauver's roster of subpoenaed witnesses was broadcast live, and the few folks with televisions invited neighbors over to watch the grilling of Marcello, Clancy and

many others. The Sheriff mentioned that he would certainly put a stop to any gambling that might come to his attention, and Marcello mostly mentioned the Fifth Amendment.

Soon enough, as some remember it, Sheriff Clancy did become aware of out-of-state "influences" infiltrating the local clubs and the days of wide-open gambling in Jefferson

▲

The "In the Line of Duty" Memorial in Metairie pays tribute to the police and firemen of Jefferson.

PHOTO BY THE AUTHOR.

Above: A Look Magazine article of February 29, 1964, chuckled over Gretna's police headquarters surrounded by Mafia-owned enterprises.

Below: Shortly before his death in 2007, Sheriff Harry Lee, famous throughout the state, was inducted into the Louisiana Politics Hall of Fame/Museum in Winnfield. His statue (right) at Veterans Memorial Park was unveiled October 1, 2008, one year after his death.

Parish came to an close, although as late as 1964 a *Look* magazine crime story included a full-page aerial photo showing the river and first four blocks of Huey P. Long Avenue, declaring that fourteen of the buildings surrounding police headquarters, mostly bars, were owned by Cosa Nostra members.

From the Clancy era till 1980 only one sheriff served more than a single term, that being Alwynn Cronvich who held office from 1964 to 1979, but on April 1, 1980, the newly elected young Chinese-American who took the oath to uphold the law in Jefferson Parish was destined not only to occupy the office for life, but to become perhaps the most universally beloved public figure in Louisiana history.

Harry Lee was a large man, and he "lived large," as the saying goes, revelling in every opportunity to fish, hunt, feast on spreads of Chinese and Louisiana foods, ride in Carnival parades, sing with Willie Nelson or throw his famous "Chinese Cajun Cowboy Fais-dodo" birthday bashes. He died of lukemia at age seventy-five, on October 1, 2007, just days before winning his eighth term of office, and if a man could live forever, that is how long most observers believe he would have served. His friend and longtime assistant Newell Normand, whom Lee had for years groomed to be his successor, was sworn in as acting sheriff, and, as a final tribute to Sheriff Lee, Jefferson Parish handed Normand the victory on election day with 90.8 percent of the vote.

CHAPTER VII

HEALTHCARE HISTORY

In the mid-1950s, as though guided by premonition, men of medicine on both sides of the river created hospitals in the nick of time. The beginnings of the sudden transformation of Jefferson from rural to urban was still more than a decade away, time enough for fledgling medical institutions to grow from modest beginnings into the major modern institutions that the future would demand.

Ochsner Clinic was founded on Prytania Street in New Orleans in 1942, and young Dr. Alton Ochsner and his associates chose wisely, a dozen years later, when they located their now world-famous Ochsner Foundation Hospital on the riverside grounds of Claude Dubreuil's eighteenth-century land grant and plantation. The property would allow expansion, and the Jefferson Highway/Claiborne Avenue corridor would provide access from New Orleans as well as from the scattered towns of East Jefferson that soon would be, in effect, one giant, seamless city. In 1963 the clinic itself made the move into a new wing of the hospital, thus consolidating all Ochsner activities at Jefferson Highway.

▲

The Ochsner Foundation Hospital/Clinic's riverside complex sprawls across the lands of eighteenth-century planter Claude Debreuil.

PHOTO BY JACKSON ELLISOR,
OCHSNER MEDIA PRODUCTIONS

SOUTH TOWER

DIABETES CLASSROOM

EXIT

↑ Physicians Center Main Entr

▲

A lobby statuary group, The Consultation *by J. Seward Johnson, Jr., at West Jefferson Hospital.*

Opposite: A surgical team in action at East Jefferson Hospital.

But not for long.

First came satellite clinics on the Eastbank, Westbank and Northshore, and then came Hurricane Katrina. Ochsner managed to remain functional throughout the storm and its aftermath, and as hospitals throughout the metro area struggled to regroup staffs, repair physical plants and resume services—be it one bed at a time, one floor at a time or one facility at a time—Ochsner's modest pre-storm expansion program took off as though blown by the storm winds.

When the dust settled, old Ochsner Foundation Hospital and Clinic were the center of a regional network of major medical facilities that includes Kenner, Gretna, New Orleans and Raceland hospitals, plus Ochsner Health Centers in Metairie, Kenner, Marrero, New Orleans and New Orleans East, Algiers,

Destrehan and Lockport. And Ochsner's roster continues to expand, with its network for home-health services now in operation; with the number of its Children's Centers (operating separately or within other facilities) nearing twenty; with specialty centers providing physical therapy, fitness regimens and breast treatments; and with its new Sports Medicine Complex on South Clearview Parkway coming on line in 2009.

Meanwhile back in the '50s, years of planning by physicians, businessmen and community leaders paid off for the Westbank when West Jefferson Hospital opened its doors in Marrero in April 1960. Now grown into a full-service 451-bed medical center, the hospital and its attached office/clinic wing occupy a twenty-acre campus strategically situated at the midpoint of the Westbank Expressway and at

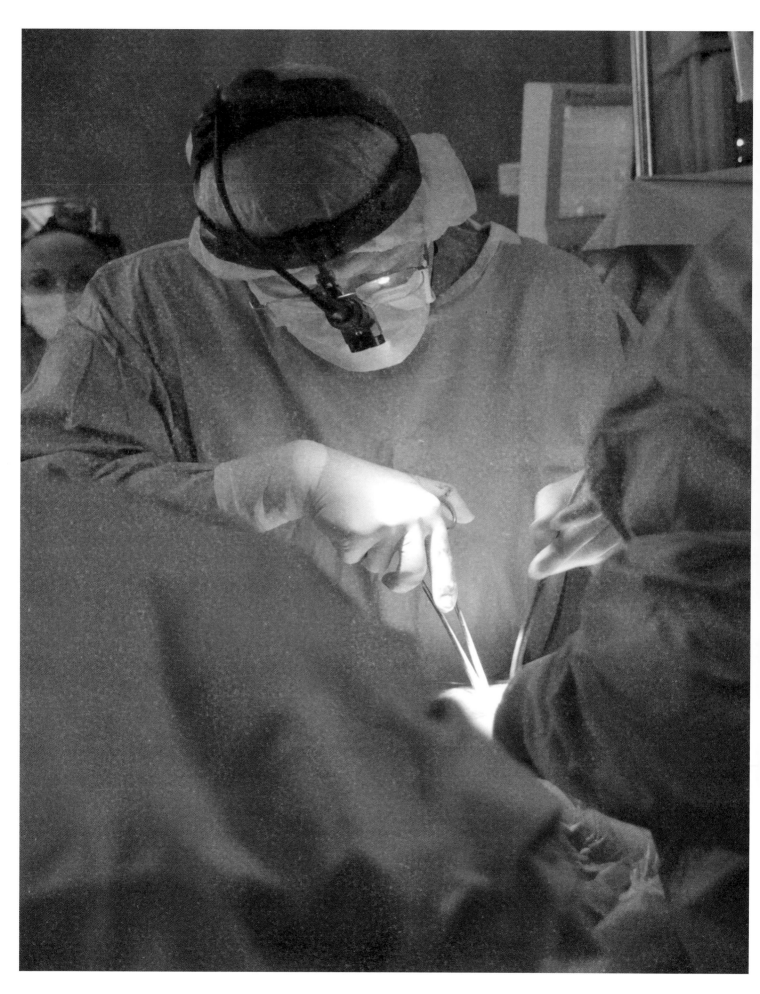

the head of the primary access route from the south, Barataria Boulevard.

West Jeff routinely appears on national "best-of" lists for overall performance, frequently receiving special recognition for such specialties as its programs for digestive care, neurology and neuroscience, stroke care, pediatic emergency care, joint replacement and overall orthopedic care. Its "Family Doctors" clinics provide essential services in the neighborhoods, and its state-of-the-art Fitness Centers provide total-wellness regimens at their Marrero and Oakwood locations.

Steadfast old Lakeside Hospital, famed since 1964 for its specialty care of women and newborns, provided the perfect match when world-famous Tulane Hospital and Clinic of New Orleans made its post-Katrina decision to create a healthcare center in Metairie. Now, in addition to its original obstetric and gynecology services, the facility is able to provide round-the-clock urgent care, family practice, and specialty care in urology, breast cancer, gastroenterology, internal medicine, orthopedics, opthalmology and non-invasive cardiology.

River Oaks Hospital in Harahan has been providing psychiatric care for adults, adolescents and children of the entire metro area since 1970, with special programs for trauma-based disorders and eating disorders, and big East Jefferson General Hospital took healthcare practically to the Pontchartrain shore when it opened on West Esplanade in Metairie in 1971.

With its famed cardiovascular unit, plus regionally respected specialists in diabetes, breast cancer, joint, pulmonary and child care, the 525-bed full-service East Jefferson Hospital has in its nearly four decades demonstrated a respect for the dignity and individuality of each patient, employing a holistic approach—physical, emotional and spiritual—to the analysis and treatment of every malady presented.

Thus the citizens of Jefferson, despite or perhaps even because of the changes wrought by Hurricane Katrina, can now enjoy a full contingent of physical and mental healthcare facilities within reach of every part of the parish. The north-south Hickory/David/Power connection, east-west Airline Drive link and Clearview/Huey Long jump to the Westbank make River Oaks everyone's neighbor, and with Ochsner now established in Raceland and Lockport, even Grand Isle falls within a relatively short radius of emergency and routine care.

CHAPTER VIII

A PRIMER IN EDUCATION

▲

Harahan Elementary School, complete with curving staircase and two-story rotunda, has been providing education and care since 1926 and was listed on the National Register of Historic Places in 1983.

PHOTO BY ERIC LINCOLN.

Although next-door neighbor of the colonial capital of Louisiana, the lands that would become Jefferson Parish remained strictly agricultural for many decades, with each landowner responsible for teaching or hiring private instructors for his own family. In the early 1830s, Jefferson received a few meager checks from the State of Louisiana to be used for educational purposes—one earmarked for the lone schoolteacher at remote Cheniere Caminada—and that begins the story of Jefferson's parish school system, a system which incidentally has always ranked in Louisiana's top three by every measure of organization, progress and supervision.

The saga of the first century of struggle is told in two master's theses that were shelved for forty years in the Tulane University library until resurrected in 1980 and 1981 as Monographs III and V of the Jefferson Parish Historical Commission. In the first of those, *The Public Schools of Jefferson Parish before the Civil War*, Lemuel W. Higgins, who himself would soon become Jefferson's Superintendent of Schools, lists four types of educational systems that preceded "true" public schools: church-maintained schools, private schools, private schools receiving public funds (subsidies for those unable to pay tuition) and private classes taught by hired tutors. The first so-called true public schools in the state, meaning no tuition regardless of any student's financial means, were opened in Jefferson and Orleans parishes in the early 1840s, and by 1851 (the first year of reliable state statistics on parish activities) Jefferson reported six operating schoolhouses plus the semi-public Gretna Academy.

In 1875, after years of disorganization and neglect due to a dual police jury system in Jefferson (enacted in 1858), years of war and Reconstruction and, as a final blow, the massive Mississippi River flood of 1874 which damaged or destroyed many schoolhouses, ten schools were operating on the Westbank and three on the Eastbank. School terms changed from year to year, cashflow from the State and police juries was unreliable, and attendance was sporadic. George Daul, author of *The Administration of the Public Schools of Jefferson Parish Since the Civil War*, records however that new taxation options and the consolidation of all Jefferson schools under one board in 1877 proved to be pivotal events. Five black schools and eighteen white schools were in operation by the early 1880s and new school buildings continued to be rented or built, including two financed in 1891 by the will of famed philanthropist John McDonogh: McDonogh No. 26 at Anson and Jefferson

Streets in McDonoghville (burned and rebuilt at Virgil and Jefferson Streets), and McDonogh 27 on Front Street in McDonoghville (damaged by Hurricane Betsy and eventually demolished).

In 1908 a new superintendent of education was named, J. C. Ellis, who served until 1940 and oversaw the expansion of the system which followed the growing population and new revenue sources—not only from taxes and, after 1922, healthy bond issues, but even windfalls from successful oilwells drilled on school board properties.

Upon the retirement of Superintendent Ellis in 1940, Lemuel Higgins, having understudied the role as assistant superintendent since 1935, took the helm and steered the system through a quantum leap in Jefferson Parish population, total urbanization along the river and lakeshore, and, before his death in 1964, the dawn of racial desegregation.

The opening of West Jefferson and East Jefferson High Schools in 1955 anticipated the population shift to the suburbs, and that growth with its requisite demand for larger and more modern facilities has continued through the second half of the twentieth century and into the new millennium, with parochial and private schools struggling alongside the public school system to keep pace. Through it all Jefferson's school system has maintained its leadership role among Louisiana parishes in terms of growth, quality and innovation, and analysis by the Jefferson Parish Economic Development Commission (JEDCO) reveals long lists of recent accomplishments and goals set for the immediate future. Six magnet schools plus a number of "academically themed" schools have broadened the choices available to Jefferson families, and six schools have adopted the demanding new International Baccalaureate curriculum and earned accreditation in that arena. A $20 million grant from Sisco Systems has provided state-of-the-art educational technology on sixteen campuses (including interactive Promethian Boards to create a "more engaging" classroom environment), and attractive bonuses have been made available to high-performing

A statuary group by Angela Gregory depicts grateful schoolchildren laying flowers before early school-financing philanthropist John McDonogh.

PHOTO BY THE AUTHOR.

teachers and principals who agree to transfer to academically lower-performing schools.

New assistance centers are available to students and families with unique needs, newcomer centers are in place to ascertain the appropriate grade level for incoming Hispanic children, and other special centers are providing rigorous academic assistance to students with learning levels two years or more behind their grade levels.

To increase access to higher education the Jefferson Chamber of Commerce has instituted a national-award-winning Dollars for Scholars program to provide financial assistance and ACT preparatory courses, and, for students whose performance levels and achievement areas lie outside the regular school system, the Chamber's strategy involves securing grants and workplace partnerships to maximize training potential and future job placement.

Meanwhile Jefferson schools are enjoying reduced student-to-teacher ratios and the curriculum at every level now emphasizes core academic skills with sharp focus on reading and math. Standardized "interval tests" are given seven times a year to pinpoint deficiencies for immediate remediation. Exacting standards and tracking systems are in place to evaluate the success of school principals, and newly established relations with teaching colleges are helping the Parish recruit the best young teachers.

New and continuing projects of the Parish are aimed at increasing the number of magnet and themed schools, launching a major capital campaign to renovate and replace school facilities where necessary, expanding public funding of "alternative schools" for children with discipline problems, and involving trade unions and businesses in preparing non-college-bound students for smooth transition into the workforce or into post-high-school training and apprenticeships. An active outreach program is being planned to provide direct school guidance to parents heretofore uninvolved in their children's schoolwork, the continuing education program for Jefferson teachers is being analyzed in concert with the Jefferson Federation of Teachers, and the business community is being challenged to assist teacher recruitment by providing such inducements as reduced rents and mortgage terms.

CHAPTER IX

DIVERSIONS

Court, diamond, gridiron, racetrack, and stage, Jefferson has had top sports and performing arts to enjoy for nearly two centuries.

Modern-era theatrical activities began here in the mid-twentieth century with struggling but determined neighborhood theaters and dinner theaters, the most opulent of which was the Beverly in Metairie (a gambling emporium turned dinner theater in the 1970s). Today the small-theater tradition continues, but it has been joined by high school performances that entertain swelling audiences as part of T. H. Harris Middle School's Academy of Performing Arts program, plus enticing schedules at the Westwego Performing Arts Theater and Rivertown (which is also home of celestial "shows" at the palatial Louis J. Roussel, Jr., Laser Planetarium).

Finally, after three decades, the Jefferson Performing Arts Society is nearing completion of its dream theater first conceived in 1978. The state-of-the-art Jefferson Performing Arts Center is rising on Airline next door to Zephyr Field, scheduled for completion in 2009 or 2010, where the Society will continue its ambitious annual schedules of plays, concerts, opera and ballet.

The sporting history of Jefferson began with horseracing in all its forms, a highpoint coming in 1838 when Duncan Kenner became a founder and first president of the Metairie Jockey Club, whose course dictated the oval configuration of today's Metairie Cemetery. "Sports" came by steamboat and train from around the country to see and be seen at the Metairie Race Track, and at the adjacent Oakland Track and various greyhound courses.

The Metairie Track closed in 1872 (and the cemetery is now part of Orleans Parish), but in 1917 another race course opened in Jefferson at a site near today's Ochsner Hospital. Like the Metairie Track, the new Jefferson Park would be known far and wide, even hosting the venerable Louisiana Derby from

▲

The Louis J. Roussel, Jr., Laser Planetarium in Kenner's Rivertown.

PHOTO BY THE AUTHOR.

1920 to 1929, won in 1924 by the famous Black Gold whose gravemarker can be seen today in the infield of the Fair Grounds Race Course.

By 1934 Jefferson Park was also closed, but at the site of today's Lafreniere Park a sulky-racing course called Magnolia Trace opened in 1954 which in 1959 would be renamed Jefferson Downs and converted to thoroughbred "flat racing" (no wheels). In 1971 Jeff Downs moved to the lakefront where racing continued until 1992.

Jefferson has never been a boxing mecca, but as a momentary diversion from the rigors of Reconstruction, in the predawn hours of May 10, 1870, a chartered train chugged up to Kenner from the city, filled with local gents, off-duty military men and well-heeled enthusiasts from around the country, all come to witness a sporting event that would give Jefferson bragging rights forever: the first world championship heavyweight match ever held in the United States. The contest took place behind the sugarhouse of William Butler Kenner's Oakland Plantation just upriver from today's Rivertown district, where a statue memorializing that history-making bare-knuckles fight now stands at LaSalle's Landing Park.

Both fighters were British-born, but Tom Allen held the current American heavyweight title and his opponent, Jem Mace, "father of modern boxing," was the current English champion and reigning world champ. The announcement of the bout, four months in advance, made world news, as did Mace's tenth-round victory.

Great local high school sports rivalries enliven every season of every year in Jefferson, but the fun actually begins years earlier, for the kids and their families and neighbors, when "players" toddle out to their first Parks and Recreation Department tee-ball fields to begin their multi-sport pre-high "careers."

The parks actually provide the first away-from-home experiences of many children and create, in the process, lively spectator sports for the neighborhoods. It all began with individual tax districts created to finance individual playgrounds, beginning on the Eastbank with Metairie Playground which opened in 1951, followed in the 1950s by Jefferson, Harlem (now Lemon), East End, Delta and (with a $25,000 grant from Jefferson Downs) Cleary Playground. Early coaches around the league were Sal D'Amico, Burdette Medlin, Doris Pete, Louis Girard, Harry Glover, and Bob Habisreitinger.

When the Parish Council system replaced the Police Jury in 1958, the parks and gyms were consolidated into a single department, first directed by Harry Glover, which opened the way for the establishment of parks in the 1970s on the booming but previously less-populous Westbank. Waggaman was the first, in 1974, followed by Avondale, Kennedy Heights, M.L. King, Nicholson, Belle Terre and Harvey.

Then along come the high school years and, for some players, college teams and even the pros, which brings to mind two great Jefferson names from the early days of baseball, Gretna's J.B. Spencer and Mel Ott.

Joseph Spencer played for eight teams in three Negro leagues—including the Homestead Grays (two championship seasons in 1943 and '44), Birmingham Black Barons (including its 1945 championship season), Baltimore Elite Giants, Harlem Globetrotters, New York Black Yankees, Pittsburgh Crawfords, and Seattle Steelheads—plus five seasons in the minor leagues. After a fourteen-year career, playing every position except pitcher, he returned to Gretna to supervise the playground that would one day bear his name. He died in 2003 at age 83, leaving a legacy still remembered by every kid who swings a bat at J. B. Spencer Park on Fried Street.

Melvin Thomas Ott began his pro career in 1926 as the youngest-ever major leaguer when he vaulted to the "bigs" at age 16 from a life of high school ball in Gretna and semi-pro ball in the St. Mary Parish town of Patterson. The semi-pro team was sponsored by the Williams Cypress Company, and there Harry P. Williams (also co-founder of the famed Wedell-Williams Air Service) bought Mel a ticket to New York and arranged a tryout for him with the New York Giants.

Ott was signed immediately and after 22 seasons retired from the San Francisco Giants in 1948 with 511 home runs (six seasons as National League home run leader, despite frequent intentional walks) and souvenirs from eleven all-star games and three World Series. He was inducted into the Baseball Hall of Fame in 1951 and the New Orleans Pro Baseball Hall of Fame in 2005, the year of that Hall's creation by the New Orleans Zephyrs.

The Zephyrs came to town from Denver in 1993 and now, as the Triple-A Pacific Coast League affiliate of the New York Mets, wow the crowds at the sprawling stadium that fans like to call the "Airline Shrine." That diamond, incidentally, has proved its potential as a prime venue for college ball as well, breaking Super Regional single-date and total three-game attendance records with its LSU-Tulane matches in 2001, and drawing enthusiastic crowds when the two schools met there again in 2003 to vie for the trip to Omaha. The field has also hosted a number of

▲

Above: Bare-fist history: Allen versus Mace.
PHOTO BY THE AUTHOR.

Below: The 2007 season opener at the Zephyrs' "Airline Shrine."
PHOTO BY JOE MAITREJEAN.

regular-season college games through the years, most notably the annual Wally Pontiff, Jr., Classic.

The Pontiff Classic honors a young man who grew up playing ball at old Metairie Playground before his memorable baseball years at Jesuit High School and LSU, where, as team captain and all-Southeastern Conference third baseman, he died of a heart abnormality in 2002, in the summer after his

junior season. Today his childhood ballpark in Metairie bears the name of Wally Pontiff, Jr., Memorial Playground.

Jefferson is also the longtime home of New Orleans Saints training activities, the team's old David Drive location now replaced by snazzy facilities (complete with a fully enclosed practice field) near Zephyrs Field. It is there that the minicamps and "organized team activities"— often open to the public—begin each spring before the out-of-town training camp.

CHAPTER X

CABBAGES & KINGS

Snakes would return to Ireland and fava bean bushes would wither in Italy if our cabbage-tossing floats and pucker-prone marching clubs did not hit the streets of Jefferson to honor St. Patrick and St. Joseph each spring, usually just days after Mardi Gras.

After Carnival and the Irish-Italian festivities of March, the old German tradition of Mayfest is observed in Gretna and the age-old World Championship Pirogue Races return to Jean Lafitte. Folks arrive by cars and boats to enjoy the food and big-name music groups at the Lake Pontchartrain Basin Foundation's big Back to the Beach Festival, at the Kenner lakefront in June, followed by a busy schedule of festive fishing tournaments like July's giant Grand Isle Tarpon Rodeo.

When fall rolls around, October brings twenty square blocks of fun at the Gretna Heritage Festival—complete with German Beer Garden, bandstands, Italian Village, arts, rides and games—while just upriver, Monsignor J. Anthony Luminais's annual Bridge City Gumbo Festival (the man and the event that put the place on the map and Holy Guardian Angels Church in the black in the 1970s) is still dishing out two thousand gallons of gumbo and dozens of other Louisiana delights in the shadow of the Huey P. Long Bridge. The good monsignor retired in 2008 but the tradition is forever.

Then it's time to welcome a brand new year and with it, of course, another Mardi Gras.

"The world loves a parade," as the saying goes, and we witness the truth of that every year as the world comes visiting in the days before Lent to see how the masters do it. No brag, just fact: nobody

▲

Jean Lafitte's annual World Championship Pirogues Races.

COURTESY OF THE LOUISIANA OFFICE OF TOURISM.

does it better, from the geographic top of the parish to the bottom—from the giant floats of the Metairie parades, just blocks from Lake Pontchartrain, to that carefree and laid-back

procession at our southernmost tip, the Grand Isle Independent Mardi Gras Parade, with its walking groups, cool cars, decorated boats (trailered) and home-crafted floats, all passing

in review to delight the islanders as it has for a half-century.

Observation of Fat Tuesday and the Carnival season began unselfconsciously in Jefferson— groups of friends here and there deciding to throw together some funny costumes and stroll the streets, eventually forming into informal "clubs" like the Owls, the Big Fifties and the Phunny Phorty Phellers in Gretna (as recalled in the writings of Henry J. Thoede). Then came larger and more organized groups like the Gretna Carnival Club (which met regularly in the old David Crockett Fire Hall), followed in 1948 by Jefferson's first full-fledged parade as the krewe of Grela rolled through GREtna-LA in 1948.

On the Friday night and Saturday afternoon of the first parade weekend each year, two reliable old guests of West Jefferson from neighboring Algiers, Cleopatra's all-female krewe founded in 1972 and the venerable 1939 Choctaw krewe, march across the parish line to entertain residents and visitors lining

the streets of Terrytown, followed by West Jefferson's own Mystic Knights of Adonis on that first Saturday night. Grela, now with nearly 30 floats and upwards of 400 members, parades at midday on Mardi Gras, winding through the Gretna Historic District followed

▲

Above: Grand Isle Tarpon Rodeo.

COURTESY OF THE LOUISIANA OFFICE OF TOURISM.

Below: Dan Kelly and Sal Gambino, kings for a day at the Irish-Italian Parade.

PHOTO BY DENNIS GUIDRY,
JEFFERSON PHOTO LAB.

The Parade of Caesar.
COURTESY OF THE JEFFERSON CONVENTION &
VISITORS BUREAU.

by the colorful and ingenious truck floats of that city's own Elks Parade.

Zeus, the oldest parade on the Jefferson Eastbank and oldest night parade in the parish, lumbered up Metairie Road for the first time in 1958. The great old Krewe of Atlas began parading on Veterans Memorial Boulevard in 1970, and Zeus's switch to that route in the early '70s firmly established Veterans as the Eastbank's standard parade route.

East Jefferson actually begins its Carnival parades a week early, thanks to the Metairie Children's Carnival Club and its Little Rascals Parade (begun in 1983 and now the longest-running children's parade in Carnival history), which follows the Veterans route three Sundays before Mardi Gras. Atlas and King Arthur's own krewe of Excalibur provide a double-feature

Friday night to launch the first big parade weekend, followed by the giant parade of Caesar on Saturday night and two Sunday parades, the ladies' daytime procession of Rhea and the old Harahan-River Ridge Carnival Club's night parade called Centurions.

The god who gave us Thursdays seems to prefer Wednesdays, and after the mid-week march of Thor (Jefferson's first combined-gender krewe), the second parade weekend begins with the male-female krewe of Aquila on Friday night. Saturday brings the time-honored Kenner ladies krewe of Isis and the Little General's big parade of Napoleon, and Sunday is a day of rest before Fat Monday.

As Westbankers are celebrating "Lundi Gras" by feasting and dancing with Carnival royalty at the Gretna Market, Eastbank revelers gather at Kenner's historic Rivertown to be entertained by bands and street performers until King Argus arrives for his traditional toast by the mayor. Argus then greets his regal guests, King and Queen Zulu, honoring them with a second-line send-off for their boatride to the New Orleans riverfront to greet Rex. Mighty Zeus, Jefferson's oldest parade, ends Lundi Gras with his dazzling night parade on Veterans, and then comes Mardi Gras when the street belongs to Argus and upwards of 150 floats of the Eastbank's two truck parades, the Elks Krewe of Jeffersonians and the Krewe of Jefferson.

As if a couple of dozen parish parades (depending on the weather) weren't a big enough bash, the Jefferson Parish Convention and Visitors Bureau in recent years has begun sponsoring giant three-day concerts billed as Family Gras, which began as an annual Eastbank event but now takes place on both sides of the river, always on the Friday, Saturday and Sunday of the first big parade weekend each year. With their high-quality Louisiana-style food booths and non-stop music by local and national stars, these events actually fit the definition of big free-admission festivals, designed to entertain locals and lure out-of-towners to spend a day or two in the parish when they come for Carnival.

The Westbank and Eastbank Family Gras locations are convenient to parade routes (www.familygras.com), and the music stops for every passing parade.

CHAPTER XI

KATRINOVATION

Summer was over when *Picayune* travel columnist Catharine Cole visited Grand Isle and Cheniere Caminada. The tourists were gone and the men were leaving for their winter fishing grounds. The articles of September 25 and October 2, 1892, record that the writer visited the ladies of Caminada (known in that time and place by their husband's names—Madame Pierre, Madame Emile, Madame Clement), enjoying coffee, breads and conversation in their pristine but weather-gray cottages, which stood shoulder to shoulder behind little yards alive with zinnias and marigolds, their outdoor bread ovens shaded by orange trees.

Caminada Pass, she wrote, was lined with schooners and luggers bearing names like *Buffalo Bill* and *John L. Sullivan*, and here and there around the peninsula were nine grocery stores, each with a ballroom where villagers went to dance and eat boiled mullet or gumbo. Over this community of thirteen hundred people rose the Gothic spire of Our Lady of Lourdes, and on its cemetery gate hung the sexton's sign: "He who is in want of a grave must come to me."

One year after the articles appeared, the *Picayune* reprinted the Grand Isle piece as a memorial. Death and destruction had visited Grand Isle during the hurricane of October 1, 1893, and the village of Cheniere Caminada had vanished.

Jefferson has taken many straight shots and glancing blows since the colony's first recorded hurricane in 1722—a twelve-foot surge at Grand Isle in 1915 with flooding throughout the parish and region, general flooding in the 1930 storm, the 1947 "Rigolets storm" that swept the lake into

▲

Katrina makes landfall, August 28, 2005.

COURTESY OF THE NATIONAL OCEANIC AND
ATMOSPHERIC ADMINISTRATION.

Kenner and Metairie, the notorious Betsy in 1965 and Camille's grizzly near-miss in 1969. And winding through it all was the moody Mississippi, with its floods of 1891 and 1927 and its disturbingly regular levee breaks called crevasses, each one starting with a trickle and ending as a miniature Niagara Falls, sweeping homes, crops, livestock and sometimes people to watery oblivion: the Little Farms Crevasse of 1849, the awesome Ames Crevasse of 1891, and a 1913 Gretna crevasse locally famous for sweeping away the pegleg of one poor fellow who was manning the pumps.

So brawny old punch-drunk Louisiana stayed pretty well braced for a blow, but then came the one-two punch of 2005, starting with Katrina on August 29, which killed 1,000 Louisianians as it smashed the metro area with 125 mph winds and 10- to 20-foot coastal storm surges that sent tidal waves through navigation channels, all of which soon overstressed and undermined the walls of key drainage canals.

Then on September 22-23, Grand Isle, already splintered and saturated by Katrina, caught the northern edge of Hurricane Rita's

180-mph winds as that storm traveled westbound through the Gulf and hooked north to smash southwest Louisiana and Texas.

Despite Jefferson (as the most populous parish) being the hardest hit in terms of displaced citizens, and despite months of frustrated efforts to rebuild homes and businesses in the face of material and labor shortages, the U.S. Department of Labor reported "substantial recovery" by the third quarter of 2006, back up to 82 percent of its pre-Katrina employment numbers.

Now all eyes are on the two categories of protections required to prevent catastrophic results of rainfall and surge when future storms strike: "internal" networks of drains, canals and pumps, all overseen by the Jefferson Drainage Department, and the "external" system of levees and surge control structures overseen by the East and West Jeff Levee Districts and the new Southeast Louisiana Regional Flood Protection Authority.

"EXTERNAL IMPROVEMENTS"

Progress since 2005 has been significant, with dozens of vital projects completed and dozens more funded and in progress. Highlights on the Eastbank include raising of levees to alltime highs, with sheet-pilings driven to new 53-foot depths along some floodwalls, surge barriers installed at the Seventeenth Street Canal and under I-10 (at the West Return Canal). Then came the upgrading of pumping stations and the installation of backup pumping systems, to be followed by the replacement of Eastbank I-walls with sturdier T-walls, plus permanent improvements at the West Return Canal's levee and floodwall and a permanent pump station with floodgates for the mouth of the Seventeenth Street Canal.

Hurricane Gustav left record floodwaters in Barataria towns and Grand Isle was hammered by Gustav and Ike in 2008, but the Jefferson Westbank had actually suffered no surge damage in 2005. Nevertheless, the Westbank's floodwalls were quickly strengthened after Katrina, with surge gates installed and interim floodwalls heightened on the Harvey Canal at LaPalco Boulevard. Then, with I-wall toughening accomplished along the Cousins Canal and other locations, and a "barge gate" installed to block storm surge at the present head of the Company Canal (which had been filled through Westwego in the 1950s), there followed a roster of twenty-plus other

▲

Like many other Jefferson sites, Wally Pontiff Park's surrounding berm can transform it to a flood-water retention pond when pumps are overworked.

PHOTO BY THE AUTHOR.

Westbank projects (including hundred-year-storm-rated surge protection on the east side of the Harvey Canal) with projected completion dates ranging from 2009 to 2011.

"INTERNAL IMPROVEMENTS"

Thirteen new "safe houses" at pump stations around the parish can now protect operators in winds up to 250 mph. All major stations now have stand-by generators, and air-suppression systems have been installed at nine pumps to further restrict backflow and allow extended functioning after power loss.

Every drain line in the parish has been cleaned, storm-water holding ponds in multiple locations now assure street drainage even at times of maximum pumping capacity, and flap gates have been added to Seventeenth Street Canal outfall pipes to prevent backflow into low-lying areas (with additional hydraulic-driven pumps to improve drainage of the "Hoey's Basin" area).

Permanent backflow prevention is coming soon for all parish pump stations, and further automation and stormproofing of the stations is in progress with Corps of Engineers funding.

THEN WHAT?

Achievement of total hundred-year-storm protection is a great first step, but only one

step, in the direction of the real issue: 500-year protection.

The Jefferson Economic Development Commission (JEDCO) points to the Netherlands, with its 10,000-year surge protection, as a role model for all surge-prone states and nations, urging the public and all political entities to take up the 500-year cause.

Other shortlist items on JEDCO's analysis of realistic and vital goals are a pump-to-the-river system for the Hoey's Basin area, a call for federal assistance to improve outdated "local" drainage, automated "climber screens" to clear accumulations of debris from pumps during storms, and a "polder system" of compartmentalized flood protection. Polders are Dutch-concept units with secondary, individual levee protection (now under study by the Southeast Louisiana Flood Protection Authority) meant to isolate an engineering failure at the trouble spot and thus avoid the "profoundly widespread flooding" that can follow such an event.

Finally, JEDCO urges systematic independent reviews of Corps of Engineers projects (with independent assessments of design and construction), and an outreach campaign to provide the public with clear and straightforward planning-through-completion flood control progress reports.

▲

A "safe room" (below) and state-of-the-art generator (above) at Bayou Segnette, for storm-condition pumping operations.

COURTESY OF JEDCO.

CHAPTER XII

GIFTS OF GEOGRAPHY

Water might be the greatest concern in Jefferson when it comes to planning and preparedness, but properly controlled it provides the type of surroundings that landlocked folks can only dream of. Lakes, river, bayous, swamps, marsh, bays, beach and Gulf: water defines Jefferson's concept of outdoor activity.

Grand Isle beach.

COURTESY OF THE LOUISIANA OFFICE OF TOURISM.

PONTCHARTRAIN LAKEFRONT

The same pumping stations that take center stage when analyzing the safety of their home and lives become little more than points of casual interest when a couple takes a jog or hike along the Pontchartrain lakeshore through Kenner and Metairie. "There they are. That's good."

With occasional detours around levee-raising projects—which never cause complaints—the lakefront trail now stretches all the way to the St. Charles Parish line, past walkers, joggers, stroller-pushers, skaters, bicyclers, kite-fliers, kids casting from the riprap and, likely as not, a conventioneer or two who've moseyed up from the snazzy Pontchartrain Center for a leveetop view of the lake.

The gazebos and piers of palmtree-shaded Laketown Park can tempt the most serious hikers to buy a beverage at the new concession building and sit awhile, watching "steamboat gamblers" hustling over to the Treasure Chest Casino and boaters embarking at the launch, some enroute to

▲

Oysters, blue crabs, shrimp, crawfish, plus freshwater and saltwater fish, straight from local waters to outlets like this fisherman's market in Westwego, or your favorite restaurant. Life is good.

PHOTOS BY ERIC LINCOLN.

favorite fishing spots and others just out for a sightseeing cruise up the lakeshore toward the Bonnet Carre Spillway or down toward the big bridge. A twenty-eight-acre land reclamation project adjacent to Laketown is being transformed into Environmental Park, complete with marshgrass, tidal ponds and appropriate flora and fauna, all surrounding a new wetlands interpretive center.

The leveeside restaurants are now more numerous than ever along the Bucktown lakefront, and Metairie's old Bonnabel boat ramp has blossomed into the new Burk-Kleinpeter-designed Bonnabel Recreation Complex, complete with calm-water launch lanes, big T-shaped fishing pier, perimeter-access piers for bigger boats and lots of green space.

At the Causeway, about 8 o'clock each evening in spring and fall, joggers arriving from either direction can join locals and tourists who gather there to greet thousands of purple martins as they circle in for a good night's rest. More than 8 million of the mosquito-devouring birds fly through the area every time migration season rolls around, and about 200,000 of those, like their ancestors before them, have made the south-end understructure of the bridge a routine overnight stopover.

That phenomenon has inspired the creation of a National Wildbird Refuge at the place (soon to include a five-acre freshwater lagoon and twenty-acre brackish-water marsh to attract other species), not to mention the creation of a Purple Martin Cocktail at Bar 38 in the nearby Lakeway Center's Marriott-Metairie Hotel.

The twin spans of the old Causeway, viewed with almost wonder-of-the-world awe by visitors throughout its half-century history, still hangs tough as the longest bridges in the world. The latest challenger, a futuristic S-shaped bridge over Hangzhou Bay between the Chinese cities of Cixi and Zhapu, came in at a lackluster twenty-two miles in 2007.

BAYOU SEGNETTE STATE PARK

Beloved Bayou Segnette, discovered by Westwego-area canal builders 250 years ago to be a natural link in their manmade routes to Caminada on the Gulf and even west to Bayou Lafourche, is now the centerpiece of one of Louisiana's most versatile State Parks. Overnighting can mean rustic tenting, RV camping with hookups or even waterfront vacation cabins, and recreation ranges from wavepool and conventional swimming pool to wooded trails and wilderness exploration.

Through the centuries the old water route to the Gulf has introduced enough saltwater intrusion to give fishermen a choice between freshwater and saltwater fishing, and for nature photography or simply observing wetland birds and wildlife, the park offers access to species that favor swamp, marshland and open-water habitats, from common cardinals and red-tailed hawks to noble bald eagles, from relatively bold raccoons to elusive mink.

For boaters the choices range from canoe explorations in and about the State Park to motorboat excursions down the bayou and historic canal into Lafitte National Park's wilderness area, called the Barataria Preserve, where other small waterways provide connections to big Lake Catouatchie and big-big Lake Salvador.

BARATARIA PRESERVE

Lafitte National Park's sprawling Barataria Preserve lies totally within Jefferson Parish, below Marrero and extending south to Bayou Barataria. Surrounding the Visitor Center with its intriguing film and interactive displays—describing the history and complex ecological balance of Barataria—are twenty thousand acres of typical Louisiana wetlands, "logged out" in the 1920s but now fully recovered.

Acres of marsh grasses lie in close proximity to classic moss-draped swamplands, and through it all run more than two miles of raised boardwalks, about six miles of ground-

▲

The Butterfly Dome on Grand Isle blows away with every storm, but admirers from around the nation always build it back.
COURTESY OF THE JEFFERSON CONVENTION & VISITORS BUREAU.

level trails, nine miles of bayous and
waterways reserved for canoe traffic and
twenty-odd miles open to boats of all types.
The waters are teeming with the predictable
fur-bearing mammals, the ever-popular
reptiles and, especially in spring, wading
birds; the dry spots are thick with cypress and
palmetto and blanketed in ferns; and low-
hung branches are often strung with the webs
of spiders that come in all sizes and
dispositions. Rangers lead guided canoe tours
on Sunday mornings and moonlight tours on
the night before each full moon.

The Marsh Overlook Trail is especially good
for gator watching, the Wildflower Trail is a
good one for butterfly watching, and all trails
are open seven days a week.

GRAND ISLE

Of course, to see indigenous butterflies
without a swampland trek, the place to be is the
famous Butterfly Dome on Louisiana's own little
laid-back resort island of Grand Isle. Most folks
come for the fishing, but Hurricanes Katrina,
Rita and now Gustav have produced evidence
of the little dome's incredible popularity, with
previous visitors from around the nation and

world sending individual donations and grants
from their organizations to replace its shredded
exterior, replant the colorful flowers, and
restore its population (with the help of butterfly
safaris undertaken by Grand Isle and Bayou
Lafourche school groups).

Nesting waterfowl are plentiful throughout the region, and spring and fall bring the migratories, so take binoculars, camera and a copy of the "America's Wetland Birding Trail" booklet, available free from the Louisiana Office of Tourism (800-227-4386). One of the island's big annual events, in fact, is the Migratory Bird Festival in mid-April, but any day is a good one in those seasons, when visiting birdwatching organizations have been known to spot as many as 170 different species of songbirds in a two-day "count."

Fishermen who trailer their boats to the island would do well to set aside a half-day or so to visit old Fort Livingston on neighboring Grand Terre Island, and perhaps to venture into lower Barataria Bay (land of the shrimp-drying platforms of the nineteenth and twentieth centuries with their stilt villages, now vanished) to see such sights as Queen Bess Island, that almost other-worldly nesting ground of the brown pelican, four miles due north of the barrier islands.

As for the fishing, Grand Isle and Caminada are home of several major fishing "rodeos" each year, the grandpappy of which is the world famous Grand Isle Tarpon Rodeo in July, but regardless of the rodeo calendar, every year offers at least 365 shots at the tarpon, redsnapper, marlin, speckled trout and other 275-or-so species of the Gulf and bay.

No boat? Two choices: shore fishing or charter boats. The sand beach destroyed by Katrina and Rita at Grand Isle State Park had been completely replaced before the visits of Gustav and Ike, but resanding after storms is routine, and fishing from piers, jetties and the surf for redfish and speckled trout is productive. And don't forget the simple pleasures of crab-netting from the jetties and the evening adventure of wading the surf to gig flounders.

CHARTERS & GUIDES

With or without fishing/hunting gear, a lease, ATV, trained dog or even a fillet/skinning knife of your own, Jefferson residents and visitors are just a phone call away from a memorable day in a duck blind or fishing boat, thanks to the parish's abundance of skilled and licensed hunting guides and

▲

Beach camping at Grand Isle State Park.

charter captains. Gretna, Westwego, Jean Lafitte and Grand Isle information centers are the best sources of current listings.

Chartering is the no-hassle way to have a great day of boating, and experienced captains take the guesswork out of picking locales for particular species as conditions change from day to day. Most of the boats, incidentally, are available for charter during the region's twenty-or-so annual fishing rodeos.

Grand Isle is the obvious departure point for lower Barataria Bay and for a wide radius of offshore-rig opportunities, and for fishing the bay some captains "mother-ship" their clients to a productive area and then provide kayaks for navigating tight spots.

A boat tour at Bayou Segnette State Park.
COURTESY OF THE LOUISIANA OFFICE OF TOURISM.

Farther inland, a charter trip from the Jean Lafitte/Bayou Barataria area to the day's recommended hotspot can, in effect, double as a tour of the wetlands that are sacred to the memory of generations of pioneering hunter/trapper/fishermen who wrested livelihoods and raised families in those harsh but beautiful environs. Some captains, in fact, offer special nature and photo excursions for observing the wildlife and habitat.

THE HERITAGE

Reminders of the history and traditions of Jefferson Parish are everywhere, but most particularly in the special collections of museums that tell the story of this place through actual tangible objects from the past, and in the surprisingly rich assortment of film and literary works that have captured elements of its scenery and personality. And through it all runs the most dramatic landmark of the Jefferson story, the Mississippi River itself.

CHAPTER XIII

THE RIVER ROADS

Leveetop joggers, bicyclers and even horseback riders are a routine part of River Road scenery as the Mississippi winds through Jefferson, and hikers like the well maintained public-access stretches of the levee that run from Westwego's river-watching pavillion to the Gretna ferry on the Westbank and, on the Eastbank, from LaSalle's Landing Park in Kenner to the Orleans-Jefferson line. Eventually, though, every Jeffersonian has to take the driving tour of both River Roads, on two different occasions or (with crossings at the Luling and Crescent City Connection bridges) up one side and down the other.

▲

A view from the leveetops.

PHOTO BY ERIC LINCOLN.

EASTBANK

An upriver drive on the Eastbank begins at the Jefferson-Orleans line (the railroad tracks and Monticello Avenue) and leads a few blocks up to a true twentieth-century landmark, DeWitt's Fruit and Vegetable Shed, then passes giant Ochsner's Hospital and, soon after, the local headquarters of the American Cancer Society and Alzheimer's Association at 2605 River Road.

The road passes the Seventh Ward World War II memorial at the river end of Causeway Boulevard, with its historical marker for nearby Camp Parapet, and a few blocks farther along, facing the river just past Central Avenue, stands the 1857 mansion called Whitehall with its imposing 53-foot gallery. This was the manor of the old Labarre family plantation until 1892, and since has served as a casino, Jesuit retreat house and, until recently, the Magnolia School for mentally challenged children.

Just upriver from the Huey P. Long Bridge is Elmwood Estates, its modern homes and lots shaded by the massive oaks of old Elmwood Plantation, and a bit upriver, in Harahan, the River Road becomes Riverside Drive and ends at Colonial Country Club, which occupies the lands of old Tchoupitoulas Plantation. Here Colonial Club Drive leads out to Jefferson Highway, which continues upriver through Harahan to Kenner, and there Jefferson (alias Louisiana Highway 48) falls in beside the river again and leads to LaSalle's Landing Park and the other attractions of Rivertown. At its intersection with Williams Boulevard, Jefferson Highway becomes Third Street and passes historic Kenner High School on its way to the St. Charles Parish line.

WESTBANK

An upriver drive on the Westbank should begin at McDonogh Cemetery, where Hancock Street and Franklin Avenue cross the Jefferson-Orleans line, to see the first tomb of philanthropist John McDonogh (since reinterred with his family in Maryland). Following Franklin upriver, turn right on Weidman and then (pausing to see McDonogh No. 26 School at Weidman and Jefferson) left on Washington, which leads along the river to become First Street in Gretna.

Lost Plantation
THE RISE AND FALL OF SEVEN OAKS

MARC R. MATRANA

▲

The long-lamented Seven Oaks lives on in the pages of Westbank history.

Follow First past the Zatarain's plant (a Louisiana culinary landmark), jog one block left on Lafayette to see the Gretna Historical Society's museum complex, and then continue on First to Huey P. Long Avenue to visit the Welcome Center (Fourth at Huey P. Long) for a walking-tour brochure of the riverfront and Historic District.

Just upriver on Fourth, take the quick detour on Derbigny to pass the Thomas Jefferson statue and Jefferson Courthouse, then continue up Fourth (crossing the old Harvey Canal bridge with its good view of the locks) to

Barataria Boulevard. Fourth jogs left at Barataria and then continues upriver through Westwego to the corner of Sala Avenue, where the little outlets of the new Wego Market were inspired by the historic storefronts and True Vine Church of old Salaville. Visit the Westwego Museum, housed in the historic General Merchandise Store at 275 Sala, and then, just past the Westwego Performing Arts Theater, climb the levee to enjoy some river watching from Westwego's "Lazy River Landing," where Confederate batteries once guarded the river.

From the nearby painted-brick remains of the historic Company Canal locks, River Road heads upriver for a half-mile, traversing the lands of lost-and-lamented Seven Oaks Plantation, to a point where Louisiana 18 forks away from the river to shortcut the dramatic Nine Mile Point bend of the river. It is better, however, to take the right fork and follow Louisiana 541 around the big bend, passing a marker at the site of Jefferson's uprivermost Confederate battery, then antebellum Derbigny and Magnolia Lane plantation homes (obscured by foliage but both marked by highway signs), and then the Huey P. Long Bridge.

A country mile upriver from the bridge is Banting Nursery Farms, which no lover of growing things can pass without browsing, and a mile or so farther along 541, ships and giant cranes begin appearing above the leveetop as you approach the historic shipyards of Northrop Grumman's "Avondale Operations." At the "T" intersection with Louisiana 18, turn right to follow 18 past the remainder of the shipyards, railyards and offices, on the former lands of George Augustus Waggaman's Avondale Plantation. A bit upriver near the tree-shaded riverfront town of Waggaman, 18 passes old Cedar Grove Plantation. Built around 1790 by Jean-Baptiste Drouet, the plantation served in the 1960s as retirement home of the French Quarter's "Last Madam" Christine Wiltz. Converted to service as the Tchoupitoulas Plantation Restaurant in the 1960s and '70s, it now once again serves as a private residence.

Above Waggaman, the pleasant leveeside drive continues through the village of South Kenner to the big Cytec plant (a specialty chemicals producer once a division of American Cyanamid) at the St. Charles Parish line.

CHAPTER XIV

MUSEUMS & MORE

Thanks to folks like the Indian dancers at Cannes Brulees events in Kenner's Rivertown, skilled blacksmithing demonstrators at the Gretna Green smithy and simply perfect curators at a surprising variety of museums, history in Jefferson Parish has escaped the doldrums of ponderous textbooks and conventional museums to take on a whole new life. On the Eastbank are the significant and lively collections of Rivertown, and on the Westbank are two major clusters of historic landmarks that are open to the public in Gretna, an irresistible general-store/city museum in Westwego and a small but captivating Louisiana Fisheries Museum in Jean Lafitte.

These collections are designed to convey knowledge and understanding of a legacy that will make you proud, and to entertain you in the process, and the fun can begin even before you get there. The secret is, never pass a visitor information center, hereabouts, without stopping to enjoy the displays, to gather the new literature and to share the knowledge and real enthusiasm of the personnel.

GRETNA

Half of Gretna's public-access attractions are strung out along Huey P. Long Avenue, right up to the riverfront, and the other half are grouped in a delightful streetcorner complex of vintage structures at Second and Lafayette Streets.

▲

Louisiana Iris at Jean Lafitte swamp-park.
PHOTO BY THE AUTHOR.

From the Westbank Expressway, exit riverward at Lafayette Street, then turn left on Tenth (passing the historic Hook & Ladder Cemetery) and right on Huey P. Long—originally named Copernicus Avenue—a broad, shady drive lined with vintage homes and churches. Gretna flourished in the Long era, and today the avenue with its "linear park" is the central corridor of the city's big National Register historic district.

Near the river, the Gretna Visitor Center is housed in a 1906 Southern Pacific depot that faces Fourth Street from the median of Huey P. Long. A 1951 Illinois Central caboose is permanently "sidetracked" outside, and inside, around the inevitable iron stove, model trains and real railroading paraphernalia share space with the Visitor Center's maps and brochure racks. The little office also serves as unofficial fan club for the town's three favorite sons: Baseball Hall-of-Famer Mel Ott, 1950s cowboy star Lash LaRue, and rock-'n'-roller Frankie Ford. "Stills" of black-clad Lash with his lethal bullwhip share shelves with Frankie Ford CDs ('50s hits like "Sea Cruise" and "You Talk Too Much"), and at a prime spot on Fourth Street, just outside the Visitor Center's door, a lifesize bronze of Ott by sculptor William Binnings was unveiled in March 2009.

Conversation around the depot often includes reminiscences of Ott's twenty-two seasons with the New York/San Francisco Giants, complete with eleven All Star games and three World Series, as well as tales of why this German community has a Scottish name and how the city came to be formed by the merger of villages like Mechanikham, McDonoghville, Gretna, and New Gretna in 1913.

Then, with all that new knowledge in mind and a map/guide to "Gretna Historic District Attractions" in hand, a tour of the avenue's highlights can begin with a one-block walk to see the 1930s mural of Gretna river traffic by "WPA artist" Stuart Purser. "Steamboats on the River" is one of several Louisiana scenes painted in public buildings during the Depression years, funded by FDR's Works Progress Administration. Somewhat smaller than most, and framed, it was recently moved from the old Gretna Post Office to the Postal

Mel Ott by sculptor William Binnings.
PHOTO BY THE AUTHOR.

Sub-station in the Huey P. Long median at Third Street—a dandy brick 1901 Texas & Pacific depot.

Next comes the 1907 Jefferson Parish Courthouse—Gretna's City Hall since 1958—which faces the Jefferson Parish World War I memorial and the river. A climb up the steps of the levee offers three rewards: a just-for-fun round trip on the Gretna Ferry, a park-bench leveetop view of the scene muralist Purser saw 75 years ago (now with modern ships), and a dramatic look back at the classic *arch du triomphe* and the stately centenarian seat of government, with its lofty pediment and Corinthian columns. The courthouse/city hall was designed with styistic elements of the Baroque and Renaissance periods by architect W. S. Hull of Jackson, Mississippi, and visitors are welcome to inspect the interior details, where they will also find a gallery of Jefferson Parish photography and an Attilio Piccirilli bust of philanthropist John McDonogh.

A short walk from the river back to the depot/visitor center, then one block beyond it, leads to the former School Board Administration Building at 519 Huey P. Long, whose upper floors were extensively restored in

2008 to make way for the dynamic displays of a new Jefferson Parish Museum. With a welcoming speech by Thomas Jefferson himself (obviously quite proud of his namesake parish) and several large exhibit rooms—dedicated to topics like immigration/population, political memorabilia, Carnival tradition, and the Harvey Canal and other catalysts to economic growth—this thoroughly modern and interactive repository is destined to be acclaimed as one of Louisiana's top parish museums for years to come. Nostalgia trumps serious history every time, so odds are that your favorite room will be the replicated hickory-stick classroom of a century past, intended to commemorate the building's origin as a schoolhouse in 1911.

The museum's ground floor houses the German-American Cultural Center, which celebrates the heritage of so many of the parish's founders and builders—the German tradesmen (the "mechaniks" of Mechanikham) of the eighteenth century, then later generations (their own offspring and later waves of German immigrants) who would become prominent innovators, restaurateurs and businessmen essential to the growth and prosperity of Jefferson and Orleans.

Settlers of the "German Coast" in upriver St. Charles Parish are remembered with a portrait of their leader, Karl Freidrich D'Arensbourg, and copies of the German-language placards and broadsides used by John Law and the *Indianische Companie* (Company of the Indies) offering land to German farmers who would agree to grow food crops for the infant (and hungry) colony.

Today's descendants of those pioneers have filled the Cultural Center with treasures, from wooden "immigration trunks" (often containing the only possessions of Germans fleeing religious persecution and unrest that had lingered long after the Thirty Years War) to the grand china and other finery of later generations. Visitors who are on or off the wagon admire the extensive collection of elaborate German steins, and children are captivated by the many miniature steins adorned with nursery-rhyme scenes.

Needless to say, one display case is devoted to the diminutive slugger Mel Ott, whose 511 home runs earned him national fame and hometown adoration. The city park/ballpark on Belle Chasse Highway was appropriately renamed Mel Ott Park in 1959, but it was Bishop Stanley Joseph Ott whose tribute to his cousin Mel topped them all. In old St. Joseph, the big Spanish Baroque church at 610 Sixth Street, noted for its Carrara marble Stations of the Cross by Italian sculptor Luca Arrighini, one stained-glass window bears the bishop's coat of arms, to which was added at his request a tiny glass baseball honoring Melvin Thomas Ott.

▲

The Westwego Museum preserves memories of Salaville, Cheniere Caminada and the old Company Canal.

PHOTO BY THE AUTHOR.

Old David Crockett No. 1.

steam fire engine, a big-wheeled hand- or horse-pulled beauty that would inspire most anyone to chase it to a fire. Patented by R. J. Gould, it rolled out of the B. F. Nichols manufacturing plant in Burlington, Vermont, in 1876, served the Crockett firehouse until 1928, and now, restored to shiny brass and copper perfection, it is the only known Gould or Nichols machine still in existence.

Parked nearby in the main room are two other big-wheeled rareties, one bearing a fancy tank for transporting a product called Foamite (for spraying trouble spots to smother flames), the other a giant and ingeniously simple portable spool for quickly transporting and unrolling extra canvas hoses. Dozens of smaller accouterments of early-day firefighting are displayed with almost military precision around the room, including vintage alarm boxes, rows of firmen's hats with their big brass "D. Crockett" crests, the ornate ring-net for catching terrified jumpers and, of course, the long-poled hooks and beautifully polished wooden extension ladders that in a later age would be carried by, yes, hook-and-ladder trucks.

Through the years the firehouse has been the scene of dances, political rallies and Carnival krewe meetings, from time to time even providing space for city government offices, and one room now contains exhibits honoring Gretna founders and statesmen. Another traces Louisiana's "Path to Statehood" from colony to U.S. territory, in 1803, and finally to its 1812 induction as the eighteenth American state.

The nextdoor cottage at 201 Lafayette was built about 1845 by Claudius and Catherina Strehle whose nine children included legendary Kittie Strehle, a first-grade schoolteacher for 57 years and lifelong resident of this home. The furnishings are modest (teacher pay, you know), but the bookcases, easel and upright piano bespeak culture. Nearby, an embroidery frame and seamstress's form for sewing female clothing remind us that hers was an era of self-reliance, and the larder, piesafe, churn, ironware and woodburning stove in the kitchen indicate a proper reverence for Southern cooking.

Directly behind Miss Kittie's home, an 1860s cottage built by her brother Ignatius faces Second Street and now contains the

A few blocks away, at Lafayette and Second Streets, the Gretna Historical Society has assembled a complex of vintage buildings that ranks among Louisiana's most casual and fun-loving museums: an antebellum firehouse surrounded by a working blacksmith shop and three classic end-gable Creole cottages.

The David Crockett Volunteer Fire Company No. 1—revered as the oldest continuously active volunteer fire company in the nation and Louisiana's official State Fire Museum—was built in 1859 with an open-air Greek Revival cupola/belfry, plenty high enough for keeping a watchful eye on the shops and cottages of early-day Gretna. The landmark is filled with treasures of firefighting history, but star of the show is its Gould #31

Local History Museum, featuring arts and items relating to politics, law enforcement, religion and other aspects of Nineteenth-Century life. The "Mayors Room" honors civic leaders from the time of the city's founding, including family descendant Edward Strehle who was mayor from 1933 to '41, and the first mayor, John Ehret, 1913 to '17.

The cottage at 209 Lafayette is the birthplace of another teacher, Lily White Ruppel, whose blacksmith father built the cottage in the 1840s. The William D. White House is now the Historical Society's reception center, and behind it stands a working smithy that not only honors White's profession but bears a sign that commemorates the odd story of Gretna's naming: "Weddings done here...only till the fire is out."

It is here, with their hammers and "hardies" and anvils and forge, that volunteers preserve the craft and art of ironwork and tell a tale of a long-ago blacksmith who lived and plied his trade in the Scottish town of Gretna Green. Smiths, in that time and place, were empowered to perform civil ceremonies, and this one inspired a popular play by befriending and marrying runaway British teenagers, too young to be wed in England without parental permission. And Mechanikham, it seems, had a judge or justice of the peace who also gained fame for accommodating young elopers, so many that it earned for his community—after the road-show version of "Gretna Green, or a Trip to Scotland" had come to town—the nickname of Gretna Green, later shortened to Gretna and made official.

In that tradition, the local blacksmith shop is now made available for weddings and "reaffirmations of vows," for which the smith's role is to add a ceremonial reading of an old Gretna Green proclamation and make the anvil ring with a stroke of the hammer to symbolize, like the joining of metals, a strong bond between man and wife. "We used to have two or three couples a month, and couples would come all day long on Valentine's," recalls John Borel, the builder and inspiration for other volunteers of the Gretna Green Blacksmith Shop. "Of course it dropped off after Hurricane Katrina, but we were back up to 23 ceremonies for Valentine's last year (2007) and 22 this year."

LAND OF LAFITTE

Crossing the great Harvey Canal at dizzying heights, or gliding under it by way of the Harvey Tunnel, the Westbank Expressway leads from Gretna to Barataria Boulevard, which earns its name by leading south to the wetlands. The old road (alias Highway 45) essentially follows Bayou des Familles to and through Lafitte National Park, with the new Lafitte Parkway (Louisiana 3134) forking away to provide a straighter route to the town of Jean Lafitte.

An enthusiast can spend days hiking and canoeing the trails and waters of the park's vast Barataria Preserve, and most anyone would enjoy spending an hour or so at the National Park Visitor Center, with its ingenious interactive displays that introduce the wildlife and ecosystems of Louisiana's swamps and marsh. Youngsters can pop open the "lid" of a cypress stump and find the swamp's tiniest denizens burrowed inside, while parents press the selection buttons of video kiosks to gain a better understanding of coastal erosion and land-loss restoration projects. Then, when a ranger announces the start of "Wings over the Wetlands" in the center's theater, take a seat for an IMAX-quality introduction to the indigenous and migratory birdlife of the Louisiana Gulf Coast.

▲

The sole surviving fire engine of its kind, on display at Old David Crockett No. 1.
PHOTO BY THE AUTHOR.

The town of Jean Lafitte, home of the World Champion Pirogue Races each June, is only a block wide but meanders several miles alongside Bayou Barataria. As Highway 3134 descends from the big Bayou Barataria bridge and loops back to the bayou's east bank, the Lafitte Welcome Center is waiting to guide new arrivals, of course, but, more than that, to thoroughly entertain them. There are bayou-cruise, airboat and fishing-guide brochures by the dozen, as one would expect; the small theater's short introductory film is lively and informative; the local art and photography gallery is worth your attention; the welcoming staff is a font of Baratarian lore...but then comes the town's pride and joy, the little show that never fails to astound the unexpecting: the Welcome Center's twelve-stage perpetual-motion puppet play that tells the story of Jean Laffite and the Battle of New Orleans as you have never imagined it.

This is a Disney-quality presentation that "played" the French Quarter until 2001, when it was purchased and given this most appropriate home, and every single scene could stand alone as a facinating diversion. Pirates ransack flaming ships, landlubbers gather 'round to bid for loot, Jean Laffite rallies his rowdies to rout the Redcoats, Andy doffs his hat and rears his steed in the precise pose of his Jackson Square statue, and even the poor wretch taking that saber through the belly seems to accept his fate with a show-must-go-on attitude.

Downstream via Jean Lafitte Boulevard, a left turn on City Park Street leads to a pristine forty-acre swamp that you can explore on a first-class mile-long boardwalk. Maintained by the local Better Swamps and Gardens Club, it is a highlight of the town's Louisiana Iris Celebration each April, complete with pleasant benches and gazebos for observing the egret rookery.

Thanks to the allocation of space in a portion of the town's new Multipurpose Building near City Hall in 2008, the Louisiana Fisheries Museum—nutured through its first seven years of growing pains in a 1900 one-room schoolhouse by retired swampman Ray Romagasse and his "assistant" Ray Jr.—can look forward to a future of ample climate-controlled space for the protection and display of the priceless arts and items donated to this collection by individuals and organizations thoughout the state. Shrimp seines hang from the ceiling above well-crafted boat models, net-knitting and fur-drying displays and vintage duck decoys—in short, the entire history in capsule form of man's reliance on the fish, reptiles and fur-bearing critters that have provided livelihoods for this region's Acadians, Islenos, Chinese, and Croatians for three centuries.

One giant diorama presents a shrimpboat and wharf scene, complete with seascape backdrop, surrounded by smaller but equally dramatic displays of authentic cypress pirogues, otter and mink pelts from the Louisiana Fur Council, an Indian skiff, a twelve-foot stuffed alligator and, of course, exhibit cases filled with colorfully labeled cans of dried shrimp, baked oysters and other delicacies produced in Louisiana for the grocery shelves of America.

Norman Ulrich heats iron at the Gretna Green smithy.

PHOTO BY THE AUTHOR.

Jean Lafitte's historic Fleming Plantation Cemetery (also known as the Berthoud Cemetery) and Perrin Cemetery are nearby, both occupying the heights of ancient Indian burial mounds. The Perrin was famous among writers and photographers of the mid-twentieth century as setting of a popular fable that it was site of the unmarked graves of Jean Laffite, John Paul Jones and, yes, Napoleon. Many locals swore by the legend, including at least one member of the Perrin family who maintained the cemetery for decades, and while many other citizens of the community smiled, they did not disagree.

WEST WE GO

From Barataria Boulevard in Marrero, the Westbank Expressway leads upriver to the Westwego Tourist Center at the corner of Louisiana Street. A few blocks north on Louisiana and three blocks right on Short Street is Sala Avenue, which leads past the new Wego Market (its little facades commemorating the old storefronts of Westwego's historic Salaville district) to the old general General Merchandise Store at Sala and Second Street, built in 1907 by Duroc Terrebonne to replace the earlier Fishermen's Exchange when it was destroyed by fire. In recent years, Monograph 14 of the Jefferson Parish Historical Series (entitled *Westwego, from Cheniere to Canal*, by Daniel Alario, Sr., and William Reeves) has captured the attention of Westwego and inspired the City to purchase and restore the landmark to house today's Westwego Historical Museum.

Aisles and display cases still contain vintage merchandise, from jars of jawbreakers to loops of barbed wire, and one room is dedicated to community history. There reposes a twelve-foot stuffed gator dubbed, of course, Salagator, and a nearby display case holds memories of the commerce that grew up along the Company Canal between Cheniere Caminada and Westwego after the Civil War, and the hurricane that destroyed Caminada it in 1893.

Upstairs rooms are furnished to re-create their role as the owner's home, and the

backyard cistern and privy also remind us that the old structure housed a family as well as a thriving business.

▲

A pirate's tale in puppetry at the Jean Lafitte Welcome Center.

PHOTOS BY THE AUTHOR.

RIVERTOWN

Between Airline Highway and the Mississippi in Kenner, the Rivertown historic district, defined by the final blocks of Williams Boulevard and its crossing streets, is a pleasant mix of shops, restaurants, Planetarium/MegaDome, art gallery and repertory theater. Two of the district's buildings are listed on the

National Register of Historic Places—the old Kenner Town Hall at 1903 Short Street and the Felix-Block Building, a handsome Italianate commercial structure at 303 Williams—and interwoven in the fabric of the district are stitches of history presenting what must be the most eclectic museum mix in the state.

Indoor exhibit and performance spaces, after some post-Katrina rearrangements, feature such specialty collections as a Science Center and "Space Station Kenner" (full-scale replica of a NASA space station), dazzling Mardi Gras exhibits, nostalgic toy train collection and the Renaissance-flavored Children's Castle. Native American groups from Louisiana and surrounding states present their storytelling, cooking, dancing and crafts traditions at a re-created Eighteenth-Century Cannes Brulees village almost every weekend, with two especially large and festive gatherings twice a year, the spring Powwow and fall Crafts Day.

In the center of it all, Heritage Park recaptures the spirit of early-day Kenner with "old-timey" gas station, packing shed, icehouse, blacksmith shop and white-spired church, all situated around a fountain and idyllic village green.

At the levee where Williams meets the river, the Rivertown district is anchored by LaSalle's Landing Park, where a lifesize carving of that great explorer (commemorating his stopover in the vicinity in 1682) stands near a perfect replica of a ten-pounder Parrott cannon of the sort manufactured in the early months of the Civil War by the Coleman Foundary of Kenner. The leveetop here is a fine spot for watching the ships go by, with the plaza's cluster of American flags popping in the river breeze, or for watching one moment, captured in bronze, of the world championship heavyweight bout between English champion Jem Mace and American champ Thomas Allen, which occurred just upriver on May 10, 1870. Commissioned by the Kenner Lions Club and created by sculptor Paul Perret, the statue was dedicated in 1988.

▲

Heritage Village at Kenner's Rivertown.

PHOTO BY ERIC LINCOLN.

CHAPTER XV

LITERATURE & FILM

Abe Lincoln said "Give me a man who loves his own place," so it's all right: don't deny the little rush you get when you come across a local reference in some national best-seller, old or new, or find some local character or piece of locale woven into the plot of an old movie or a brand new feature down at the theater.

Grand Isle alone has given us three important American novels. *Chita* (Harper & Bros., 1889) by the great Lafcadio Hearn is not one of them, even though it begins with beautifully descriptive passages about Grand Terre and Grand Isle, because it quickly moves on to that novel's chief concern, the hurricane of 1856 and its destruction of the Last Island resort hotel in Terrebonne Parish waters. No, the world would have to wait another decade for Kate Chopin's acclaimed story

Between the two of them, the major film versions of the Jean Laffite story spun off a paperback, a comic book, and a "Big-Little Book."

PHOTO BY THE AUTHOR.

of desire and dispair called *The Awakening* (Stone & Co.), set in Grand Isle and New Orleans, published in 1899 and still frequently reissued. Heck, you know it's important when it gets its own *Cliff Notes*, and it was filmed as *The End of August* in 1982 and for television as *Grand Isle* in 1991.

James K. Feibleman was a Tulane philosophy professor and four-time novelist whose *The Long Habit* (Duell, Sloan & Pearce, 1948) was a not-surprisingly philosophical story of the resort community and villagers of 1940s Grand Isle, which he renamed Isle Cheniere in "Hamilton" Parish for purposes of his tale-telling.

Ten years later, Shirley Ann Grau, Feibleman's wife and later a winner of the Pulitzer for her *Keepers of the House*, used the island as setting for *The Hard Blue Sky* (Knopf, 1958) but called it Isle aux Chiens (Isle of Oaks) and, to establish more remoteness for purposes of her plot, moved it a bit farther out to sea.

The 1920s brought the black-dialect stories of R. Emmet Kennedy of Gretna, an author honored by a memorial gathering at the Gretna Market on May 19, 1995, where members of the Westbank's black community voiced appreciation for Kennedy's works as the only record of the lives and folkways of their early-twentieth-century Westwego and Gretna ancestors. The 1920s and '30s was the age of dialect literature, when, for example, Roark Bradford's several best-selling stories of black culture and religion in Louisiana were spawning a Pulitzer-winning play and Academy Award-winning film, and Kennedy's short stories of Gretna's River Road in *Black Cameos* (Boni, 1924) and *Gritny People* (Dodd Mead, 1927) also captured the interest and affection of America. His final work of local fiction was a novel set along the river in today's Westwego, *Red Bean Row* (Dodd Mead, 1929), named for the neighborhood established by former Seven Oaks house and field workers whose Baptist church, called True Vine, occupied two of the first lots sold by Pablo Sala in historic Salaville.

Harnett Kane's novelized biography of John McDonogh, *Pathway to the Stars* (Doubleday, 1950), was one of that perennially best-selling historian's few departures from straightforward documentary presentation. McDonogh was a nationally well-known character in his day, and remains so in Louisiana and Maryland, but Kane's popular novel gave the philanthropist a personality and revived nationwide consciousness of his achievements exactly one century after his death. The setting, appropriately, is divided almost equally between the westbank McDonoghville plantation and the French Quarter and old business district across the river.

A small library would have trouble containing all the published accounts of pirate/patriot Jean Laffite, of which the non-fiction works range from history to misguided history to blatantly bad history. Then there are the sensationalized accounts created purely for entertainment value, perhaps the first of which was John Holt Ingraham's ostensibly factual *Lafitte: The Pirate of the Gulf* (Harper & Bros.), presented as a novel in 1836 and as a Superior Stories comic in 1955.

Lyle Saxon, Stanley Clisby Arthur, Robert Tallant, and others authored serious attempts at reality in the 1920s and '30s. Saxon's *Lafitte the Pirate* (Century, 1930) inspired the first Laffite movie, director John Ford's *The Buccaneer* (starring Fredric March) in 1938, and Tallant's *The Pirate Lafitte and the Battle of New Orleans* is cherished because of the lively illustrations by beloved local cartoonist John Chase.

In 1943 the publishers of the great old *Jefferson Parish Yearly Review* had a brilliant concept that was executed by a dream-team of local talent: *The Land of Lafitte the Pirate*. After the foreword by Lyle Saxon comes a visual tour of the Barataria wetlands and barrier islands featuring photographs by Eugene Delcroix (still in demand today) and scenes by master

▲

PHOTO BY THE AUTHOR.

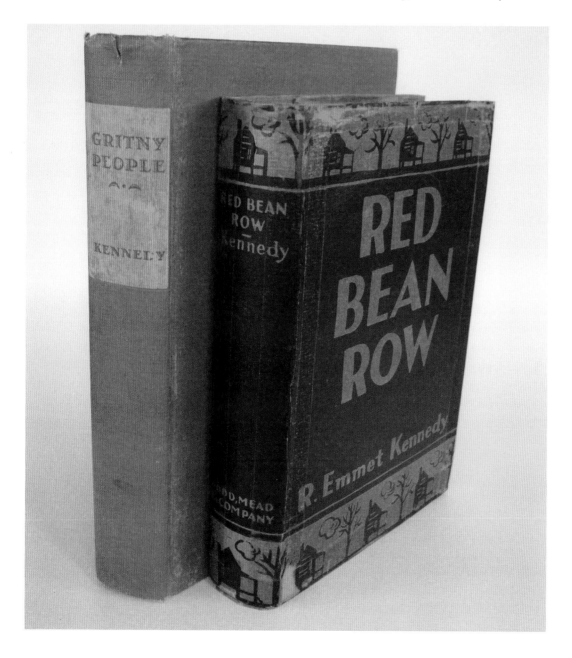

illustrator Tilden Landry, laid out so as to illustrate page by page the flow of writer Ray Thompson's story. Worth a search.

Yul Brynner is Laffite, Charlton Heston is Andy Jackson, and Charles Boyer is Dominique Youx in Cecil B. DeMille's 1958 remake of *The Buccaneer*, which spun off a Classics Illustrated comic and a paperback of the screenplay.

During her research for *Gretna—a Sesquicentennial Salute*, published as the Jefferson Historical Commission's Monograph IX in 1986, author Mary Curry, Ph.D., unearthed an early who-dun-it movie involving murder during a Mississippi River crossing of a passenger train on one of Gretna's two railroad transfer ferries. The "starring" ferry was the old sidewheeler *L.S. Thorn*,

capable of shuttling eighteen freight cars or nine passenger cars at a time from levee to levee, and the film was *Mysterious Crossing*, alternately titled *Murder on the Mississippi*. It was released by Universal in 1936 and starred James Dunn and Andy "Jingles" Divine.

THE HORIZON

With Jefferson Parish's natural assets and thriving economy, it would be easy for natives and newcomers to take their quality of life for granted, but economic stability requires the constant influx of new and high-quality corporate citizens. To that end, the Parish works with the Jefferson Parish Economic Development Commission (JEDCO), an independent agency whose main objective is to "drive wealth creation" by encouraging and channeling entrepreneurship, quality jobs and investments. That agency reports 324,500 businesses operating in Jefferson as of 2008, which represents the opening of some 2,500 new enterprises per year in recent times, but the goal is even greater increases.

For starters, Jefferson Parish, as the "economic engine" that steers the economy and redevelopment of the region, is poised and ready for such growth. Think of the location—the center of the continent and center of the Gulf Coast—and think of the infrastructure that optimizes the benefits of that location:

Within Jefferson's primary sphere of activity are the cargo-handling and warehousing assets of the Jefferson Port District, Port of New Orleans, Plaquemines Port, St. Bernard Port and Port of South Louisiana (with its 54 miles of facilities stretching through three upriver parishes), all busily shipping and receiving merchandise and commodities from and to the nation and the world, borne by U.S. and foreign flagships and by barges on the Mississippi River and Gulf Intracoastal Waterway.

Six major railroads and two strategically invaluable short-line railways exchange cargoes every day (with mind-boggling efficiency) with those ships, with air-transport facilities of Louis Armstrong International and with the nation's major motor-freight carriers whose big rigs glide through daily on that incredible 10-49-55-59 Interstate Highway network.

By all national measures Jefferson can boast a large and well-trained working population in an environment that is rich with workforce development and training programs. Some 84 percent of the parish's 18-to-34 age group has at least completed high school, and the Jefferson Chamber of Commerce provides a strong presence in the arena of matching the individual skills of workforce newcomers (graduates and non-grads) to apprenticeship and post-high-school training opportunities provided by Jefferson's famously cooperative private sector.

Almost 20 percent of the 18-to-34 population has achieved a bachelor's degree or higher. Indeed, the metro area is home of ten four-year colleges and universities, two community colleges, two technical colleges and eight law and medical schools.

▲

Major activity-and-people places like the Alario Center represent the importance of spectator, convention and tourism activities to the future of Jefferson's economy and quality of life.

PHOTO BY ERIC LINCOLN.

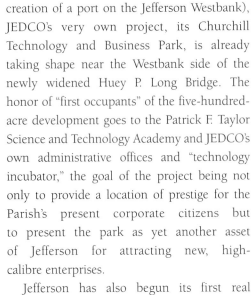

▲

Above: Land, sea, and air—interstate highways, the Mississippi River and Louis Armstrong International Airport.

PHOTO BY BRIAN LAFLEUR.

Below: The Huey P. Long, a half-century old and still growing.

COURTESY OF THE LOUISIANA TIMED PROGRAM.

Median and average household incomes are \$42,816 and \$59,191, and by early 2008 the civilian labor force numbered 232,137 with 225,758 (97.3 percent) employed.

Investment and employment opportunities can only increase as the parish looks ahead to identify projects that will strengthen the business climate of Jefferson and its neighbors. The concept of regionalizing the governance of Armstrong International is on the table, for instance, along with establishment of a "development authority" to put blighted and under-utilized properties to work. While experts are analyzing the feasibility of various plans for the strategic development of lakefront

and riverfront properties (possibly to include creation of a port on the Jefferson Westbank), JEDCO's very own project, its Churchill Technology and Business Park, is already taking shape near the Westbank side of the newly widened Huey P. Long Bridge. The honor of "first occupants" of the five-hundred-acre development goes to the Patrick F. Taylor Science and Technology Academy and JEDCO's own administrative offices and "technology incubator," the goal of the project being not only to provide a location of prestige for the Parish's present corporate citizens but to present the park as yet another asset of Jefferson for attracting new, high-calibre enterprises.

Jefferson has also begun its first real involvement in tourism promotion on the Parish level. Kenner, Gretna, Westwego, Grand Isle and Jean Lafitte tourism offices have been on the scene for some time, but the new Jefferson Convention & Visitors Bureau has hit the ground running, deftly conducting advertising campaigns, creating promotional literature, designing enticing websites and chasing potential convention customers to help fill hotels and meeting facilities throughout the cities and unincorporated areas of the parish.

Those are the things that convention/tourism bureaus typically do and the Jefferson CVB does them well, but it has not stopped there. Its own innovation, creation of the Carnival season's Family Gras concerts, not only entertains residents but tests a revolutionary concept: a bureau that not only promotes existing attractions and events but actually creates new events and pinpoints target markets for promoting them. In this case, Family Gras ads are placed in specific cities, within a predetermined radius, with follow-up analysis conducted to gauge success.

Bold exploration. Innovation. Accomplishment. The same pattern that Jefferson Parish has known since the Chauvin boys cut their first cypress trees on the Eastbank, since Claude Debreuil dug his first canal to the wetlands, since John McDonogh freed his first slave, since Louis Roundtree opened his first schoolroom on that remote cheniere called Caminada.

A TRIBUTE: THE HISTORIANS

A profile of a place becomes, pro forma and perforce, not only a present-day snapshot but a review of that region's recorded history, and the story of Jefferson Parish to be found in this volume is a survey of the works of many.

Jefferson has been blessed with a bounty of prolific writers of history, and their works offer not only a learning experience but real reading entertainment. There is adventure to be found in those pages, not to mention romance, drama, nostalgic reminiscence, soft-sell boosterism, comedy, tragedy—all the pleasures of a good story well told.

Incredibly these past and present scribes are not career historians or professional writers but a cadre of curious and literate laiety—"citizen historians"—some of whom are cited in this text (in the body of it rather than in footnotes, foregoing that formality since most "bits" of information came from so many sources that scholarly footnotes would have popped like balloons).

MAJOR WORKS

The cornerstone of this era's historical writings is *Metairie, a Tongue of Land to Pasture* (Pelican Publishing, 1973) by the late Monsignor Henry C. Bezou, whose intricately interwoven accounts of historic personalities and events produced an eminently readable text and invaluable reference, and two years later came Betsy Swanson's *Jefferson Parish: From Shore to Shore* (Pelican, 1975), which introduced the age of large text-and-illustration-packed parish histories to Louisiana but has never been equalled.

As Monsignor Bezou's *Metairie* did for the Eastbank, *Lost Plantation, the Rise and Fall of Seven Oaks* (U. Press of Miss., 2005) by a descendant of the Seven Oaks Zeringues, Marc R. Matrana, M.D., virtually tells the story of the entire Westbank. As a gallery of gripping verbal portraits it captures that major Louisiana manor at every stage and through every age, but always set against the backdrop of the external forces that drove its destiny, thus creating less a "Story of" the plantation than an important "Life and Times of."

R. Emmet Kennedy, who profiled black residents along the Gretna-Westwego riverside in his 1920s fiction, was also a musician and folklorist whose *Mellows (Chronicle of Unknown Singers)* and *More Mellows* preserved their spirituals and folksongs for the pleasure and edification of Louisianians and musicologists everywhere.

Other sources of Jefferson histories and insights are Henry J. Theode's *City Hall-Gretna* and *History of Jefferson Parish and Its People* (private, 1964 and 1976), *Kenner* by Mel Leavitt (Merchants Trust & Savings Bank, 1980), *The City of Gretna, Gateway to the Westbank* by Virgie Ott (Office of Tourism, 1995), Deno Seder's *Wild About Harry* (Dedeaux, 2001), and Catherine Campanella's *Lake Pontchartrain* and *Metairie* for the "Images of America" series (Arcadia, 2007 and 2008).

So history-minded is Jefferson that in 1974 the Parish actually created a Historical Commission, seven members appointed by the Parish Council and presently headed by retired Parish Archivist Mary G. Curry, Ph.D., who has personally authored several Jeff Parish writings and spearheaded many applications for listings of Jefferson landmarks and districts on the National Register of Historic Places. The Commission sponsors public-awareness events, such as tours of Camp Parapet, and publishes the Jefferson Parish Historical Monographs series.

To date, the monographs include, No. 1, L. G. Whitbread's *Placenames of Jefferson Parish*; No. 2, *Grand Isle on the Gulf* by S. K. Evans, F. L. Stielow, and Betsy Swanson; No. 3, L.W. Higgins' *Public Schools of Jefferson Parish Before the Civil War*; No. 4, W. D. Reeves' *De La Barre - Life of a French Creole Family in Louisiana*; No. 5, G. C. Daul's *Administration of the Public Schools of Jefferson Parish Since the Civil War (to 1940)*; No. 6, William Allan's *Life and Work of John McDonogh*; No. 7, *Elmwood: Historic Archaeology of a Southeastern Louisiana Plantation* by R. C. Goodin, J. K. Yakubik, and C. H.

Goodwin; No. 8, *Random Readings of the Jefferson Parish Yearly Review*, edited by Betsy Swanson and Monsignor Bezou; No. 9, *Gretna - a Sesquicentennial Salute* by Dr. Curry; No. 10, Monsignor Bezou's *Historical Markers*; No. 11, Betsy Swanson's *Terre Haute de Barataria*; No. 12, Edith Graham Giraud's *Growth and Change in the Public Schools of Jefferson Parish, 1940-1960*; No. 13, *Rebellion of 1768*, translated and edited by Wilbur Meneray; No. 14, Daniel Alario, Sr., and William Reeves' *Westwego, from Cheniere to Canal*; No. 15, Bernice Dormio's *Music Education in the Public Schools of Jefferson Parish*; No. 16, *Lost Plantation, the Rise and Fall of Seven Oaks* by Marc Matrana, M.D.; and No. 18, Frank Borne, Jr.'s, *Jefferson Parish Politicians of the Past and Present, 1825-2005*.

Most of the Parish Commissioners are also members of one or more public historical organizations, one of which is parish-wide in scope: the Jefferson Historic Society of Louisiana. Founded in 1977, its activities include the publishing of brief studies in its "occasional" journal, *Jefferson Parish Notebook*, on such topics as "The Great Mace-Allen Fight" by Nathaniel Belloni Jr., "Seven Oaks Plantation, a Lasting Legacy" by Dr. Matrana, Frank Borne, Jr.'s, "Avondale-Waggaman: Legacy of a Family and Its Land" and Dr. Curry's "Jefferson Parish Courthouses."

The Gretna Historic Society, founded in 1969, sponsors that city's Spring Tour of Homes and preserves the five-building museum complex that includes the old David Crockett Volunteer Fire Company No. 1.

Friends of the German-American Cultural Center, formed in 1999, maintains and staffs its Cultural Center museum, sponsors a May Fest, organizes group tours of Germany and welcomes the public to attend their meetings and hear guest speakers at 7:00 p.m. on the second Saturday of each month.

Founded in 1996 by author Daniel Alario Sr. and friends, the Westwego Historical Society has focused attention on the Salaville Historic District by its restoration of the 1907 General Merchandise Store at 275 Sala Avenue, and maintains in that landmark its Westwego Historical Museum.

CURATORS & "WELCOMERS"

Fortunately some of Jefferson's most informed "citizen historians," as museum curators and Welcome Center personnel, have the opportunity to share their knowledge daily. Kenner's Rivertown director Renee Gaitan and her *Cannes Brulees* coordinator Tracy Bruno, for instance, have to stay informed on everything from ancient Indian cultures to NASA space stations.

On duty daily at the Gretna Historical Society's museum complex is Amery Englade, the Society's "official sergeant-at-arms and bartender" who volunteered in 1993 to curate the complex for a year and just lost track of time. On special occasions volunteer blacksmithing demonstrators like Norman Ulrich and Jill Ott man the complex's Gretna Green Blacksmith Shop museum and forge, sometimes joined by the smithy's founder and inspiration, John Borel.

German-born Gisela Meyer, who met and married Gretna GI John Meyer in 1963, is the bilingual and knowledgeable curator of the German-American Cultural Center in Gretna, and the real treasure of Jean Lafitte—the Louisiana Fisheries Museum— was curated for its first seven years by Ray Romagasse and is now overseen by the enthusiastic Pam Encala. Growing up, Lori Guin, now curator of the Westwego Museum, learned Westwego and Caminada history and lore at the knees of the founders of the Westwego Historical Society, her aunt and uncle, Zenobia Rebstock "Bebe" Alario and author Daniel Alario Sr.

Westwego is also well represented by its Tourism Coordinator (and occasional museum guide) Nancy Michel, and Claudette Perrin is her city's official greeter (and frequent city tourguide) at the Jean Lafitte Welcome Center. Gretna Tourism Coordinator Virgie Ott founded her city's Spring Tour of Homes, led the effort in 1989 to preserve the Kittie Strehle Home as a museum and has now turned her Welcome Center into a veritable mini-museum of Gretna's history and personalities.

OTHER SOURCES

I am indebted to my guides to the past, historian Marc Matrana, M.D. and Jefferson Historical Commission member Frank Borne Jr., and to my guides to the future: Councilman Chris Roberts of District 1 who revealed plans for the new Jefferson Parish Museum, and, for insights on the return of Rivertown attractions still in post-Katrina flux, Mary Sharon Howland of Kenner Community Services and Kenner Information officer Emile Lafourcade.

Hours of digging by State Archaeology officer Nancy Hawkins unearthed secrets of Jefferson prehistory, Special Collections researcher Charlene Bonnett at the State Library paved the way to our history of roads and highways, and Gwen Styron and Gary Scheffler of Jefferson Parks and Recreation scored well in the field of Jefferson's athletic parks program.

Jeff Richard and Patsy David of the Louisiana Office of Tourism shared photography and vital information, Louisiana treasures were provided for these pages by Erin Rolfs and Tom Lanham of the State Museum and by Marylou Eichorn and Sally Stassi of the Historic New Orleans Collection, and John Leslie and Tim Loomis of the National Oceanic and Atmospheric Administration made time to search for the perfect Katrina image in the midst of Hurricane Ike.

Arthur Hardy (author of the encyclopedic *Mardi Gras in New Orleans* and publisher of the *Mardi Gras Guide*) was my source of Carnival history from the earliest times through post-Katrina updates, and friend and brother Jerry Volk was a tireless guide to photography and to Irish-Italian and Carnival parading lore.

Analysis and planning in the areas of economic growth and storm protection were generously shared by the Jefferson Parish Economic Development Commission, with much clarification provided by Marketing/PR Director Scott Rojas of JEDCO., President Violet Peters and assistants June Labat and Kayla Aucoin of the Jefferson Convention and Visitors Bureau shared knowledge and photography, and the Jefferson Chamber of Commerce—President/CEO Glenn Hayes, Communications Coordinator Danielle Carrigan, Program Coordinator and ace photo-scout Selva Riemann, Membership Director Pete Percopo and Coach Bob Taranto—were a source of constant support.

References not named in "The Historians" tribute include:

Becnel, Thomas. *The Barrow Family and the Barataria and Lafourche Canal*. Baton Rouge, Louisiana: LSU Press, 1989.

Conrad, Glenn, editor. *Dictionary of Louisiana Biography*., Lafayette, Louisiana: Louisiana Historical Association and Center for Louisiana Studies, 1988.,

Field, Martha R. *Louisiana Voyages, the Travel Writings of Catharine Cole*. Jack and Joan McLaughlin, editors. University Press of Miss., 2006.

Hardy, Arthur. *Mardi Gras in New Orleans, an Illustrated History*, third edition. New Orleans, Louisiana: Arthur Hardy Enterprises, 2007.,

Hirsch, Robert and Barbara Schultz. *Wedell-Williams Air Service*. California: Little Buttes Publishing, 2001.

Parkerson, Codman. *New Orleans, America's Most Fortified City*. New Orleans: The Quest, 1990.

INDEX

SHARING THE HERITAGE

Historic profiles of businesses, organizations, and families that have contributed to the development and economic base of Jefferson Parish

▲

JEFFERSON PARISH

Quality of Life

Healthcare providers, school

districts, and universities, and

other institutions that contribute to

the quality of life in Jefferson Parish

CITY OF GRETNA

Folklore has it that, in the 1830s, Gretna was a popular play, not a place.

In New Orleans, "Gretna Green or Matrimony in Scotland" was on stage with the famous actress of the day, Jenny Lind. It was a story of a romance blossomed between two lovers in eighteenth century England, where matrimony could only happen to couples over the age of twenty-one or with the permission of their parents. With a disapproving father as a catalyst, the lovers eloped across the border into Scotland to wed in the village of Gretna Green, a haven for runaway marriages.

The quickie marriage was performed by the Blacksmith, who struck an anvil with his hammer, sealing the vows and lives of lovers like the forging of two metals.

In the 1830s, New Orleans was very French, very Catholic and very strict socially. For those who were to marry, they had to do so by protocol. For those who did not wish to follow such tradition, they would elope across the river to a hamlet village known as Mechanickham to be wed by a justice of the peace.

The popularity of the play and the practice of marriages outside of New Orleans society led to the naming of "Gretna;" thus a community was born.

The St. Mary's Market Steam Ferry Company purchased property in 1839 on the "Right Bank of the Mississippi River." As a good developer, many of the jobs were located in New Orleans and a new residential area on the West Bank would provide customers for the ferry service as they had to traverse the river to live and work.

The early years saw the residents of this new community band together, for the good of all, and founded the David Crockett Volunteer Steam Fire Company in 1841. Little

did they know that their organization would fight fires and protect life and property to this present day, to become the oldest, active volunteer fire company in the United States.

On either side of the Crockett Station, Creole cottages were the homes of educators such as Lilly White Ruppel, Kittie Strehle and Helen Cox. For their life's work of teaching the youth of Jefferson Parish, schools would be named after them for their dedication and their mark on the community.

According to Gretna Mayor Ronnie Harris, there were about eighty houses in the three villages of Mechanikham, Gretna and McDonoghville in 1841. Just four years later, Gretna had hundreds of houses and hotels, stores and various types of shops. Industry grew as well to include a foundry, blacksmith shop, sawmills and even a public school with sixty students. Catholic leaders formed the first congregation on the West Bank in 1857 and the first church was completed in 1859.

The reason for the delay in the building of the church was because the Bell Crevasse had flooded the area. Crevasses are breaks in the natural levee along the Mississippi. Flooding was common and it was not until 1881 that a flood protection levee was built. It was unable to hold back the waters and the entire City of Gretna was flooded again. The last crevasse to flood Gretna occurred in 1912.

The Gretna riverfront, along with its access to two railroads, attracted industry and in 1887 the Southern Cotton Oil Company selected that area for its base of operations.

The City of Gretna borders the West Bank of the Mississippi River adjacent to Algiers (Orleans Parish, West Bank) and Harvey and has been the Jefferson Parish Seat of Government since 1884.

One would think that with the center of government, Gretna would have had the best of services to keep up with the growing community. Unfortunately, this was not the case and, in 1913, the Good Government League, or "Goo-Goos" with their brash leadership, formed its own city government with Governor Luther E. Hall's August 13, 1913, proclamation declaring the incorporation of the "City of Gretna."

John Ehret was to be the first of Gretna's six mayors to date, many of whom were called upon by the residents to serve long terms of office, each leaving a legacy for the future of the community; Ehret, founder of Gretna, Henry Viering, the shortest tenure of only two years, Charles Gelbke, who served three separate terms, Edward Strehle, serving during the depression of the 1930s, William White, post World War II boom times served for thirty-six years, and Ronnie Harris who has served since 1985.

▲

Left: David Crockett Fire Co., No. 1 was founded in 1841. Present structure was built 1859, now the State of Louisiana Fire Museum.

Below: Crockett's 1876 "Iona Iver" Steam Fire Pumper, Louisiana's only object on the National Register of Historic Places.

A number of public officials have served on the City council but the longevity of fifty-four years by Chief of Police B. H. Miller, Sr., and later succeeded by his son, B. H. Miller, Jr., serving twenty-six years overshadow the accomplishments of many. Chief of Police Arthur Lawson served for twenty-six years in the department before being elected in 2005.

Following World War II, Gretna experienced a population boom and along with it came industry. Beautification projects emerged, shopping centers were built, a modern sanitary sewerage system was built, miles of streets were paved and street lighting improved. Transportation arteries key to growth included the West Bank Expressway and first bridge span over the Mississippi River, now known as the Crescent City Connection, opened in 1958.

In 1964, when the city fathers needed a new City Hall, they chose the former Jefferson Parish courthouse. Built in 1907 in the heart of downtown, the courthouse now serves as Gretna City Hall. This structure was added to the National Register of Historic Places in 1984.

The 1970s saw improvements to the City's infrastructure and a new senior center to accommodate the aging population. Mardi Gras parades began in 1947, but Carnival Day made its way to the West Bank during the New Orleans police strike in 1979 and became a permanent fixture in Gretna in 1983.

Unfortunately, that prosperity came to a halt. The younger population dwindled as well as the economy.

When Harris was elected Mayor in 1985 he knew that he had to stem the downturn. In order for there to be a bright future, he reasoned, the City must take a look and preserve its past. As a collective, that is what the Gretna elected officials did.

They knew that preserving the downtown area would be a major component of the revitalization. Preservation continues today with the renovation of the former U.S. Post Office as the Cultural Center for the Arts envisioned to bring theater and art showings to the heart of Gretna. The German American Cultural Center contains a wonderful exhibit

▲

The 2009 leadership of the City of Gretna (from left to right): Councilman Vincent E. Cox, III, District 3; Councilwoman Belinda Cambre Constant, District 2; Councilman at Large/Mayor Pro-Tem Wayne A. Rau; Mayor Ronnie C. Harris; Chief of Police Arthur S. Lawson, Jr.; Councilwoman Raylyn Reine Beevers, District 4; and Councilman Jonathan C. Bolar, District 1.

of the history of the story of the German immigration to Southeast Louisiana. This will compliment present attractions of the Gretna Historical Society's Museum Complex that features the State of Louisiana Fire Museum. The future will see nighttime concerts at the Riverfront Amphitheater and the Jefferson Parish History Museum will celebrate our Parish's heritage since 1825.

In 2005, Hurricane Katrina devastated Gretna however it was not as catastrophic as the flooding experienced by New Orleans. Harris and the other elected officials outlined three goals for the recovery—ensure safety and security, retain the business infrastructure and have the area serve as a "headquarters" for relief agencies.

Harris believes that the excellent quality of life and deep sense of community offered by Gretna was what brought the people and businesses back. "Gretna is dedicated to bringing activities and permanent infrastructure to its people," Harris said.

With its excellent police and emergency services provided by the men and women of the Gretna Police Department, Gretna was recognized by WDSU-TV as the "Safest Neighborhood in New Orleans" in 2008. Gretna has seen a rebirth of population with renovations to homes in the local and national historic districts of Downtown Gretna and McDonoghville. Additionally, with a concerted effort toward removing blighted buildings, Gretna is experiencing new construction of homes with a historic look compatible with its older architecture.

The City of Gretna has hosted the Gretna Heritage Festival, which is sponsored by the Gretna Economic Development Association since 1991. Funds raised by nonprofit organizations at this multientertainment event provide the community with their services throughout the year. In 2008 over 100,000 attended the Heritage Festival over its three-day period with six stages providing national recording artists as entertainment.

The Gretna Farmer's Market was begun after Hurricane Katrina's devastation in 2005 giving the public access to fresh fruits and vegetables since the grocery stores were closed after the storm. Each Saturday,

vendors from Southeast Louisiana come to Gretna to sell their homegrown products to the community. Throughout the year, the Gretna Market hosts events for many nonprofit organizations as well as providing an economic impact to the merchants and restaurants in Downtown Gretna.

Each year, fall, winter and spring, on every second Saturday, the Gretna Art Walk provides the oak tree lined medians as the location for local artists to offer their works to the public.

The City is committed to working with its business community. The proposed expansion of the Westside North Shopping Center not only provides more offerings to its citizens, but expanded retail space means an increase of sales tax paid to the City.

One of the highlights of his administration, Harris said, is the clean up of the old Malter International site. He was able to secure funding from the federal Environmental Protection Agency to remove the hazards and put the property back into commerce.

In 2008 the people of the Timberlane subdivision showed a true vote of confidence in the Gretna lifestyle and exciting economic climate as they agreed to become a part of the City effective January 1, 2009.

Gretna's unique location, its historic past, great traditions and its strong sense of community gives optimism for a bright future ahead.

Please visit the City of Gretna's website at www.gretnala.com.

▲

The Gretna Heritage Festival began in 1991 and is a three-day event with entertainment by national recording artists.

JEFFERSON PARISH PUBLIC SCHOOL SYSTEM

The Jefferson Parish Public School System is one of the largest districts in the state of Louisiana and is nationally ranked in the top hundred for student enrollment. There are 87 schools located on both the east and west banks of Jefferson Parish with a total enrollment of almost 44,000 students. Jefferson Parish is extremely proud to have one of the highest percentage rates of certified teachers in Louisiana, an impressive ninety-six percent. The System also has the highest number of nationally board certified teachers in Louisiana at 123.

There is an old saying that history repeats itself and since history is a core subject...The Parish of Jefferson was created out of parts of the parishes of Orleans and Plaquemines in 1825 during the administration of Governor Henry Johnson. In 1832 a warrant was created authorizing the State Treasurer to pay the Treasurer of the Board of Administrators of the School Fund of the parish of Jefferson $400 for the last two quarters of the year 1831. Later that year, another $1,300 was appropriated.

According to the General School Act of April 1, 1833, under which the schools operated at that time, state support was given at the monthly rate of $4 per child in a school of ten or less, $3 per child in an enrollment from ten to twenty, and $2.50 per child when the enrollment exceeded twenty. At this time, there were a total of fifty students attending public school.

The first Act of the Legislature dealing directly with Jefferson Parish school affairs was Act 47, approved March 19, 1839. It apportioned $800 for the public schools of Jefferson Parish, in addition to funds already provided and required the police jury or citizens to contribute a like amount for the same purpose. A Board of Directors was established in 1841 to manage the affairs of a projected public school. The president and

Board of Council approved an ordinance of eight Articles to create another public school. About a month later they appropriated $1,000 for the use of the proposed school. A schoolhouse was secured from the rental of Kaiser's Ball Room for $15 a month. John H. Smiley was hired as the first teacher of the Jefferson Parish Public School System at a salary of $75 per month. Those resources were immediately overwhelmed by the public's request for services. In response, the principal's salary was reduced by $15 and an assistant teacher was hired for a monthly salary of $30 but the requests for admission continued to pour in. A janitor to sweep the floors on an as-needed basis, at the principal's discretion, was added. Soon, even with the addition of a second and third assistant, the schools were still overcrowded.

By 1844 the overcrowding was so abundant that the board and council approved the building of the first Jefferson Parish Public School, the Laurel School. Original enrollment at the Laurel School was 278 students. Almost immediately it was obvious that another school was needed. Six months later the board and council purchased the necessary land. Even though this second school, Live Oak, provided some relief, a new problem was brought to light, many young men had jobs that did not allow them to attend regular school, thus the creating a need for night school. The Board appointed a night school teacher to hold classes at the Laurel School. The teacher was paid $25 per month.

A third school was built and by 1851 there were 643 boys and 643 girls registered throughout the six different Jefferson Parish schools. The required subjects were: spelling, reading, writing, arithmetic, grammar, geography, history, and composition. In 1854, two more schools were added and by 1857 there were 1,071 students registered. The division between the two river banks happened in 1860. The areas were called the "Left Bank" and the "Right Bank." With the arrival of the Civil War, education took a back seat to military operations and financial support. Although the schools seemed relatively untouched, at least physically, by

the war, the acting governor of Louisiana did not formally resume operations until April 1865 even though administrative services resumed actively working in August 1864.

In 1870 the new charter of New Orleans provided for New Orleans to "absorb" 10 schools, 35 teachers, and 1,243 pupils from Jefferson Parish. Then, in 1877, New Orleans absorbed students from Jefferson Parish yet again. A yellow fever epidemic in 1878 claimed 668 Jefferson Parish Public School children. But the bad news was not over. In 1879 a new Louisiana constitution "limited salaries, restricted taxation to support

schools, and limited expenses that could be used for education."

Eventually education in Louisiana received good news. Governor Nicholls was elected to his second term in office in 1888 and focused his attention on education. He created the State Board of Education and by 1896, Jefferson Parish ranked fourth in the percentage of educational funding within the state of Louisiana.

Citizens approved another first for Jefferson Parish Public Schools in 1906, a special tax, dedicated to the improvement of conditions of schools. The first superintendent of Jefferson Parish Public Schools, J. C. Ellis, began work in 1907 and continued until 1940. Under the direction of Ellis, the system went through an era of organization and development including the building of many more schools.

An epidemic of measles, whopping cough, pink eye, and colds caused some impact from World War I on the Jefferson Parish School System. The next big change was the introduction of physical education in 1920. Bus transportation was introduced that same year.

By the start of the school year in September 1925 the number of students in the Jefferson Parish Public School System had swollen to five thousand. Teacher salaries stabilized and revenues became steady. Then, just as plans were being made for another school building program, the Depression hit. Schools were closed and teacher salaries were cut in half.

The board went to the people in September of 1935 asking for a special four-mill tax for one year to provide financial relief for the schools. Toward the end of the Depression, 11 schools were built in the Jefferson Parish Public School System in 1940.

The school system experienced extraordinarily rapid growth from 1940 to 1960. Returning soldiers from World War II, the industrialization of Jefferson Parish, construction of Veterans Boulevard, the Causeway in 1956, and the Westbank Expressway in 1957, the opening of the second Mississippi River Bridge in 1958, and construction of numerous subdivisions along Airline Highway brought more families and their children into the school system. In 1940 there were 8,511 children in schools. By 1950 the number had risen to 11,596, an increase of almost seventy-five percent. In 1960 more than 32,900 students were enrolled in 39 schools. Three bond issues totaling more than $17 million had been voted to build forty-three new schools and greatly enlarge the existing ones. This growth brought changes to the system's transportation facilities, school personnel, curriculum, and administration departments.

The school system continued growing at a rapid pace from 1960 to the mid-1980s.

Following the oil bust, the school system underwent difficult budget cuts in the 1990s. Enrollment rapidly declined and then leveled off at approximately fifty thousand students; however, the system remained the second largest system in the state. On August 29, 2005, Hurricane Katrina damaged some of Jefferson Parish, but devastated Orleans Parish and wiped out St. Bernard and Plaquemines Parishes. The system's administration regrouped in Baton Rouge within five days of the deadly storm and reopened eighty-one schools just five weeks later on October 3, 2005. That stunningly quick reopening allowed Jefferson Parish to rebuild and prosper faster than any surrounding parish.

The system continues to improve education with its creation of a magnet school program, development of successful alternative education programs, and large investments to renovate existing facilities.

Magnet schools are schools designed for student that are academically advanced. There are six magnet schools in Jefferson Parish: Metairie, Haynes, Gretna and Ruppel Academies for Advanced Studies, Patrick F. Taylor Science and Technology Academy, and Thomas Jefferson Academy. Admittance to these schools is by testing. The Jefferson Parish Public School System also offers advanced programs in Montessori, arts, and French and Spanish language immersion.

Two of JPPSS' ten public high schools recently won approval from the International Baccalaureate Organization to issue I.B. diplomas starting in the 2006-2007 school year. The International Baccalaureate (I.B.O.) curriculum prepares students for competitive college environments.

The Jefferson Parish Public School System believes in well-rounded individuals. There are athletic and art programs as well as academics. There are football, baseball, track, and soccer teams as well as choir, band, theater, chess, Beta Club, and a host of other extracurricular activities to help the children of Jefferson Parish become well-educated and well-rounded individuals who will succeed in our modern world.

Plans for the future include remaining loyal to the core commitment and mission

while increasing student engagement and achievement as well as upgrading, teaching, and using more and better technology. These plans are driven in part by CISCO systems via funding and expertise. The Center for Leadership in School Reform and the Schlechty Group are also providing assistance in this quest for improvement. As the students continue to grow, so must the School System. For that effort, the Jefferson Parish Public School System definitely gets an A-plus.

For more information about Jefferson Parish Public Schools, please visit www.jppss.k12.la.us.

JEFFERSON PERFORMING ARTS SOCIETY

The Jefferson Performing Arts Society (JPAS) serves the state of Louisiana, several counties in Mississippi and communities throughout the Gulf South. Through its diverse programming and over 150 annual performances that include Grand Opera, Broadway Musicals, Symphonic and Choral Concerts, Children's Choirs, Louisiana Renaissance Festivals, Ballet, Modern Dance and distinguished guest artists of all genres from around the world, JPAS has rightfully earned the reputation as "Louisiana's Cultural Leader." A nonprofit organization founded in 1978 by Dennis G. Assaf and Hannah Cunningham, JPAS is dedicated to the artistic and cultural enrichment of the Gulf South. Its mission is to support, produce and promote the performing arts in Jefferson and its surrounding areas.

JPAS created the cultural climate in Jefferson Parish. It can be said with great pride that even with the catastrophic weather events of Hurricane Katrina in 2005, JPAS has never missed a single season. Prior to its inception, professional arts offerings were virtually nonexistent in Jefferson Parish. Additionally, citizens had no real venue in which to enjoy the arts in their home parish. Dennis G. Assaf and Hannah Cunningham realized the serious artistic void that existed in this community, which relied on neighboring Orleans Parish

Right: Maestro Dennis G. Assaf (left) with State Senator John A. Alario, Jr., at the Westwego Performing Arts Theatre and on the set of Return to the Forbidden Planet, c. 2008.

PHOTOS BY JOHN J. VOLLENWEIDER, SR.

Below: State Senator Ken Hollis, Chairman and co-founder Hannah J. Cunningham, and JPAS co-founder Maestro Dennis G. Assaf, c. 2008.

PHOTOS BY JOHN J. VOLLENWEIDER, SR.

for its cultural diversions. Together, they set out to make a change.

Thus a critical element of JPAS' mission to support and promote the arts in this area was and is today "to be the catalyst to build a true performing arts facility for Jefferson Parish." Since 1978, JPAS has led the charge for a state-of-the-art performance venue in Jefferson Parish. JPAS has championed the positive economic impact and quality of life that a viable arts presence contributes to the community and continues these efforts today.

In 1998, JPAS sought and secured $15 million in state funding for a new performing arts venue in Jefferson Parish through the dedicated leadership of State Senators Ken Hollis, the late John Hainkel, John A. Alario, Jr., and Steve Scalise. Groundbreaking for the new Jefferson Performing Arts Center took place in February 2007 at LaSalle Park in Metairie, a location recommended by the efforts of JPAS. Expected completion is fall of 2010.

JPAS' outreach and service extend to both banks of the Mississippi River. Performances on the East bank are currently held at the Jefferson Performing Arts Center, occupying the East Jefferson High School Auditorium in Metairie. Performances on the West Bank are held in the Westwego Performing Arts Theatre and Teatro Wego! Dinner Theatre in Westwego.

In 2000, after twenty-two years of proven arts leadership in the community, JPAS was chosen by then State Representative John A. Alario, Jr., the mayor and city council of Westwego to manage the soon to be constructed Westwego Performing Arts Theatre (WPAT). The grand opening of the theatre took place in October 2004 with nine performances of the Broadway hit *Chicago*. Sold-out audiences continued to greet the premiere season of seven JPAS productions that included a visiting performance by the Japanese Noh Theatre on its American tour. Never had the West bank of Jefferson Parish experienced such quality and variety of arts programming that JPAS brought and continues to bring each year since.

In 2005, Hurricane Katrina severely damaged WPAT and the Jefferson Performing Arts Center on the East Jefferson High campus. Despite the tragedy and frustrations brought by this storm, Katrina sparked a renaissance for JPAS. With damage to both venues, JPAS was compelled to focus on the remaining viable venue—a recently renovated historical building in the city of Westwego. Officially the city's Community Center, Teatro Wego! Dinner Theatre was born. This venture revived the lost offerings of dinner theater in the metropolitan New Orleans area and further extended the JPAS cultural portfolio.

Dedicated to arts education and enrichment for the region, JPAS offers a plethora of arts programs and activities for all ages. The JPAS Symphony Chorus is the founding affiliate of JPAS. Originally recruited in 1978 from seven Old Metairie churches to perform "Handel's Messiah" with the New Orleans Symphony, this fine ensemble has achieved an impressive record of accomplishments including its Carnegie Hall Debut in 1993 with Maestro Assaf. With performances yearround, it continues serving and enriching the community under a new name—The Jefferson Chorale.

The JPAS Children's Chorus and Youth Chorale were formed in 1984. Prior to Katrina, it consisted of eight different ensembles of students in grades one through twelve from over five parishes. These award-winning choirs have toured the USA, performed with the New Orleans Opera Association and JPAS and recorded two CD's. The JPAS Children's Choirs continue to foster music

▲

Above: Maestro Assaf conducts the JPAS Symphony Chorus and others in their Carnegie Hall debut, 1993.

Below: JPAS Youth Chorale on Tour at the Empire State Building, 2004 (top), and in Concert at Washington Cathedral, 1999 (bottom).

Above: JPAS presented Disney's Beauty and The Beast in 2004.
PHOTO BY MARK EDWARD ANDREWS.

Below: Grand opera debuted in Jefferson Parish in 1994 with Rigoletto starring Metropolitan Opera star baritone Ted Lambrinos and soprano Nancy Ross.
PHOTO BY MARK EDWARD ANDREWS.

appreciation in young people through music theory and performance. Each year the choirs perform throughout Jefferson and Orleans and tour to regional and national festivals.

JPAS provides several arts outreach programs that serve students of varying socio-economic backgrounds. At the forefront of this effort is JPAS' Arts Adventure Series for Students (AAS), Cultural Crossroads and Stage Without A Theatre (SWAT).

JPAS Arts Adventure Series (AAS) program presents kid-friendly main stage productions especially for student groups at heavily discounted rates during the weekday. JPAS provides free study guides and cross-curricula lesson plan materials to coordinate with every AAS performance. These early-morning

weekday matinees allow students to experience the arts in action and give educators an easy way to teach across the curriculum by integrating the arts into their lesson plans. Since starting this program in 1989, JPAS has provided thousands of local area students the opportunity to experience professional-grade theatrical productions and learn with the arts.

Another important branch of JPAS' arts outreach is the Stage Without a Theatre program. This program identifies and works with at-risk youth in South Louisiana, presenting the arts as a positive alternative to street culture. These students are "on the brink of promise," poised for brilliance if given the opportunity to channel their energy into activities that will enhance their lives and lead them towards brighter futures. JPAS Cultural Crossroads provides this opportunity by integrating art and cultural experiences into a student's core curricula. It is a cross-disciplinary program that connects the arts with subject areas measured by the LEAP Test. Artists from various disciplines hold residencies at participating schools and work in tandem with classroom teachers to co-create lessons.

JPAS Cultural Crossroads currently serves students in schools throughout four parishes. On average, African Americans make up ninety percent of participating students. Ninety-five percent of the participating students receive free or reduced cost lunches. Additionally, thirty percent of these youth are special needs students. Participating students are pretested and post-tested by JPAS arts educators to track changes in learning. JPAS is proud to report that overall, students who participated in this program have shown a positive increase between twenty and eighty percent in test scores.

Similar to Cultural Crossroads, Stage Without a Theatre (SWAT) enriches the educational experience for underprivileged students by providing arts-based instructional opportunities that link directly with core academic subjects. By doing so, SWAT improves student academic achievement while assisting the students to overcome potential obstacles of race and socioeconomic status. With many schools across the state of Louisiana constantly facing funding cuts that translate into the elimination of arts-based instruction, JPAS strives to preserve this important aspect of education.

The success of Stage Without a Theatre is measured in such cases as Lincoln Elementary School for the Arts in West Jefferson. In the 2007-2008 school year, during which the school participated in Stage Without a Theatre, Lincoln Elementary received recognition from the Jefferson Parish School System for its significantly positive performance on standardized tests. The students achieved a passing rate of ninety-three percent, seven percent higher than the state average.

Since 1995, JPAS has offered Summer Musical Theatre Camps for youth entering grades three through twelve. Local theatre professionals provide training in voice, dance, acting, costuming and technical theatre. This culminates in full productions of Broadway Musicals like *Cats, Les Miserables, Annie Get Your Gun, Disney's High School Musical,* and *Aida*. The continuing success of this youth program has led to the expansion of the JPAS youth theatre. JPAS Theatre Kids! was created in the fall of 2008 and offers year round theatrical activities for young people.

The diversity of JPAS is second to none in both programming and outreach. Throughout the years, JPAS has collaborated with major cultural institutions from around the globe including the French consulate; the Korean Society; and the consulate general of Japan; Tulane University's Amistad Research Center; the Sofia Philharmonic of Sofia, Bulgaria; the

Houma Terrebonne Civic Center; Gulf Coast Performing Arts at the Biloxi Saenger Theatre; the Grand Casino Biloxi; and the Pensacola opera, not to mention every professional arts organization in New Orleans. In a given season, patrons experience the broadest array of cultural offerings found anywhere, prompting one critic to comment, "JPAS is your one stop shopping source for all your cultural needs."

Since 1978, JPAS has grown into an engine of economic activity for the region annually impacting the local economy at a rate close to $5 million. The Jefferson Performing Arts Society is honored to serve, enrich and lead the cultural life of Jefferson Parish. JPAS welcomes the support, investment and participation of the community in their multi-faceted organization.

▲

Above: Kenneth Beck in the tragic ballet Giselle, c. 2000.

PHOTO BY MARK EDWARD ANDREWS.

Below: Sheriff Harry "Santa" Lee and Maestro Assaf prepare for the Christmas concert in 1986.

Jefferson Parish Sheriff's Office

Since being founded in 1825, Jefferson Parish has grown from a rural farming community to the sprawling suburban "metropolis" that exists today. Over these 183 years, there have been thirty-one sheriffs in Jefferson Parish. These individuals have seen enormous changes in their duties, the size and makeup of their offices, the parish citizenship, and the types and numbers of crimes they face each day. Some have been more effective than others and some have been more "colorful" than others. Some made great advancements during their terms and others crumbled under the weight of the responsibility. Through it all, the Jefferson Parish Sheriff's Office has emerged as one of the premier law enforcement agencies in the state of Louisiana.

Throughout Louisiana's history, local sheriffs have typically been very powerful within their parish. This is probably why this office is so highly sought after. Even today, with all of the checks and balances in place in governments, many view the Louisiana Sheriff as a "king" in certain respects. While this may a bit of a stretch, most sheriffs today do command a certain amount of respect and carry a certain amount of political clout in their respective parishes. This has been true, in most cases, for the thirty-one sheriffs of Jefferson Parish.

Jefferson Parish was formed on February 11, 1825, as a result of a dispute among plantation owners in the New Orleans area. Early documentation shows that the first sheriff was Andres Valsin de la Barre. The de la Barre family members were dominant players on the Parish Police Jury in 1825 and most likely controlled the Sheriff's Office at that time. In the early years the Parish was sparsely populated and relied heavily on the neighboring city of New Orleans for support and commerce.

In the early 1900s, the Parish was frequently referred to as the "Free State of Jefferson" and probably resembled most small rural communities in the old west. In its early days, Jefferson Parish was gaining a reputation for its free-wheeling ways and lackadaisical enforcement of gambling laws. If things were too "hot" in New Orleans, gambling proponents and the like could simply go across the river and set up shop in Jefferson Parish.

In the late 1800s, the Marrero family began to emerge as one of the more dominant families in the Parish. Being a landowner and a businessman typically translated into power on the police jury. Louis M. Marrero, Sr., fit this mold nicely. He parlayed his family's stature in the parish into service on the Parish Police Jury and then in the Louisiana Senate from 1884 through 1896. He became sheriff in 1896 and served through 1920. In keeping with Louisiana tradition at the time, Sheriff Marrero kept the "power" within the family, by having his son, Louis, Jr., serve concurrently as the Parish District Attorney from 1904 until 1916.

Gambling continued to be a problem in the early 1900s in Jefferson Parish and then Governor Luther E. Hall threatened to impeach Marrero for failing to uphold the gambling laws. He was defeated in 1920 and died the following year. Despite his defeat, his name has lived on in the Parish and one of the largest unincorporated areas of the Westbank is now named after him.

The longest-serving sheriff in parish history took office in 1926 and served for twenty-eight years. Frank James Clancy served as the City Attorney for the City of Kenner and as the Jefferson Parish Clerk of Court before

Leo M. Marrero, June 9, 1896, to May 20, 1920.

Perhaps the most colorful of all the sheriffs was Harry Lee, who served for twenty-seven years until his death in 2007. The first Chinese-American sheriff in the United States, Lee soundly defeated his predecessor, Alwynn Cronvich, and took office in 1980. From the beginning, Lee had a penchant for being a "straight-talker." One of his favorite sayings was "it is what it is." While Lee's straight talk shocked and angered some, as evidenced by the election results over the years, it mostly seemed to endear him to his loyal constituents. This endearment was evidenced by the fact that throughout his years, only one serious challenger, in 1987, ever took him on. In all other elections, he soundly defeated his opponents, usually with more than seventy percent of the vote.

Lee was always a staunch defender of his deputies, as long as they acted in the best interest of the citizens or the office. He was also known to be a very generous person; having raised and donated enormous sums for various charities. His rags-to-riches story is known throughout the Parish and, apparently, guided his generosity to those less fortunate.

Sheriff Lee's annual fundraiser, the "Chinese Cajun Cowboy Fais Do-Do," was one of the biggest social events of the year and was regularly attended by more than five thousand supporters and well-wishers. In the end, he would give most of his political war-chest away to charities, hospitals or schools, especially if it benefited children.

You really know you have made it in the New Orleans scene when you are able to have your own Mardi Gras float. Each year, Sheriff Lee and his guest riders would toss thousands of refrigerator magnets with his likeness on them. Never afraid to make fun of himself and his love for good food, his magnets chronicled his own personal "battle of the bulge" with some depicting "Fat Harry" and others, "Skinny Harry."

▲

Harry Lee, April 1, 1980, to October 1, 2007.

becoming Sheriff. During those twenty-eight years, the population of the parish exploded, especially after World War II.

Gambling continued to be a major issue; so much so, it brought Clancy into the national spotlight in 1951. Accused of having ties to organized crime, he begrudgingly testified before Congress and promised that he would shut down gambling operations throughout the parish. After being forced to do the unthinkable, Clancy was asked if he could win reelection in 1952. He testified under oath that he did not think he could win reelection without the gambling establishments behind him. His decision to close down the gaming establishments cost him valuable support in both the business community and among the populace. Apparently, the perception of the parish being like the "wild-west" was still alive and well.

Up until the end, Clancy enjoyed widespread popularity and strong political power. With the Parish's rise in population, his power also began to spread outside of the parish. This was evidenced by his being the founder and first president of the Louisiana Sheriff's Association, a statewide association of sheriffs.

It was under Lee that the men and women of the Jefferson Parish Sheriff's Office faced their greatest challenge. On August 29, 2005, Hurricane Katrina, the worst disaster in U.S. history, devastated New Orleans and the surrounding parishes. Although spared the kind of damage seen in New Orleans and St. Bernard, Jefferson Parish was still greatly affected by the storm. The citizens were evacuated for weeks and widespread flooding caused damage in many neighborhoods.

Living in southeast Louisiana, the department had planned and prepared for many hurricanes, but in the aftermath of Katrina, the department was confronted with many unanticipated and, in some cases, unimaginable obstacles.

Frustrated by the lack of a speedy and coordinated federal or state rescue effort, Lee made a public appeal asking anyone with a boat to meet him in the parking lot at Sam's on Airline Drive, to mount a local volunteer rescue effort into the neighboring parishes. Sheriff Lee was never known to have patience with bureaucracies and it was very clear early on that FEMA was definitely a bureaucracy. Within an hour, more than fifty volunteers came with their boats. By the end of the day, there were hundreds of volunteers with boats from across the state. Sheriff Lee's department provided gas, food, and directions to this "Cajun navy."

On top of rescuing the citizens, the department was called upon to address the immediate needs of its own employees, by providing food, housing, clothing, and financial assistance. By doing this, Sheriff Lee was able to keep the moral of the "troops" a top priority and to maintain adequate staffing levels both during and after the storm.

No sheriff has ever been more proud of his troops, having faced the ultimate challenge of public service. In 2007 the beloved Lee lost his battle with leukemia at the age of seventy-five.

Into this great power vacuum stepped Sheriff Lee's trusted Chief Deputy, Newell

Normand. Newell had been with the office since 1980 and had served as the chief deputy/comptroller since 1995. Recognizing his extensive law enforcement experience and his business acumen, the citizens overwhelmingly elected him to be the thirty-first sheriff of Jefferson Parish.

What was not lost on the citizens was the fact that the Sheriff's Office had become "big business" during Sheriff Lee's tenure. Jefferson Parish was no longer a sleepy rural community. The parish was now one of the leading "retail Meccas" in the state, with a vibrant economy and one of the largest populations. The number of employees had grown from a few hundred to nearly sixteen hundred. Likewise, the operating budget now exceeded $100 million.

As the chief executive officer of the Law Enforcement District, the sheriff has the responsibility for enforcing state and local laws within the parish. The Sheriff's Office provides protection through on-site patrols, investigations, etc. The Office also serves the residents of the parish through community policing details, neighborhood watch programs, and other programs.

The sheriff also administers the parish jail and exercises duties required by the parish court system, such as providing bailiffs, executing orders of the court, serving subpoenas, etc. Finally, the sheriff serves as the ex-officio tax collector of the Parish. As such, the sheriff is responsible for the collection and distribution of property taxes, sales taxes, occupational licenses, fines, bonds and costs imposed by the local district courts. In Jefferson Parish, tax collections now exceed $800 million each year. Needless to say, the citizens have placed a lot of trust in the sheriff and his staff.

The number of employees with the Sheriff's Office was 1,462 in 2007, down from its high of 1,661 in 2003. The department lost hundreds of employees following Katrina but has been able to regain some of the losses since then.

Revenues over the past twenty years have grown from a low of $35 million in 1986 to a high of $134 million in 2007. The General Fund operating budget accounts for $115 million of this amount. There was a great surge in taxes during the post-Katrina building boom, but things are starting to get back to normal. Because law enforcement is so labor intensive, salaries and benefits represent nearly seventy-five percent of the budgeted expenses.

Population estimates peaked in 1986 at 472,000, were down to 457,000 in 2004 prior to Katrina, and now stand at 442,000. In 2007 the Office handled nearly 350,000 service calls!

The Sheriff's Office consists of thirteen "bureaus" or divisions, including executive, civil, finance, fleet, tax, patrol, special ops, internal management, technical services,

criminal and special investigations, narcotics and corrections. The makeup of the office demonstrates the wide range of responsibilities placed upon the Sheriff and his staff.

The plan for the department over the next five years is to continue to provide superior law enforcement services to the citizens of the Parish. Maintaining a quick response time to calls for service and a high solve rate for homicides are priority.

Old favorites, such as the Neighborhood Watch program, the DARE program or the Young Marines program, are promoted and supported by the office. Proven crime-fighting initiatives, such as the highly successful "Code-6" program, which targets violent repeat offenders, are also continuing.

Given the changing dynamics of the parish and its citizens, there are also new crime abatement initiatives, such as the West Bank Crime Task Force that is carried out by the Sheriff's Office and other local agencies, the blighted housing program that provides support to the parish's code enforcement section, or the support provided to the Crimestoppers organization, which pays citizens for anonymous tips. The Sheriff is also investing heavily in technology, with laptops in every car, crime statistic databases, neighborhood and traffic cameras, license plate recognition technology, etc.

Sheriff Normand is also reaching out to the schools to try to reach the children when they are still young. This includes programs such as Characterlinks, which tries to instill a moral compass in students during their formative years.

In 2008 the Sheriff's Office began the largest capital improvement program in its history. Plans include a new state-of-the-art crime lab building at a cost of nearly $24 million. Construction of two new district stations at a cost of $2 million each is also underway. The total capital improvement program is expected to cost over $30 million. Most of these facilities are expected to be completed in 2009 or 2010.

With all of these responsibilities in mind, the focus of the Office remains the same today as in 1825, keeping Jefferson Parish a safe place to live, work and raise a family.

CITY OF KENNER

During the famous French explorer LaSalle's expedition down the Mississippi River from Montréal, he stopped and named present day Kenner as "Cannes Brulees," meaning burnt cane after the method he saw Native American Indians use as a hunting technique. Kenner officially became a city in 1855. A gentleman named Minor Kenner founded the city on land purchased by his family in the Cannes Brulees area. Kenner was one of four brothers, all of whom contributed to the prosperity of Kenner. When the city of Kenner began it consisted of three plantations, Belle Grove, Pasture, and Oakland. The rest of Kenner was nothing but swampland.

One plantation was owned by Jean Baptiste Martin d'Artaguiette, a French naval commissioner. Martin provided many services for the French government and in exchange for his services he was awarded the land of his plantation. Over the years, the Cajuns developed a saying, "Ca date du temps d'Artaguiette." The translation is "it goes all the way back to the days of d'Artaguiette." meaning that something is as old as all of Louisiana history.

Another plantation belonged to Joseph Montespuiou, the Count d'Artagnan, as in the Musketeer d'Artagnan. The Count's family name of d'Artagnan "had come to be associated with loyalty and bravery and was borrowed by Alexander Dumas when he wrote *The Three Musketeers*." The city of Kenner truly has a rich foundation of literature and honor!

The last plantation was owned by a gentleman named Louis Trudeau. Eventually Trudeau sold his plantation to Kenner brother William Butler Kenner. Williams Boulevard, the major North-South artery in Kenner from river to lake was named for him. These three plantations started the booming economy of Kenner. In 1850 the youngest Kenner brother, Duncan, recorded sales of 1.5 million pounds of sugar. That is more than a century ago and the gentleman sold a million and a half pounds of sugar! This entrepreneurial spirit seems to have become part of the residents of the city of Kenner that is still prevalent today.

During the early 1900s the Orleans-Kenner or the "OK" streetcar line ran from Rampart Street and Canal all of the way to Williams Boulevard and Jefferson Highway, where Rivertown is today. By the 1950s word of Kenner's reasonable prices and land availability caught the attention of developers. The developers began subdividing, draining, and filling the swampland and turning it into sites suitable for building. During the 1960s Interstate 10 was built and Veterans Boulevard was improved. These two significant changes made the city of Kenner much more accessible and desirable to families and businesses. By 1960, Kenner had grown from three plantation homes to a population of 17,037. By 1979 the city had grown to a population of 60,524. In the 1980s Kenner was the fifth largest city in the state of Louisiana. By the U. S. census of 2000 the population had expanded even further to a population of 70,517. Then Hurricane Katrina hit. Many people moved to Kenner in lieu of returning to Orleans Parish.

Louis Armstrong International Airport started as Moisant Stock Yards, hence the initials MSY. The airport grew and during World War II the airport served as a government air base. Commercial service began at MSY in 1946. Kenner cooperated with New Orleans in the 1990s to expand the east-west runway. The name was changed from Moisant to Louis Armstrong on July 11, 2001, on the centennial of Armstrong's birth. Remarkably, the airport had "no significant airfield damage and had no standing water in aircraft movement areas" and opened for humanitarian efforts a mere two days after Hurricane Katrina. MSY served 7,525,533 passengers in 2007. The airport offers incentives to airlines and passengers. Among international airports in the United States, MSY is known to be one of the safest.

In the city of Kenner, on the banks of the famous Mississippi River, sits Rivertown. Only two minutes from the airport, Rivertown boasts a repertory theater, fine arts gallery, planetarium, Mardi Gras museum, and even a toy train museum.

Another charming part of Kenner is Laketown. A traditional boat launch site and fishing piers provide easy access to Lake Pontchartrain. There is a beautiful gazebo and places for picnics all set on over thirty picturesque acres. Environmental Park is a new preservation project in Kenner. Reclaiming the lakefront with its "grassy marshes and tidal ponds with indigenous flora and fauna" and building the Pontchartrain Environmental

Center is anticipated to begin soon. Plans for the Environmental Center include educational and informative presentations about Louisiana's wetlands as well as shelters, walking paths, play areas, a boardwalk, pavilion, and piers.

An interesting contrast to this is the Treasure Chest Casino, located on the Lake at Williams Boulevard. Gambling is only part of the entertainment provided by the casino. The frequent concerts, a fabulous buffet, an intimate café, and valet parking all help to create a delightful experience.

Not only does Kenner boast many recreational options but there are also plenty of facilities for conventions. There is the Pontchartrain Center, a convention center of 73,243 square feet plus numerous hotels with meeting rooms of varying sizes, all within a few minutes of the airport. In fact, the Pontchartrain Center has a hotel right next door and is walking distance to the Casino. Kenner is also a retail destination highlighted by The Esplanade mall anchored by Dillard's on one end and the newly renovated Macy's on the other end.

Minor Kenner's dream of turning Cannes Brulees into a city has come true. The city of Kenner has become a thriving city known for recreation, enterprise, commerce, community, and congenial family life.

For more information on the City of Kenner, please visit www.kenner.la.us.

EAST JEFFERSON GENERAL HOSPITAL

In the mid-1960s, community leaders saw the increasing need for a healthcare facility to serve the burgeoning population of the East Bank of Jefferson Parish. One of those leaders was the late Dr. Isadore Yager. He forecasted rapid growth in this part of Jefferson Parish and as an internal medicine physician; he understood the need for additional healthcare facilities in the area.

In 1965 the Jefferson Parish Council passed an ordinance creating a hospital service district on the East Bank and a bond issue was put before the residents. Dr. Yager, with tremendous help from his colleagues, Dr. Henry Threefoot and Dr. John Rourke, business leaders Joseph Domino, Joseph Bautsch, Frank Cicero, Harry Collins, Nicolas Gagliano, Richard McCarthy and John McCloskey, Jr., along with hundreds of volunteers, developed a grassroots effort to educate the voters and pitch their idea. They spoke to civic groups, sent mailings, worked closely with Parish President Tom Donelon, Parish Council Chairman C. J. Eagan and Joseph Yenni, slowly building their case.

All of their hard work paid off. In November of 1965, Jefferson Parish voters said "yes" to East Jefferson General Hospital.

Once the bond issue passed, officials broke ground on twenty acres of undeveloped swampland that would become East Jefferson General Hospital. Now it was time for the real work to begin. Plans would need to be finalized and the actual construction would soon follow.

Architect Jim Blitch was chosen to design and build the 250-bed facility. For the Blitch family, East Jefferson General Hospital began as any other project, but by the end it became a tremendous source of pride.

With the area just having gone through Hurricane Betsy early that year, every detail of the hospital was geared to make the building not only the best medical facility, but as hurricane-proof as possible. The hospital was built at a much higher elevation than originally planned; windows were narrow, bolted in and had working shutters; a generator was installed in case of electrical outages; and a well was dug to ensure a potable water supply. One of the most important details was the placement of all lifesaving departments, including the Emergency Department, on the second floor or higher, in case of rising floodwaters.

These design elements proved critical during and after Hurricane Katrina. As the storm bore down on EJGH, more than 1,500 physicians, team members and their families braced themselves to care for the 300 patients who remained under their care. While the neighborhoods surrounding the hospital took on water, EJGH stood strong, becoming one of only three hospitals in the area to never close their doors. Not one patient was lost to Hurricane Katrina and since then, the hospital has emerged as an even greater partner to the community it serves.

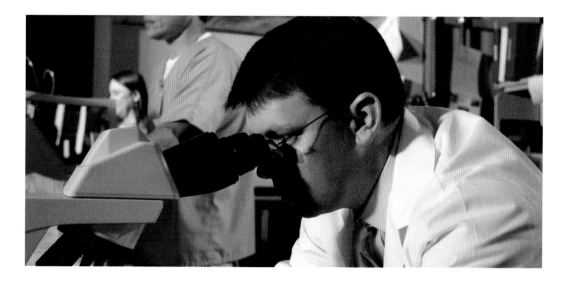

EJGH has been the recipient of many honors since its inception and stands out as a state-of-the-art healthcare facility not just in Jefferson Parish, but also at a state and national level. The independent healthcare rating system, HealthGrades, named EJGH a five-star hospital in the areas of cardiovascular and pulmonary services, including special recognition as "Best in Louisiana for Cardiac Surgery," "Top Five Percent in the Nation for Cardiac Surgery," and "Top Five in Louisiana in Pulmonary Services."

In 2002, EJGH became the first hospital in Louisiana to earn the prestigious Magnet Status for nursing excellence from the American Nurses Credentialing Center. And in 2006, EJGH was one of only a handful of hospitals able to raise their standards high enough to earn the distinction of being renewed as a Nurse Magnet Hospital.

Most recently, East Jefferson General Hospital announced its affiliation with M. D. Anderson Physicians Network®, giving it access to the evidence-based treatment protocols, credentialing guidelines and treatment processes,

developed by the University of Texas M. D. Anderson Cancer Center.

To EJGH patients, affiliation represents new hope for cancer care. With more than one hundred detailed regimens for the diagnosis and treatment of almost every type and stage of cancer, affiliation gives EJGH the tools necessary to provide a broad range of cancer services to the residents of Southeastern Louisiana, close to important support systems, such as family, friends and primary physicians. With this affiliation, local patients will also have access to M. D. Anderson Cancer Center in Houston, when appropriate.

EJGH is the highest volume birthing center in Southeast Louisiana and has won numerous awards for cardiology, pulmonology, orthopedics, and surgical services. It also hosts one of the most advanced diagnostic and treatment technologies in the region.

East Jefferson actively supports the community they serve with a wide variety of outreach programs. Some of these include free and discounted healthcare screenings, seminars, weekly Healthy Lifestyles segments on WWL-TV, the Healthy Lifestyles for Kids initiative designed to educate children in the Jefferson Parish schools and Healthy Lifestyles magazine, a quarterly publication to inform members of the community about important healthcare issues and community offerings.

Today, East Jefferson General Hospital has 450 beds and a medical staff of over 700 physicians. With over three thousand team members, the hospital is one of the largest employers in Jefferson Parish.

▲

Above: East Jefferson General Hospital lab.
COURTESY OF GLADE BILBY, II.

Below: Nurse Jamie Reyes, RN, BSN, cradles a member of the East Jefferson General Hospital family.
COURTESY OF GLADE BILBY, II.

CITY OF WESTWEGO

"All aboard! West we go!"

That is one version of how Westwego got its name. Legend has it that the conductor would shout that phrase as the west-bound train was leaving the station.

The city of Westwego began when Seven Oaks Plantation owner Camille Zeringue left a will stipulating that his land not be split during his widow's lifetime. Widow Zeringue had other plans, soon selling a portion to the railroad. The rest remained Zeringue-owned until 1892 when it was sold to Pablo Sala and became known as Salaville.

On January 18, 1919, Salaville became the Village of Westwego. On September 16, 1919, it became the Town of Westwego. Finally, on October 23, 1951, the town became the City of Westwego.

In the early days, the cheniere, salt dome, and river levees formed the natural landscape of the bayous. Cheniere means "a place of oaks." It is a word heard often in Westwego's history. According to Daniel P. Alario, Sr.'s book, Westwego from Cheniere to Canal, it is from "Cheniere Caminada that Westwego acquired its soul." From the beginning, French was spoken in most of the homes in early Westwego. Even the homes of "immigrants learned French from their Acadian wives."

Originally, the main industry of Westwego was seafood. As far back as 1803 Surveyor Carlos Trudeau noted that shellfish were "so abundant that the different tribes that inhabit these lakes make it their principal diet." However, before the Civil War, hunting, farming, and logging were the main occupations. Then, by 1895, the seafood industry returned as the primary occupation and has remained prominent ever since.

The Hurricane of 1893 formed rapidly on a Sunday and brought devastation to Cheniere Caminada. After the eye of the storm, a giant tidal wave destroyed virtually every structure in its path. Within twenty-four hours, the storm had come and gone. Unfortunately almost all buildings on Cheniere Caminada were also gone. The scene was even worse than the carnage left by Katrina. Bodies and houses broken like kindling were left behind floating in craters left by the crashing waves. Those that survived moved by boat to Westwego in order to continue their fishing trade within a safe harbor away from the Gulf of Mexico.

The beginning, growth, destruction, and return of Westwego seems to have established a pattern. Each time Mother Nature wreaks havoc on this gem of a city, she bounces back even better than before, testifying to the

indomitable spirit of her people. Those fortunate enough to have visited Westwego know there are no strangers here only friends you have yet to meet.

The Westbank and city of Westwego are in full bloom with development projects right now. Westwego is certainly building, growing, and progressing to become better than many larger cities. Some of the delights that await tourists include the new Farmers & Fisheries Market, Bayou Segnette State Park, TPC of Louisiana Golf Course, the Westwego Performing Arts Theatre, The Alario Center, Westwego Historical Museum, the Westwego Art Center, and, of course, the famous Shrimp Lot.

Plans for the future are extremely exciting. The city purchased a former sea-plane airport and plans to convert it into a recreational facility. This facility, the Wetlands Harbor Activities Recreational Facility (WHARF) is unique in that everything is designed to be accessible to the physically and mentally challenged. Plans for the WHARF include rental cabins, fishing, and places to visit wildlife.

The Farmers & Fisheries Market amphitheater can accommodate spectators for major concerts and other entertainment events along with other amenities for fans to enjoy. One enchanting facet of this project is that each building will be named after a historically accurate Westwego business.

The Lazy Riverboat Landing destroyed by Katrina will be rebuilt and there are also plans for construction of a new government building. The new construction is intended to house City Hall, the Westwego Police Department, and the Department of Motor Vehicles.

This charming city, so close to the huge metropolis of New Orleans, is like an oasis. It is like being able to return to a simpler, friendlier, less stressful way of life. Yet it offers all of the advantages of modern technology, positive growth, and financial opportunity.

There is a lot of information available on the City website www.cityofwestwego.com.

All of the progress in the city of Westwego, would not have been possible without the help and support of Senator John Alario; State Representative Robert Billiot; Jefferson Parish officials and past and current City Council Members Councilman John "Johnny" Shaddinger, District 1; Councilman Ted J. Munch, District 2; Councilwoman Lisa H. Valence, District 3; Councilman Melvin J. Guidry, District 4; and Councilman Larry Warino, District 5; and, of course, Chief of Police Dwayne J. Munch, Sr.

It is easy to see that Westwego has kept up with the times and not only embraces the future but is preparing to meet it with open arms. Those same open arms are waiting for new citizens to join the city of Westwego.

According to Mayor Daniel P. Alario, Sr., "The possibilities for Westwego are endless. We are stepping out of the past and into state-of-the-art. The potential of this community is unbelievable!"

JEFFERSON PARISH

▲

Zephyr Field, "the Shrine on Airline" in Metairie, Louisiana, home of the New Orleans Zephyrs, the Triple-A affiliate of the Florida Marlins.

Jefferson Parish was established by Legislative Act on February 11, 1825, during the administration of Louisiana Governor William C. Claiborne. It was named after President Thomas Jefferson in honor of his role in the Louisiana Purchase in 1803. The first census was taken in 1830 and it showed a total population of 6,846.

The Parish originally extended from present day Felicity Street in New Orleans to the St. Charles Parish line. As Orleans Parish grew it annexed from Jefferson Parish such established areas as the Garden District, Lafayette, Jefferson and Carrollton. The present boundary was set in 1874 and the seat of Parish government was transferred to the West Bank along the Harvey Canal. A decade later, parish government moved downriver to Gretna, where it has remained.

When New Orleans was captured during the Civil War, Jefferson Parish was also under military occupation. The Parish was able to take over its own civil affairs in 1877 and its boundary was established as the 17th Street Canal where it stands today.

Jefferson Parish's economy until the twentieth century largely was agrarian and its population was sparse. Between Jefferson's small communities were large plantations, dairies, farms, swampland, and otherwise undeveloped tracts of land until the first great migration of middle-class families and urban-dwellers from the 1940s to the 1970s. In the early part of the twentieth century, manufacturing plants and industry found a home along the West Bank of the Mississippi River. The Harvey Canal, which leads from the river to the Gulf of Mexico, became the site of Jefferson's major manufacturing and shipping center.

From farmland to thriving suburb, Jefferson Parish has a colorful history. The 2005 hurricane season was a defining event.

"We learned that flood control and emergency preparedness are critical to protecting Jefferson Parish and its citizens and have made substantial progress in these areas," said Jefferson Parish President Aaron Broussard. "During future emergencies, our essential personnel will remain within the parish."

According to Broussard, thirteen safe rooms to protect public works employees have been constructed near the pump stations. Most importantly, work continues on the hundred-year hurricane protection plan that reinforces the levees. The parish is promoting funding to protect the wetlands and improve drainage.

Jefferson Parish has charming neighborhoods, lush waterways and enhanced green spaces with projects to beautify major thoroughfares. To preserve its outstanding quality of life, Jefferson has strengthened environmental and housing regulations.

Diversity, variety, choices are words that describe real estate in Jefferson Parish. From the East Bank to the West Bank and from the shores of Lake Pontchartrain to the waters of Grand Isle, the housing ranges from mansions to weekend camps.

High quality healthcare can be found at Jefferson Parish's two not-for-profit hospitals. East Jefferson General Hospital has received top ratings for both its cardiac and pulmonary services, is the first hospital in Louisiana to achieve Nurse Magnet Status and in 2008 became an M. D. Anderson Physicians Network affiliate hospital.

West Jefferson Medical Center is known for its excellence in cardiology, cardiovascular care, neuroscience, orthopedics, spine care and oncology. The facility has operated its Air Care aero-medical flight service and EMS program since 1979. The Air Care program serves the Gulf South.

Business is booming in the parish. Jefferson continues to lead the state in population, workforce size, and economic viability. As further evidence of Jefferson's positive business climate, more than five thousand new businesses have opened in the parish since 2006. There are now over thirty-five thousand businesses currently operating within the parish.

The advantages of doing business in Jefferson Parish are numerous. Educated workforce, excellent healthcare and proximity to several distinguished colleges and universities are just some of the benefits.

By offering incentives to movie and television production companies, Jefferson now plays a big part in "Hollywood South." In addition, it offers infrastructure for sound stages, twenty-four hour, seven days a week film and law enforcement liaison, experienced film crews, film-friendly government and much more. It has become a much desired movie location for films including: Runaway Jury, Ray, DejaVu, All The King's Men, K-Ville (the series), Cirque du Freak, and many more.

Residents enjoy premiere shopping, recreation and cultural activities. The Clearview Mall and Lakeside Mall are located in the heart of Metairie featuring numerous stores, boutiques, food courts and restaurants. The Oakwood Center in Gretna boasts over seventy stores and at The Esplanade in Kenner shoppers can experience a two-level enclosed shopping mall with a large food court.

Jefferson Parish is home to parks and recreational facilities for all ages with some of Louisiana's most picturesque wetlands, parks, campgrounds, beaches, bird watching trails, and fishing spots. Beautiful Lafreniere Park covers 155 acres and is the largest park in Metairie.

The waters that surround the parish contain hundreds of species of fish, making it one of the nation's top fishing spots, and home to some of the oldest fishing rodeos in the country.

For a day of fun, families can head over to Zephyr Stadium, "the Shrine on Airline;" for events, game schedules, team stats, and much more, visit www.zephyrsbaseball.com. Or visit the John A. Alario, Sr., Event Center at the Bayou Segnette Sports Complex. The complex is a multipurpose facility located on the West Bank of Jefferson Parish in Westwego. The Alario Center was designed to host athletic events, trade shows, concerts, graduations and other events. For more information on the John A. Alario, Sr., Event Center visit www.alariocenter.com.

The Jefferson Performing Arts Society is dedicated to the arts, education and cultural enrichment of the New Orleans region. A new performance arts center with 1,050 seats will soon open.

Traveling to the parish is easy. Louis Armstrong New Orleans International Airport located in Jefferson Parish serves as the gateway to the region's tourism industry. More importantly, the economic activities directly related to the Airport generate hundreds of millions of dollars of economic impact and thousands of jobs.

Additional information about Jefferson Parish is available at www.jeffparish.net.

▲

Lafreniere Park, Metairie, Louisiana.

OCHSNER HEALTH SYSTEM

Founded as a single clinic in uptown New Orleans in 1942, the Ochsner Health System today includes seven medical centers in southeast Louisiana and more than thirty-five neighborhood health centers, along with four Elmwood Fitness Center locations.

Ochsner is named for one of its founders, Dr. Alton Ochsner, who was among the first researchers to link tobacco with lung cancer. In 1941, Dr. Ochsner and four of his colleagues from the Tulane University School of Medicine (Drs. Edgar Burns, Guy A. Caldwell, Francis E. LeJeune, and Curtis Tyrone) established the first multispecialty group practice in the South, following the models of the Cleveland Clinic and Mayo Clinic.

When word got out that a private multi-practice clinic was in the works, the New Orleans medical community was outraged. The standard model at the time was a single practice, and many physicians felt that a group practice posed unfair competition. On Holy Thursday night in 1941, each founder received a small leather bag containing thirty silver dimes and a note that read: To help pay for your clinic. From the Physicians, Surgeons, and Dentists of New Orleans. The Biblical reference implied that the founders were Judases who had betrayed their colleagues in the local medical community.

They also encountered financial obstacles. Local philanthropists were reluctant to fund a clinic, and banks were equally unenthusiastic. The clinic was eventually funded thanks to an intervention by a well-connected patient of Dr. Caldwell's. Each of the founders also contributed $4,300 of their own money to the endeavor (about $64,000 in today's dollars). The first Ochsner

Clinic opened on January 2, 1942, in a five-story building on Prytania Street in New Orleans. The staff consisted of nineteen physicians and surgeons.

In 1944 the Alton Ochsner Medical Foundation was founded, and, in 1946, the Foundation Hospital opened in a former army barracks. The hospital was nicknamed Splinter Village by the nurses, who would take off their shoes during the hot New Orleans summers—and would often find splinters in their feet from the hospital's wood floors as a result.

The hospital quickly outgrew its first home, so the Riding Academy on Jefferson Highway was purchased as the future site of Ochsner Foundation Hospital. When the hospital at 1516 Jefferson Highway opened on June 12, 1954, physicians used their own vehicles to transport patients from Splinter Village. The Brent House Hotel also opened for the convenience of patients and their families. In 1963 the Ochsner Clinic moved to the Jefferson Highway campus, bringing the clinic and hospital together in one location.

The 1970s, '80s, and '90s were a period of significant growth for Ochsner. A highly specialized group practice, it was also a teaching hospital involved in medical research. Ochsner saw many milestones during this period, including the first heart transplant in the Gulf South, which was performed by Dr. John Ochsner, a son of Alton Ochsner, in 1970. During this period,

▲

Above: The original Ochsner Clinic building located at the corner of Prytania and Aline Streets in uptown New Orleans.

Below: Ochsner's five founders. Back row, (from left to right): Drs. Francis LeJeune, Curtis Tyrone, and Alton Ochsner. Front row (from left to right): Drs. Edgar Burns and Guy Caldwell.

Ochsner was also the site of Louisiana's first heart-lung transplant; the birth of Louisiana's first surviving set of quadruplets; and the first successful adult and pediatric kidney transplants in the Gulf South. The organization expanded its presence with neighborhood clinics staffed with primary care physicians, as well as branches in Baton Rouge and on the North Shore.

Until August 31, 2001, the Ochsner institutions consisted of three separate companies that operated in conjunction with one another: Ochsner Clinic, Ochsner Foundation Hospital, and the Alton Ochsner Medical Foundation. In order to create an integrated healthcare provider, the physician partners of Ochsner Clinic voted to merge these companies into a single nonprofit entity.

The institution now known as the Ochsner Health System is headquartered in New Orleans and is one of the largest healthcare systems in the region. Ochsner is also one of the largest non-university-based teaching hospitals in the country, conducting more than three hundred ongoing research trials annually.

In the aftermath of Hurricane Katrina, Ochsner has continued its commitment to excellent healthcare in southeast Louisiana. In 2006, Ochsner acquired three new hospitals in the New Orleans area: Ochsner Medical Center-West Bank, Ochsner Baptist Medical Center, and Ochsner Medical Center-Kenner

(formerly Meadowcrest Hospital, Memorial Medical Center, and Kenner Regional Medical Center, respectively). Additionally, Ochsner acquired St. Anne General Hospital in Raceland, Louisiana, which now provides specialty care in Lafourche Parish as Ochsner St. Anne General Hospital.

In 2007, Ochsner treated more than 38,000 inpatients (hospital) and more than 1.5 million outpatients (clinic services) throughout the system. Ochsner employs more than 10,000 employees and 600 physicians in 80 medical specialties and subspecialties.

Ochsner was ranked one of the "Best Places to Work" by *New Orleans CityBusiness* in 2005, 2006, and 2007 and received the "Consumer Choice for Healthcare in New Orleans" for twelve consecutive years. Ochsner was chosen as one of the nation's best hospitals by *U.S. News and World Report* in July 2007.

▲

Above: In 1952, Dr. Alton Ochsner surveys the groundbreaking ceremony for the new Ochsner Foundation Hospital on Jefferson Highway.

Below: Ochsner Medical Center, the headquarters of Ochsner Health System, at 1514 Jefferson Highway as it looks in 2007.

JEFFERSON PARISH FORENSIC CENTER

The Jefferson Parish Forensic Center, located in Harvey, Louisiana, is home to the Jefferson Parish Coroner's Office and the Helpern-Eckert Institute. The Coroner's Office provides technologically advanced methods for death investigation, toxicology screening, sexual assault services and mental health services. The office also serves the public through programs presented in its state-of-the-art, multimedia educational facility.

The Coroner's Office was established in 1805, and, until 1845, the governor made appointments for the office. In 1845 coroners were elected to two-year terms. In 1879 the term was increased to four years and the qualifications were altered to require a candidate to be a licensed doctor of medicine unless no doctor ran for the office.

Records indicate that the earliest known coroner of Jefferson Parish was Robert L. Milling who served from 1834 until March 18, 1836. The current Jefferson Parish Coroner is Dr. Robert Treuting, who was elected in 1988 and is the second longest serving coroner in parish history.

Dr. Treuting immediately recognized the need for a modern forensic facility. In passing and renewing a property millage, he was able to bring the coroner's office from its then existing primitive state at the old Jefferson Parish jail to the current facility.

Louisiana law mandates that the Office of the Coroner perform death investigations, mental health exams for involuntary commitments and sexual assault exams on all persons in cases under police investigation.

To fulfill its mission in death investigation, the Coroner's office employs forensic investigators, forensic pathologists, toxicology lab personnel and support personnel. Scene investigation combined with medical examination through autopsy yields a determination of cause and manner of death. Other services include identification of remains, notification of next of kin and delivery of personal effects of the deceased and bereavement counseling.

The Mental Health Services Division is primarily engaged in the involuntary commitment of individuals suffering from substance abuse or mental illness who are deemed dangerous to self or others or gravely disabled.

"We serve as a resource center for concerned families and friends seeking help for those suffering from mental illness and substance abuse problems," said Dr. Treuting.

The division coordinates services with Elderly Protection and Child Protection Services as well as private and public hospitals throughout the region. Educational programs are offered to local law enforcement and medical personnel in mental health laws and procedures.

The Mental Health Task Force was formed by the Coroner's Office and conducts monthly meetings with all affected agencies involved in mental health services including the district attorney, sheriff's office, hospitals, and social service agencies. Common mental health issues are presented and legislation is pursued on topics affecting the community.

The Sexual Assault Division focuses on exams and reports for all alleged victims of sexual assault in cases under police investigation. This division provides personal support to all alleged victims from the initial report through any testimony in cases which are prosecuted.

In conjunction with the overall investigative function of his office, Dr. Treuting saw the need for a working DNA lab. He enlisted the support of the Sheriff and the District Attorney of Jefferson Parish to form a cooperative endeavor agreement which funds

The breezeway entrance to the Forensic Center.

and maintains the nationally accredited Jefferson Parish Regional DNA Laboratory.

Community participation is an important aspect of the Coroner's Office. "We offer the services of the Jefferson Parish Forensic Center to various civic and government organizations by hosting educational and community meetings on our campus," he said.

The Coroner's Office offers advanced forensic training to pathology residents of the local medical schools and hosts and maintains the Helpern-Eckert Institute, a forensic research facility housing educational materials dating from the 1920s.

This commitment to the community was never more evident than before, during and in the long aftermath of Hurricane Katrina. The storm tested all of the resources of the Jefferson Parish Coroner's Office. Due to the storm's path, the Coroner's Office was spared a direct hit which allowed its personnel to work during and immediately after the storm. In its aftermath, Katrina left the metro area of New Orleans and those who remained behind in a flooded, wind damaged city with little or no outside help for many days. Prior planning in the construction of the Forensic Center provided a generator for power. The men and women of the Jefferson Parish Coroner's Office responded to the challenge by performing many individual acts of courage throughout metro New Orleans in the recovery, identification and storage of those who died during the storm. Coordinating its efforts with the Federal D-Mort team in St. Gabriel, the Jefferson Parish Coroner's Office helped families in their search for loved ones and maintained the dignity of the deceased by insuring proper identification, storage and transport. For all who stayed, worked and cared for their fellow man, both alive and deceased during this aftermath of Katrina, history will surely note that it was their finest hour.

▲

Above: Post mortem surgical suite.

Below: Toxicology laboratory.

JEFFERSON CHAMBER OF COMMERCE

The Jefferson Chamber of Commerce is one of the leading business organizations in Jefferson Parish. The organization was recognized as Louisiana's Chamber of the Year in August 2006, given a four-star accreditation in 2005 by the U.S. Chamber of Commerce, and most importantly, the Chamber continues to grow in membership and community involvement.

Founded in 1997 the Jefferson Chamber of Commerce is a private, nonprofit member organization managed by a voluntary Board of Directors, with committees to initiate programs, activities and a staff to support the daily affairs of the Chamber.

The Chamber has set high goals and accepted greater responsibility as a leader in Jefferson Parish, helping the area to become highly recognized as a progressive Parish with limitless success opportunities. The Jefferson Chamber is a zealous community partner and remains constant in its dedication to the betterment of the Parish and the region.

Committed to the cultural, civic and economic improvements within Jefferson Parish and the Region, the Chamber has worked diligently towards its Mission: "Improving Business, Improving Lives." Through the organization's voice in government, its commitment to workforce development, and many high impact programs and events, the Jefferson Chamber has cemented itself as leader within the region.

The Chamber's Board of Directors has taken active stances on an array of issues ranging from the consolidation of levee boards to high-rise development. Another avenue that Chamber leadership utilizes to remain active in government is the PAC (Political Action Committee). The PAC is established as an independent, not-for-profit organization for the purpose of endorsing and supporting political candidates who demonstrate, through their actions, interest in the private enterprise system.

The Chamber empowers its membership to be politically involved with VoterVOICE, which provides Internet-based tools that allow the Chamber to launch and manage grassroots, lobbying campaigns and governmental affairs activities. The software, through e-mail action alerts, informs Chamber members of current political activities affecting the Parish and Region and connects them directly with their local, state and federal Representatives.

Business luncheons, the Annual Day at the Legislature, and the Washington Fly-In provide other opportunities to connect to Chamber membership and the community with elected officials on crucial issuesfacing Louisiana.

The Chamber steadfastly believes that through education and experience, individuals will be the force behind the Parish's continuous forward movement. Leadership Jefferson, a prestigious program developed in 2002, is a year-long opportunity for a class to learn about crucial community issues (healthcare education, law enforcement, diversity, quality of life and economic development).

Participants are encouraged to use the knowledge and resources gained in the sessions to become an involved and active community member. The 126 graduates who have taken the program have already taken two dozen board and other prominent positions in various businesses, civic and political organizations through the region.

Young, motivated students have also benefited from the Chamber's leadership initiatives. The Jefferson Chamber Youth Leadership Program, connects students from Jefferson Parish public, private and parochial schools, develops leadership skills and inspires future community involvement.

The Chamber has much to be proud of as a recognized leader in Louisiana. Not only was

the organization awarded the state's Best Large Chamber of Commerce by the Louisiana Association of Chamber of Commerce Executives, but also had individual members recognized at the State level. For the second year in a row, six of eight nominated Chamber members have been selected statewide as Small Business Award Recipients.

Members are more enthusiastic than ever to learn about available resources. The Chamber caters to this desire for more information by providing seminars, workshops and networking events.

An alternate avenue for leadership development, available to all members, is committee involvement. The Chamber's seven different committees provide countless opportunities for members to become active in the community—wherever their interests might be. The committees, all working to meet the mission of civic, cultural and economic advancement, include: Business Development & Growth, Community Affairs, Communications, Education, Government, Membership and Special Events.

Babe Ruth once said, "The way a team plays as a whole determines its success. You may have the greatest bunch of individual stars in the world, but if they don't play together the club won't be worth a dime."

The Jefferson Chamber partners with organizations and companies across the area, including Algiers Economic Development Foundation, Crimestoppers, Dollars for Scholars, Elmwood Business Association, East Jefferson Business Council, GNO, Inc., Harvey Canal Industrial Association, Hispanic Chamber of Commerce, Jefferson Business Council, Jefferson Convention and Visitors Bureau, Jefferson Council on Aging, Jefferson Economic Development Commission, Kenner Professional Business Association, New Orleans Chamber of Commerce, Slidell Chamber of Commerce, South Louisiana Economic Council and many more, working together to ensure Jefferson Parish and the Region continue to flourish.

To be a well-rounded organization, the Chamber has established relationships with other entities and companies committed to the advancement of Jefferson Parish. The Board of Directors includes nonprofit organizations, large corporations (e.g. Cox Communications New Orleans, Northrop Grumman Ship Systems, Atmos Energy, East Jefferson General Hospital, West Jefferson Medical Center, Harrah's New Orleans Casino & Hotel and Entergy Louisiana), parish government representatives, and small business owners. The Board meets once a month and allows local leaders to discuss and take action on pertinent issues.

Along with entities devoted to economic development, parish advancement and government, the Chamber maintains a strong relationship with the local education system. Understanding that the future of the community depends on the development of tomorrow's leaders, the Education Committee is a constant supporter of the Jefferson Parish Public School System and works closely with the local colleges and universities.

In January 2007 the Jefferson Chamber of Commerce established the Jefferson Chamber Foundation. The goals of the Foundation are to work to improve education in Jefferson and the surrounding area, and elevate the competency of the regional workforce. During its first few months of operation, the Foundation has received federal, state and regional funding to assist in stemming the dropout rate and improve worker core competencies.

In summary, the Jefferson Chamber will always work to fulfill its Mission Statement: to work for the business community; to enhance the economic, civic, and cultural environment; and to advance the quality of life in Jefferson Parish.

PARISH MANAGEMENT CONSULTANTS, LLC

Parish Anesthesia Associates, Ltd., a private practice anesthesiology group, was formed in 1987 and is known today as Parish Management Consultants, LLC (PMC). The mission of PMC is to provide the best quality anesthesia as defined by national benchmarks, supported by results-oriented and quantifiable management services. PMC will aggressively pursue growth, retention, and differentiation strategies that will result in PMC becoming the number one anesthesia company in the United States. In addition to providing anesthesia services, PMC will investigate and implement other healthcare management strategies that bring value to the company.

PAA was actually the result of a merger of two groups, Parish Anesthesia and Metairie Anesthesia. Parish Anesthesia included the following doctors: Charles Schroeder, Melvin Triay, Stephen Blatt, and Louis Levin. Metairie Anesthesia included Doctors Rama Edupuganti, Neal Comarda, and Rao Kata. These groups merged and became Parish Anesthesia Associates. Shortly thereafter, the group recruited the following doctors: Ron Bernard, Joseph Spalitta, Mark Henson, David Shawa, Charles Eckert, and David Dodd. In 1989, with these new recruits in place, the group's clinical coverage included: Doctor's Hospital, Houma Outpatient Surgery Center, Browne McHardy Clinic, East Jefferson General Hospital and Lakeside Hospital.

During the early years, like most anesthesiology groups, there were few exclusive contracts with hospitals. Often, competing groups worked in the same facility. PAA, from its inception, promoted the care team model in the delivery of anesthesia relying on their certified registered nurse anesthetists (CRNA) to assist in providing quality care to their patients.

In the mid to late 1990s, the Group began to feel the financial pressures generated by national and local physician and CRNA shortages. Due to this shortage, the Group was competing for physician and CRNA recruits as salaries and benefits were continuing to escalate. To compound this problem, the Group's revenue stream was declining primarily due to reduced payment from both Medicare and insurance companies. Faced with these challenges the PAA Board hired the Group's first full time professional administrator in 2001, T. Steven Martin. Under Martin's direction, the Group recruited a management team with the expertise to meet the demands associated with maintaining and supporting a large physician practice. The management staff was responsible for business operations including but not limited to: hospital contracting, cash management, human resources, payroll, billing and collection and managed-care contracting. This component of the practice was organized under a limited liability company, Parish Management Consultants, LLC. This entity became the practice management side of the practice and eventually absorbed the original company, Parish Anesthesia Associates. As a combined entity, the physicians assumed responsibility for the clinical services and the management company was responsible for the business aspects of the practice.

PMC's operational acumen was challenged dramatically by Hurricane Katrina in August of 2005. At that time, the company's operations were statewide with anesthesia groups in Lafayette, Baton Rouge, and Monroe, Louisiana. The business' corporate office at 3510 North Causeway Boulevard became unavailable so PMC quickly established a temporary home office in Lafayette. The establishment of this office along with the outstanding efforts of individual staff members ensured that no payroll was missed and that the physicians and CRNAs were reassigned to areas where patient care need was greatest. Many of Parish's CRNAs and physicians staffed facilities in Jefferson Parish that had remained open during the storm to serve the people left stranded by Katrina. The hardships faced by these healthcare providers were tremendous.

One of the more important milestones in the new company's development was the negotiation of a five-year exclusive contract with East Jefferson General Hospital. This contract and the subsequent business relationship established between PMC and EJGH became the template for future growth. Over the next five years, the business grew to include thirteen hospitals and eight outpatient centers. Today, PMC is recognized as the tenth largest physician-owned anesthesia group in the country.

Another major development in PMC's growth was the addition of an Anesthesiology residency training program with Tulane University. Dr. Frank Rosinia of Parish became the chairman of the Department of Anesthesiology at Tulane's School of Medicine while also providing the medical directorship at Tulane Medical Center and Tulane-Lakeside Hospital. This contract represented the first true integration of an educational residency program with a private practice in Louisiana. It also marked a change in PMC's original mission. By entering into this relationship and by supporting anesthesiology residency training, PMC became an active participant in the healthcare recovery process for Louisiana.

PMC's future growth and development in anesthesia is focused on nationally benchmarked quality measurement, integration of anesthesia electronic records into its practices, and increased responsibility for the management of its facility's operating rooms. Furthermore, the PMC management team has the depth, training and experience to take on new healthcare management ventures in Radiology, Emergency Departments, and in any number of hospital ancillary services. PMC's original mission and values remain intact; and the success is based on Parish's ability to blend excellent management with quality clinical services.

▲

Opposite, top: PMC Board of Directors: Standing: Neal Comarda, M.D., Melvin Triay, M.D., Frank Rosinia, M.D., and Mark Henson, M.D. Seated: President and CEO T. Steven Martin.

Opposite, bottom: Top to Bottom: Charles Schoeder, M.D., Stephen Blatt, M.D., and Charles Eckert, M.D.

Below: PMC Executive Team: Standing: Robert Wright, Carolyn Wooton, and T. Steven Martin. Seated: Bridget Galatas and Kathy Pratt.

HOPE HAVEN

Hope Haven was founded in 1925 by the Very Reverend Monsignor Peter M. H. Wynhoven. The original facility was a trade school for boys and at one point, included an excellent dairy farm and book bindery among other trades. In 1930 the Saenger Gymnasium was added and in 1932 Madonna Manor became part of the complex to house younger boys and girls.

The Jewish community was very generous in helping to build the Hope Haven campus. In fact, several buildings are named in honor of persons of Jewish heritage in appreciation of their generosity. Throughout the years, other buildings have been added and there are now twelve buildings in all. During its history, Hope Haven has become the home of many ministries of the Catholic Charities Archdiocese of New Orleans.

The future of the Hope Haven campus is bright. The Archdiocese has concluded that there are different ways in which the Hope Haven campus can be of greater benefit to the community.

The many ministries of Hope Haven touch all segments of the community. Foster children learn the skills needed to live on their own through the Independent Living Skills Program. Graduates of the program may also participate in the Hope Chest; a program that allows graduates of the Independent Living Skills Program to select gently worn clothes and household items as they go out on their own.

Embracing the family who find themselves without a roof over their head is the calling of the Jefferson CARE Center. The Center is a shelter for families in need. This unique program allows the entire family to remain together without separating the men from the women and children.

Hope Haven has programs to help seniors live life to the fullest in their golden years. Food

for Families/Food for Seniors distribution center is a government sponsored program that distributes food to those in need.

The Program of All-Inclusive Care for the Elderly, also known as PACE, is a new program that provides daytime care for the elderly (fifty-five and over). PACE centers include adult day care that provides nursing, physical, occupational and recreational therapies, meals, nutritional counseling, and personal care; medical specialists may also be on staff. Medication costs, home healthcare, social services, respite care, hospital and nursing home care are also coordinated by PACE.

Hurricane Katrina spared the dorms and cottages on the Hope Haven campus. As part of its commitment to the entire community, the campus houses volunteer groups from around the country who come to help build homes.

According to Heidi Hillery of Catholic Charities Archdiocese of New Orleans, the campus of Hope Haven will remain dedicated to the citizens Jefferson Parish and surrounding communities for a long time.

Additional information is available on the Internet at www.ccano.org.

West Jefferson Medical Center, a community hospital, founded in 1956, is dedicated to quality patient care provided in a comforting and cost-effective manner.

In the 1950s, a group of citizens led by the late Dr. Joseph Massony and George Fonseca embarked upon a journey to develop a hospital on the West Bank of Jefferson Parish. In those days, the West Bank was cut off by water from access to the medical facilities located on the East Bank in New Orleans except by ferries and the narrow Huey P. Long Bridge. A trip to New Orleans for routine check-ups could easily consume most of a day. This could be an insurmountable trip during an emergency.

A Hospital Service District was created under Louisiana Statutes. Bonds were then passed to finance a 150-bed facility to be named West Jefferson General Hospital. Names of the first hospital committees and members of its board can be found today in West Jefferson's Hall of History.

From the humble beginning the hospital grew to the 451-bed nationally recognized facility renamed West Jefferson Medical Center, which serves the community today. In 2007, West Jefferson was the Louisiana hospital to receive the Outstanding Achievement Award of the Commission on Cancer of the American College of Surgeons.

The first hospital executive, David Smith, retired with nearly forty years of service. At the time of his retirement, Smith was the longest serving administrator of a major hospital in the United States. The second administrator, Gary Muller, was at the helm of West Jefferson during Hurricane Katrina. The third administrator in West Jefferson's history

is Chief Executive Officer Nancy R. Cassagne. Appointed in 2007, Cassagne is a native and life long resident of the community. Governed by the Jefferson Parish Council, the hospital has a ten-member appointed board of directors. The chairman of the board in 2008 is Louis Thomas, a local businessman.

West Jefferson Medical Center currently has 1,846 employees including nearly 600 nurses, over 400 physicians, and a dedicated Auxiliary which formed in 1959. The chief and vice chiefs of staff are Doctors Jonathan Boraski and David C. Treen, Jr.

West Jefferson provides emergency, acute, outpatient and rehabilitative services. Its centers of care include heart care, neuroscience with a dedicated Stroke Unit, oncology, orthopedics and spine care. West Jefferson's motto "We're about Family" is advancing the medical center's trademarked 'Our Family Caring for Your Family' slogan. From the Family Birth Place to Family Doctors clinics, to Business Advantage and outpatient programs such as a Sleep Disorders Center, Breast Care Center, EMS and Air Care, Imaging, Diabetes Services, Fitness Centers, CyberKnife Center, Return to Work Center, and Hyperbaric and Wound Care, West Jefferson is known throughout the region.

West Jefferson Medical Center is located at 1101 Medical Center Boulevard in Marrero, Louisiana, and on the Internet at www.wjmc.org.

▲

CEO Nancy R. Cassagne.

WEST JEFFERSON MEDICAL CENTER

Archbishop Chapelle High School

The first freshman class of 236 girls walked onto the campus of Archbishop Chapelle High School in the fall of 1962. Founded by the Archdiocese of New Orleans and named after the sixth Archbishop of New Orleans, the Most Reverend Placide Louis Chapelle, it is a Catholic college preparatory high school serving young woman in grades eight through twelve.

Chapelle was originally staffed by five nuns from the congregation of the Sisters of Charity of the Incarnate Word and by four lay faculty members. Greeting the girls on the first day in 1962 were a classroom building, the cafeteria and the convent. All physical education classes were held in the parking lot, and school assemblies were held in the cafeteria.

By the time that class was ready to graduate, the student population had swelled to 1,057 students taught by 50 faculty members.

In the early years, the girls shaped the school's image that is still seen today. Chapelle students proudly wear the green and white school colors and loudly cheer for the Chipmunks—the school mascot. In the 1965-66 school year, Chapelle's first class approached graduation without an alma mater. Legend has it that Sister Maria Goretti, the choral instructor, composed the music.

The lyrics were then added by Patsy Seamster, a member of the Class of '66.

The founding principal of Archbishop Chapelle High School was Sister Beatrice Hogan. She served from 1962-68 and again from 1971-1974. Five other dedicated men and women led Chapelle to make it what it is today. Chapelle's current principal is Mary Beth Drez and the president is Jane Ann Kuckelman Frosch, Class of '74.

ACHS has weathered the two major hurricanes that have hit the area since its inception. The gymnasium was completed in August 1965, just in time for the roof to be blown off by Hurricane Betsy.

After Hurricane Katrina, Chapelle hosted as many as 450 "transition school" students for several months while their schools were involved in clean-up and repair.

ACHS was the first school in the area to implement seventy-five minute classes to help meet the different learning styles of all students. These classes provide time for lecture, group interaction, research and independent study.

Archbishop Chapelle High School was named a Blue Ribbon School of Excellence three times by the U.S. Department of Education in 1987, 1991, and 1996.

In its history, Archbishop Chapelle High School has educated over ten thousand young women, many of whom have remained in the area and have made an impact on Jefferson Parish. They are doctors, lawyers, judges, accountants, teachers, nurses, business owners, mothers and volunteers, helping to make the community a better place in which to live.

In 1959, thirty-five Jefferson Parish physicians realized that the patients and physicians of Jefferson Parish needed to have their own voice in Louisiana's medical affairs. This group of physicians petitioned the Louisiana State Medical Society to charter the Jefferson Parish Medical Society (JPMS). At the same time, Jefferson Parish was building West Jefferson Medical Center on the Westbank and East Jefferson General Hospital was a distant dream. The goal of the organization was and remains to provide a strong, unified voice for patient advocacy and professional development for the physicians in Jefferson Parish.

From the core of thirty-five physician members, the Jefferson Parish Medical Society now has 450 actively practicing physicians, 105 retired physician members, 227 physicians participating in specialty training as medical residents, and 35 medical student members.

According to Executive Director Charlene Baudier, the organization exists to assist in the advancement of medical science; to improve the delivery of medical care in Jefferson Parish; to provide timely health education and information to the people and physicians of Jefferson Parish; to render medical services to the people of Jefferson Parish in times of disaster; to further medical education; and to work with and support other medical societies of the State of Louisiana, the Louisiana State Medical Society, and the American Medical Association.

JPMS provides physician referrals, member information, educational meetings, quarterly newsletters, and an annual directory. An important function of the organization is acting as liaison with other professional medical associations such as the American Medical Association (AMA) and Louisiana State Medical Society to provide government/industry leaders with impartial information relevant to Louisiana physician/patient issues.

Some issues this group has tackled are: JPMS endorsed water fluoridation and the K.O. polio immunization drive that resulted in ninety percent of children and adults being vaccinated in the early 1960s. The excess funds from that drive were used to underwrite D-T immunizations. In 1993, JPMS worked with the Parish Council to pass a smoking ordinance for Jefferson Parish. After Katrina, the JPMS helped members rebuild their practices so Jefferson Parish residents could have access to medical care.

The organization is a not-for-profit with a nonprofit charitable subsidiary called the Jefferson Physician's Foundation (JPF). Both organizations raised funds and contributed volunteer hours to Jefferson Parish Drug Free School programs, educational displays for the Louisiana Science and Nature Center, Second Harvest Food Bank and Teen Life Counts (a suicide prevention and awareness program).

In April 2009, Jefferson Parish Medical Society will celebrate fifty years as the major advocate for Jefferson Parish physicians and their patients.

Jefferson Parish Medical Society is located at 4937 Hearst Street, Suite 2B, in Metairie and at www.jpms.org.

▲

The 2008 JPMS Board of Directors. Seated (from left to right): Brian M. Bourgeois M.D., treasurer, and Kathleen S. Schiavi, M.D., member-at-large; Back row (from left to right): Robert J. Chugden, M.D., chairman, board of censors; Mohammed Suleman, M.D., vice president; Emery A. Minnard, M.D., president; Carlos Rodriguez-Fierro, M.D., immediate past president; and Robert W. McCord, M.D., secretary. Not Pictured: Sidney H. Raymond, M.D., member-at-large.

ACADEMY OF OUR LADY

In 2007 a new school for young women was created on the Westbank of Jefferson Parish that drew upon the strong foundations and deep traditions of Archbishop Blenk High School and Immaculata High School. Academy of Our Lady lives the Salesian family spirit of reason, religion, and loving kindness and instills in young women the values to live as Catholic Christians, the drive for life-long learning, and the skills to succeed as responsible citizens in society.

Immaculata High School opened in 1956 and was served by the School Sisters of Notre Dame. Since 1979 the Salesian Sisters of Saint John Bosco have been the heartbeat of the school.

Archbishop Blenk High School, dedicated to the life and memory of Archbishop James Hubert Blenk, opened in 1962. Blenk was originally staffed by Marianite Sisters and was eventually led by lay personnel until the Salesian Sisters accepted the administration in 2006.

Although the two schools were spared the physical wrath of Hurricane Katrina in 2005, the aftermath of the storm and the overall effects on the Archdiocese of New Orleans led to the decision to join the two schools.

In its inaugural year, Academy of Our Lady maintained a student population of nearly 700 students. Its first graduating class numbered 177 seniors.

Under the Salesian Sisters, the Academy educates the whole person, using the educational philosophy developed by St. John Bosco and St. Mary Mazzarello. Academy of Our Lady challenges young women, according to the teachings of Jesus Christ, to develop their God-given gifts and talents so as

to assume their religious, academic, social, moral and civic responsibilities.

Academy of Our Lady is at the forefront of utilizing technology. At the Academy, tablet laptop computers for all students and faculty, and wireless Internet access in every classroom and throughout the campus, allow students and faculty to share information on the server creating paperless classrooms. Academy of Our Lady recognizes the importance of complementing this strong academic program with extracurricular clubs, activities, and athletics.

The new Academy of Our Lady High School will create a learning community comprised of students, teachers, families and community members of the Westbank. Plans for the new buildings include an auditorium and chapel. Educational programs will reach beyond traditional academics and offer students the opportunity to engage in pre-professional study in fields such as medicine, technology, and the arts.

Academy of Our Lady High School will be a center of spirituality, education, culture, athletics, and outreach services for the community of the Westbank.

The temporary location of Academy of Our Lady is 537 Avenue D in Marrero. Please visit www.theacademyofourlady.org for more information.

The Jefferson Convention & Visitors Bureau (JCVB) was established in 2000 so that the parish could take an active role in marketing Jefferson as a tourist destination.

The Jefferson Chamber of Commerce and its then Chairman of the Board Philip Rebowe recognized the economic impact of tourism and its potential for growth. Jefferson Parish was ranked as the number two parish in Louisiana for domestic travel impact according to studies commissioned by the Louisiana Office of Tourism. Parish hotels received overflow occupancy from conventions and citywide events that were being held in downtown New Orleans. In the mid-to-late 1990s, Jefferson no longer received the high levels of overflow due to the ever increasing supply of hotel rooms being built in downtown New Orleans and realized the need to create its own destiny.

The JCVB's mission is to actively support the growth of Jefferson Parish tourism through promotion and marketing of its natural and developed resources for the economic benefit of the community and the enjoyment of residents and visitors.

In the early days, the JCVB operated with one employee, the first Executive Director Lance Broussard, and an active volunteer board of directors. The Bureau had no dedicated funding, so it held its first fundraiser in 2003 in conjunction with the Thomas Jefferson exhibit, Jefferson Parish's namesake, at the New Orleans Museum of Art.

The Jefferson Parish Council assists the JCVB with funding and a permanent revenue source was established in 2004. The JCVB and Jefferson Parish were successful in lobbying the Louisiana Legislature in increasing the hotel occupancy tax by one percent and dedicating it to tourism promotion. Therefore, the funding of Jefferson destination marketing comes from the industry it promotes.

The membership based organization provides meeting planners as well as visitors with comprehensive information as to where to stay, what to see and where to eat. Jefferson Parish features two convention facilities, nearly 7,500 hotel rooms, historic districts, outdoor adventure, world class cuisine and gaming. Jefferson Parish is the retail capital of Louisiana with shopping styles from malls to boutiques, not to mention antiquing.

In 2007, the JCVB created and produced Family Gras, a three part festival that encompasses Mardi Gras parades, costuming and free outdoor concerts. In its first year, Family Gras generated over $550,000 in local and state tax revenue and the 2008 event generated over $3 million in local and state tax revenue.

In 2008, the JCVB was proud to be a part of the grand opening of the Westwego Farmers & Fisheries Market that is a versatile venue supporting local merchants, artisans and entertainers.

Jefferson Parish offers a unique visitor experience that can be coupled with the traditional visitor amenities of New Orleans. Jefferson…so close and yet a world away. The JCVB website, www.experiencejefferson.com, offers additional information.

▲

Above: Lafreniere Park.

Below: The Barataria Swamp.

Jefferson Parish Convention Center.

THE MARKETPLACE

Jefferson Parish's service industries

and retail establishments provide the economic

foundation of the parish

COX COMMUNICATIONS

What started as an entrepreneurial solution to a reception problem became one of the most influential mediums of the twentieth century. Cable television, an industry more than sixty years old, continues to develop and impact daily lives.

Cable originated in the 1940s and 1950s as a means of enhancing poor reception of over-the-air television signals in mountainous or geographically remote areas. By erecting "community antennas" on mountain tops or other high points, and then connecting homes to the antenna towers to receive the broadcast signals, television could be viewed by all. Decades later, cable systems would evolve by connecting homes with the coaxial cable line.

In 1978, Cox began work building a system in Jefferson Parish to bring cable television to the Crescent City and its surrounding areas. By 1980 local subscribers were enjoying the benefits of cable.

When Cox first began offering service, employees fondly remember having to type orders on typewriters using carbon paper in order to make multiple copies. On the Westbank, Cox initially had about twenty-five employees working out of the office and only twenty-three channels were being offered. Back then, customers would refer to getting cable service as simply getting HBO.

Jefferson Parish residents became part of this universal information outlet that allowed local communities to connect in ways never imagined. Major events in local, national and world history have been viewed by subscribers from all over the country because of the power of cable.

As Cox invested locally in upgrading the system and extending services to adjoining parishes, the company steadily grew. By the early 1990s, Cox expanded its lineup to include extended basic cable, and by 1995, Cox was able to offer an unprecedented fifty-five channels to subscribers.

The local advancements continued. By 1999, Cox was able to offer customers Digital Cable and High Speed Internet. In 2002, Cox was truly a multi-system operator with the launch of phone service. And with the introduction of High Definition Television (HDTV) in October 2003, Cox remains committed to offering variety of channels for viewers. Cox Communications is proud of its past and excited for its future in Jefferson Parish.

The company is committed to providing people with services that impact their daily lives. Whether it is sending family pictures to friends, automatically recording their favorite television series, or checking voicemail from any location, customers are able to simplify their lives and have the convenience of enjoying their most precious asset—time.

Post-Katrina, Cox Communications made a significant investment of $550 million in Jefferson Parish and the surrounding area.

Cox Enterprises pledged $10 million in both cash and in-kind donations with the bulk going to nonprofits including the American Red Cross, United Way of New Orleans and United Way of St. Charles, Habitat for Humanity and Boys and Girls Clubs of Southeast Louisiana.

But financial assistance proved just one example of the company's ongoing work to rebuild the area better than before.

Getting the word out to the rest of the country that the greater New Orleans area was open for business was critical following Katrina. Many began to forget the plight of the Gulf Coast region two years post-Katrina, yet affected communities continued to suffer.

Adding to the difficult circumstances, negative media coverage had left the New Orleans tourism market in vital condition. Cox rose to the challenge with entrepreneurial insight and led the way by promoting tourism nationwide.

By leveraging cable as its natural resource, Cox Communications partnered with the New Orleans Tourism & Marketing Corporation and pledged to run advertisements beckoning Americans to visit New Orleans. The spots—featuring notable local celebrities such as Emeril Lagasse, Patricia Clarkson, Dan Akroyd, Wynton Marsalis and John Goodman—aired across Cox systems nationwide.

In an effort to expand the initiative, Cox partnered with other cable providers to run the advertisements; the tourism generating ads were shown in virtually every market across the United States. The campaign represented an unprecedented partnership between private industry and government. In the end, the success was staggering, with $12 million contributed by the end of 2007 and a projected $1.3 billion economic impact.

Another pressing need to be addressed was volunteerism. Cox created Volunteer New Orleans (www.volunteerneworleans.com) to encourage locals to play a key role in restoring their communities. The site also provides a one-stop online resource for those wishing to assist in the rebuilding by gathering information and links to area nonprofit organizations requesting help. By the end of 2007, Volunteer New Orleans established strong partnerships with the United Way and Volunteers of America and successfully

averaged 55,000 online visitors per month and matched countless volunteers with organizations seeking assistance.

For over twenty-five years, Cox New Orleans has committed itself to the greater New Orleans area by supporting education initiatives, community involvement, youth development and assistance to local non-profit organizations. To continue developing its charitable ventures, Cox created "Cox Charities," a 501(c)3 organization designed to fairly and efficiently distribute grants to needy nonprofits. Administered by the Greater New Orleans Foundation, Cox Charities utilizes an advisory board comprised of employees and community leaders to select recipients.

In 2007, Cox Charities awarded its first grant cycle—a total of $45,000 in grants was distributed amongst eighteen diverse community organizations. Each nonprofit was awarded $2,500 for their work with youth and education

programs. The Cox Charities initiative has been embraced by the community and employees alike, as much of the funding for the program is donated by Cox employees. Cox continues to plant its roots deeper in the greater New Orleans area and, with determination and passion, strives to rebuild the community better than before.

Cox New Orleans recognizes the necessity of private industry in rebuilding our area. Cox works tirelessly to ensure it is an active and present community partner and continuously strives to improve Jefferson, Orleans, St. Charles and St. Bernard Parishes.

Engagement in education is a company priority. Cox annually gives $25,000 in scholarships and is proud to be a charter corporate sponsor of Jefferson Dollars for Scholars. Since 1993 the company has donated well over $150,000 towards college and summer enrichment scholarships to Jefferson Parish public school students.

Engaging students with Cox creates lasting relationships and successful results. The Cox *Plugged In* television program, an energetic monthly one-hour teen talk show, features local high school students discussing educational issues and timely topics of interest. Additionally, students receive a unique production experience by observing the behind-the-scenes in making television.

Cable lends a critical resource to the learning environment. Cable in the Classroom fosters the use of cable content and technology to expand and enhance learning for children and youth. Cox provides one free cable installation and complementary monthly basic service to over three hundred public, private, and parochial schools in the four parish area.

In the wake of the 2004 Super Bowl half-time controversy, public concern about the appropriateness of some programming has become a major issue, especially for families. Cox Communications established Take Charge! (www.cox.com/takecharge) to help parents manage their kids' exposure to mass media content with easy-to-use tools and resources. Parents are able to learn online how to safely and effectively guide their children's cable, Internet and phone experience.

Cox understands recognition is important in the community. Since 1992, the annual Cox Inspirational Heroes program has honored over twenty-five hundred inspirational student heroes. Recipients are selected by school administrators for overcoming great personal adversity and challenges in their lives, whether mental, emotional, behavioral or physical.

Another significant program for students began in 1995 as the Black History Art Contest. Following Hurricane Katrina, the art contest developed into the Our History Art Contest, a program that encouraged young artists to depict their cultures, recognize significant events or people and remember historic occurrences—regardless of race or religion. Students from over three hundred public, private and parochial schools are invited to enter their artwork for scholarship dollars awarded by Cox.

Cox Communications continues to be committed to recruiting and hiring qualified local residents. With over 700 employees in the greater New Orleans area, Cox works tirelessly to serve its customers and remain the area's most trusted provider.

Cox employees engage in meaningful, fun and exciting opportunities to get involved with the community. Partnering with national cable networks, Cox employees often help in rebuilding efforts. After Katrina, Cox employees worked with CNN and KaBOOM to build a playground in Pontiff Park, helped restore McDonough 35 Senior High with several NBA All-Stars as well as completed numerous individual projects to rebuild the region.

Cox leadership is honored to serve in various capacities on local nonprofit, business and civic associations and boards. To augment Cox's commitment in the four parishes served, the company offers financial assistance to events, programs and initiatives. Through advertising, public service announcements and long-format programs, Cox is able to give added value and exposure to local events and happenings.

A trusted provider, Cox Communications is proud to serve and work in Jefferson and the surrounding parishes. Cox is a multiservice broadband communications and entertainment company serving nationally over 6.2 million total residential and commercial customers. The company is the third-largest cable television company in the United States offering an array of advanced digital video, high-speed Internet and telephony services over its own nationwide IP network. For business customers, Cox Business is a full-service, facilities-based provider of communications solutions for commercial customers, providing high-speed

Internet, voice and long distance services, as well as data and video transport services for small to large-sized businesses. When it comes to advertising, Cox Media offers national and local cable advertising in traditional spot and new media formats, along with promotional opportunities and production services.

For decades, Cox has been a corporate leader in the community. Whether it is keeping up with advancements in technology, supporting the community during times of great struggles or leveraging resources to create astounding results, Cox is a company that realizes its role not only as a trusted provider, but as an active and engaged corporate partner.

HALL PIANO COMPANY

▲

Above: The Hall Piano Company showroom.

Below: Steve Kinchen and John Wright, the current owners of Hall Piano Company.

There are some businesses that New Orleans natives have grown up knowing represent quality. Hall Piano Company is one such company. Established in 1958, Hall Piano celebrates their fiftieth anniversary with a range of services and products far greater than those offered when they first opened. The original location was on the quintessential New Orleans corner of Camp and Julia Streets. At that time, the business concentrated on "restoration of fine quality grand pianos for the discriminating pianists and reconditioning of upright pianos for students." Word spread of their wonderful craftsmanship, and the company soon had to move to larger quarters to better handle the increased work. The logical choice was to head to the biggest New Orleans suburb, Metairie. The move turned out to be a wise one, tripling their space and allowing the company to begin stocking and selling pianos. Not only did Hall Piano now offer quality new pianos, but they also continued to offer used pianos that they had refurbished themselves. Because Hall Piano Company had done the refurbishing, they knew the instruments were in excellent condition.

Hall Piano Company's mission statement expresses their commitment to the community and their craft: "To enhance the quality of life in our community by encouraging music participation. To present our product lines in a positive, honest and realistic manner that

shows respect to our customers, our store and our industry. To educate our customers on the qualitative issues that can help them make an informed buying decision. To help our customers select and ultimately purchase the piano that best meets their needs and desires."

Notice that the mission statement is not centered on sales. That is because at Hall Piano, their belief is that when you treat people fairly and your staff is knowledgeable, the sales will follow naturally and there is no need for pressure.

Embraced by both owners and employees of Hall Piano, this commitment also expresses an unwavering pledge to provide the best products, exceptional service, and the use of fair business practices in all dealings.

Louisiana's premier establishment for piano sales and service, Hall Piano Company invites customers to explore their fine line of piano products including Steinway & Sons, Steinway designed Boston and Essex, Young Chang, Bergmann and Kohler & Campbell as well as Kurzweil Pro and Home keyboards, PianoDisc and QRS player systems, and our used and reconditioned instruments.

Hall Piano Company is Louisiana's exclusive Steinway dealer, and loves to share the Steinway model of excellence. Each piano takes up to a full year to create, and owners can choose from over twelve different styles and twenty-six unique finishes for their Steinway piano. Another extraordinary feature, Steinway pianos are noted for their financial appreciation. From the beginner to the professional, there is a Steinway designed piano that is perfect for everyone's lifestyle. From the nine foot Model D Concert Series (a favorite of artists worldwide) to baby grand

installation technicians with over thirty years of experience on staff full-time.

As part of their commitment to the community, Hall Piano is pleased to connect piano students with teachers. A visit to www.hallpiano.com and the piano lessons icon will lead you to a list of teachers across our region. They are also happy to host many of the teachers' recitals each spring. From people who have never touched a piano to advanced pianists, lessons are designed with all levels of students in mind.

The "Free Piano Classes For Kids" program offers the opportunity to "try the piano" for students between the ages of six and seventeen with no prior experience in studying piano. Designed to assess a child's piano-playing interest level, all materials for the free classes are provided at no charge to the student and are conducted at Hall Piano. Classes are formed periodically, and reservations are required for the first lesson. Call 504-733-8863 today or email us at lessons@hallpiano.com.

Hall Piano Company was instrumental in establishing the Steinway Society of New Orleans, whose major contributions have assisted many nonprofit organizations in acquiring their Steinway, and Steinway Designed Boston and Essex pianos. The Society has also established the "Piano Bank" whose goal is to reach out to economically disadvantaged children who might otherwise not get a chance to study piano by providing them with a piano and/or tuition for lessons. Information on the application process is available online at www.steinwaysocietyneworleans.com.

Among their more notable clients are the Louisiana Philharmonic Orchestra, the Baton Rouge Symphony, Tulane and Loyola Universities, the Jefferson Performing Arts Society and the Musical Arts Society of New Orleans. Many of their private clients have written to share their enjoyable personal experiences. Please visit their website at www.hallpiano.com for more information.

pianos and upright models, the perfect piano is waiting for you at Hall Piano.

Kurzweil keyboards are available in an array of configurations including synthesizers, performance controllers, stage pianos and numerous other possible additions. They are available in both home and professional models.

Along with the largest selection of pianos in the gulf south, Hall Piano Company offers a wonderful array of services designed to support every piano need. Some of their services include Piano Moving, Tuning and Regulation, Repair, Rebuilding, Player Systems, Piano Upgrades, Appraisals and Consignments, Digital Instrument Services, Rentals, Restoration, and Concert Artist Services.

One of the most popular services offered by Hall Piano is player piano retrofitting. The experts at Hall Piano have over thirty years experience in creating digital player systems out of acoustic pianos. There are two

C's Discount Pharmacy

Long time locals know the Ciolinos. Founding father Felix first opened C & L Pharmacy on Broad Street in 1956 and his second C & L in 1968 on Paris Avenue in New Orleans. He made the move to Jefferson Parish and opened Ciolino Pharmacy as his first Jefferson Parish store in 1973.

Felix graduated from the Loyola School of Pharmacy after World War II and quickly made a name for himself as a qualified pharmacist and the "go to" person for medical questions and problems. He prided himself on offering personal service to all his customers. While Felix knew how to take care of his customers' pharmaceutical needs, one aspect of his business was quite puzzling.

One day a sales representative for a weight loss product visited Felix. Together they noticed that the three cases of previously ordered product had not sold. The representative came back the next week and the cases were still there. Felix thought that the only way to sell the product was to lower the price to pennies over his cost. To his amazement, the three cases flew off the shelves, then five cases and then ten cases. Two women fighting over the last six pack of the product opened Felix's eyes to the "power of discounting."

▲

Felix J. Ciolino, c. 1960.

Methodically he went through his entire inventory lowering his retail price to pennies over his cost and he was astounded at the success. "I wasn't making any money, but I sure was selling product," he said.

Shortly thereafter he lowered the prices of his prescriptions bringing business in by the droves. It was evident that his two "coffee girls" and his wife, Mary, needed additional help to handle the customer counts. Felix knew that customer counts were key.

"The more people who were talking about the great deals at the store brought in more customers. The more customers, the higher the sales and all those pennies that I made turned into a comfortable living for me and my family," Felix said.

A discount pharmacy was born!

Felix operated his first Jefferson Parish location on West Esplanade and Clearview Parkway from 1973 until 1977 when he sold to his top pharmacists. For the next ten years, he did consulting work for area pharmacies.

C's Discount Pharmacy was opened in 1987 on Veterans Boulevard by Felix along with his son, Steven. At age fifteen Steven began working for his father as a stock boy and went on to graduate from Xavier University School of Pharmacy in 1981. He currently serves as president of the organization. Steven still follows the business plan developed by his father.

"It's not about how much you can charge the customer, but about how little," Steven said. "We believe that we are unique in that way."

The personal touch philosophy is still very much a part of the C's Discount Pharmacy service. Steven's mother, Mary Ciolino, who is currently in her eighties, is at the store three days a week still greeting customers by name. The Ciolino's know that this is an important part of their business especially when dealing with something as personal as healthcare products and prescriptions.

C's Discount Pharmacy is a family run business. Steven's brother, Sal and his cousins Greg, Jane and Douglas are all involved in various aspects of the business.

By offering discounted pricing on additional lines such as greeting cards, gift wrap, candles and household items, their customers realized even more savings with every trip to the Pharmacy.

The biggest product lines include vitamins, household cleaning products, American Greetings cards and cosmetics. According to Steven, his vitamin suppliers cannot believe that the volume of vitamins that he regularly buys is only for two stores.

The original West Esplanade store became available in 1997. The Ciolinos renovated the location and reopened as C's Discount Pharmacy in 1998. Sales immediately "took off."

"The new store was cleaner, neater and offered a greater product mix," said Steven. "The neighbors were happy to have us back."

Hurricane Katrina took its toll on the West Esplanade store in 2005. Extensive flooding and vandalism forced its closure for sixteen months. After another renovation, the store opened in January 2007; once again much to the joy of its neighbors.

Before the storm with business booming, it was apparent that a central distribution warehouse was critical to continued success. After the storm in 2006, a central distribution warehouse was opened in Metairie. It not only supplies the two current stores, but will supply those planned for the future.

Steven said that the company's future will be based on the teachings of his father—superior customer service, low prices and an extensive selection.

"Our goal is to open a few more stores in the next several years," Steven added. "We want to offer more people the opportunity to shop with us and continue to make all our customers happy that they have chosen to trust C's Discount Pharmacy."

C's Discount Pharmacy is on the Internet at www.csdiscountpharmacy.com.

▲

Above: The children of Felix and Mary Ciolino seated on a Metrecal weight-loss product display, c. the 1960s (from left to right): Mary Katherine, Salvatore, and Steven Ciolino. Not pictured: David Paul and Leonard Ciolino.

Below: C's Discount Pharmacy at 1401 Veterans Boulevard in Metairie.

Bottom: C's Discount Pharmacy at 4650 West Esplanade Avenue in Metairie.

AD GRAPHICS, INC.

Ad Graphics, Inc., is the sort of company that is not only concerned with first impressions. Ad Graphics is concerned with every impression your advertising makes. They offer a wide range of services and products in order to get you from the idea stage to the finished solution in the shortest, most cost-effective way possible. The mission statement of Ad Graphics says a lot about the way the company does business: "The team of Ad Graphics is dedicated to producing products and services to fit your needs. We work hard on the details; move each job through production as quickly as possible, while setting the highest standards for quality, all at the best price possible. We promise!"

Raymond Pertuit started Ad Graphics on March 1, 1988, armed with a degree in Commercial Art and several years experience in the industry. Raymond and his wife, Sharon, started with a secretary, a printer, and a salesman. At that time, Ad Graphics primarily did screen printing. The company got a big break when a routine sales call resulted in acquiring the Shoe Town account of 114 stores.

Practically overnight the small company's output approximately doubled. Ad Graphics continued to grow steadily. Eventually, the parent company of Shoe Town filed for bankruptcy. In an odd twist of fate, Raymond ended up appointed to the committee to decide the future course of that company. After hearing all of the "big" company representatives speak, Raymond gave his opinion. "I told them that it would be better to forgive the debts, let the company continue to operate, and give them a chance to recover. That way all of their people stayed employed. The company could also continue supporting other local businesses." The other committee members considered this point of view for a little while and then agreed with Raymond and he continues to this day to "do the right thing."

Ad Graphics now has a workforce of thirteen people, a 6,000-square-foot plant that they own, plus a 1,000-square-foot showroom that they rent. The majority of Ad Graphic's customers are local companies and that is the way owner Raymond prefers it. "It allows all of the employees, myself included, to remain accessible to our clients. That's very important to the way we do business."

The range of services available from Ad Graphics has grown over the years. Screen printing, digital printing, fleet graphics, exhibits and displays, and graphic design services are all available. Each category of service works especially well with certain types of products.

Screen printing is a very flexible way to get your message across. Decals, posters, signs, banners, displays, varying types of adhesive and static-cling items can all be screen printed. Screen printed decals usually work best for equipment, OEM markings, safety, parking, identification, promotional, window, bumper stickers, and reflective graphics.

Fleet graphics concerns advertising on trucks, vans, autos, boats and public transit. Ad Graphics can produce magnetic signs, striping, and full-color photos and graphics. Fleet graphics are available either long or short term; there are many options for both durations. Either way, Ad Graphics will get your vehicle noticed.

Digital printing is available with our excellent team of graphic designers to translate your ideas into something that can be seen and touched. Digital prints tend to work best for trade show, floor, backlit, display, and courtroom graphics. Wall murals, banners, art canvas, and photo enlargements can all be printed digitally.

Point of Sale items are banners, signs, posters, danglers, menu boards, displays, window graphics, cut-outs, literature holders, and counter cards. They can be screen printed or, for smaller quantities, digitally printed.

Tradeshow displays such as tabletops, back-walls, pop-ups, hard-wall, and islands are available, all of which can be custom-made. Ad Graphics is the only authorized Downing Display distributor in the area.

Also available at Ad Graphics is a talented in-house art department. Your product will be original and fresh when designed by this team. This design team has several diverse styles all giving input into the creative process to create just the right design for you. Whether you want your design to be traditional, cutting edge, masculine, or feminine; whether you know exactly what you want, or you have no idea; Ad Graphics can make a unique design, exclusively for you, based on the information that you provide to the team. Clients can bring in completed art work or have the Ad Graphics art team work their magic.

Another testament to the integrity of the company as a whole is its incredibly low employee turnover rate. The average employee has been there for ten years. This is due in part to the fact that the company keeps up with cutting edge equipment and training for the staff. Of course, the great benefit package does not hurt either.

Ad Graphics has prospered and succeeded through the years. Raymond has shared the success of Ad Graphics with a huge assortment of charities. Some of the organizations that have benefited from the company's good fortune are the Jefferson SPCA, Special Olympics, Little Sisters of the Poor, and New Orleans Medical Mission. Contributions are sometimes monetary, sometimes in the form of donated signage, sometimes both.

As for the future, plans include to continuing the steady ten percent annual growth, continuous upgrading of equipment, and adding even more modern, updated processes.

Ad Graphics is located at 413 Commerce Point in Harahan and on the Internet at www.adgraphicsinc.net.

STUART SERVICES LLC

Stuart Services began in 1956 as Stuart Electric, Inc. Owner Carl G. Stuart employed one assistant, and the company installed circuits for window air conditioning units. Through superior job performance, Stuart Electric became the exclusive provider of this service for such New Orleans icons as Comeaux's Furniture and Levine's Furniture. Stuart Electric soon developed a reputation for superb workmanship and outstanding customer service, which expanded throughout the New Orleans community. Other New Orleans icons soon followed: Kirshman's, Schwegmann, Maison Blanche, Campo Appliance, Radio Center and Universal Furniture began utilizing Stuart Electric with confidence that the job would be done correctly.

Out of concern for his customers, Carl Stuart introduced flat-rate pricing. Carl realized that people appreciated knowing the full cost of a job before it began. This "up-front" flat-rate pricing system is still in use today at Stuart Services; and customers still appreciate knowing the cost of a job before the work is started, allowing them to make informed choices.

Between 1956 and 1961, Stuart Electric employed four people. Realizing the need for additional space, the company relocated to Little Farms Avenue in Metairie in 1964, staying within its home parish of Jefferson. At this time, the company also expanded to ten

employees. The company continued to grow and in late 1990 Carl began searching for someone to buy his company. Carl met Jude Raspino through a mutual acquaintance and they began discussing the possible sale of Stuart Electric. With Raspino's experience running his own electrical business, it was a perfect fit. In April of 1991, Carl sold Stuart Electric to Raspino. Since the purchase, the new company has averaged fifteen percent growth each year. The small company that installed window unit circuits now provides a wide range of electrical services as well as emergency generators, air conditioning, heating, and plumbing services.

November 1998 brought additional changes to Stuart Electric. The company relocated to its present location at 4724 Utica Street, the former location of a very popular night club during the 70s and 80s, known as "Frankie Brent's." The building was razed and a new state-of-the-art facility was designed to provide for the specialized needs and future growth of the company. In January 1999, other improvements included refinement of the service department equipment and a new computerized service center was added to allow accurate routing of twenty-four individual service vehicles. Wiring was added to accommodate thirty computer and phone terminals. The staff grew to 28 employees with a business plan aimed at 100 employees. With the addition of air conditioning services in June 2001, Stuart Electric Inc., was renamed Stuart Services.

Stuart Services' commitment to our community is displayed on each of its vehicles, "Committed to Rebuild New Orleans." The vehicles display the "Stuart Guy" Superhero clutching a lightening bolt…not too much fic-

tion portrayed there! Stuart Services was indeed a superhero in the aftermath of Hurricane Katrina. In fact, an employee discussed the recovery effort in an article in The Washington Post on October 8, 2005, a month after the devastation. At that time, Stuart Services was back in business serving the commercial and residential community. The company helped to rebuild lives in Jefferson Parish and the surrounding areas, including the Northshore. Stuart Services also participated in charitable work with Children's Hospital, Second Harvest Food Bank, ABC's Extreme Makeover: Home Edition and many other New Orleans institutions.

The progress and growth of Stuart Services exemplifies the progress and growth of Jefferson Parish. In early 2008 the company complimented its trade expansion with plumbing services. Now customers who are comfortable with Stuart's high level of customer service in the electrical and air conditioning field can enjoy that same level of service for all of their plumbing needs.

Stuart's commitment to their customers is evident with their participation in the BBB Care Program. According to the Better Business Bureau of Greater New Orleans, Stuart is a BBB Accredited Business in good standing. Stuart Services also received a national ranking by Nexstar Network in 2008. Having scored high marks in customer service, employee satisfaction and financial success, Stuart earned the Nexstar Select Service Seal.

Nexstar Select Service, which is considered as the "Good Housekeeping Seal of Approval" for service providers in the electrical, plumbing, heating and air conditioning trades states: "These professionals earned the right to be recommended as a trusted source; count on them to deliver quality results, fair pricing and superior treatment." Stuart has certainly lived up to its mission statement:

"To provide excellent service to our customers; to provide exciting opportunities for our employees; and to provide prosperous growth of our company."

There is a bright future for Stuart Services. Goals for the future include continued growth through trade expansion and company acquisitions, which in turn stimulate the economy of Jefferson Parish. Jefferson Parish and Stuart Services are an excellent pair.

For more about Stuart Services, to schedule a service call or read testimonies from satisfied customers, please visit the company at www.stuartservices.com.

SOUTHLAND PLUMBING SUPPLY, INC.

▲

Above: Chad Vinturella supervising the merchandise loading for a delivery.

Below: Second-generation owner, Alan Vinturella and his son, Chad, in the Kohler Premier Showroom.

Opposite, top: The Metairie showroom facility located across the street from the main sales offices and warehouse.

Opposite, middle: Southland Plumbing Supply's Mandeville showroom.

Opposite, bottom: A vast array of kitchen and bath merchandise for customers to peruse.

Southland Plumbing is the American Dream come true. It is a locally owned family business that was started by John Vinturella when he was fifty-two years old. John started in the plumbing business as a plumbing contractor. He had the foresight to see that Jefferson Parish would be the next area of growth in metropolitan New Orleans, sold his plumbing business, and bought a small branch of a plumbing supply company. The original site totaled 2,000 square feet.

Because John had been a plumbing contractor he was not exactly very welcomed by his wholesale competitors and factory representatives. They were suspicious. Perseverance paid off. A few dealers took a chance on him and it was soon evident that John was an honest wholesale plumbing supplier. Business grew and the same people that snubbed him when he started his new venture were suddenly seeking his business.

John has three sons: John, Alan, and Gary. Although he has a degree from LSU in chemical engineering, when John offered Alan a chance to join the company and grow with it, Alan went to work with his father. The business moved from the 2,000 square foot facility on Airline to a 10,000 square foot building on Metairie Road. Alan seemed to

have a knack for the business. He aggressively sought and brought the commercial end of the business to Southland. Growth became extraordinary. For the next fifteen years every month had a higher volume of product moved than the previous month!

Eventually, younger brother Gary joined the business. Then, in 1975, the remaining and oldest brother, John, joined the business. Fall of 1975 saw another big addition to the business. Southland became a distributor for plumbing giant Kohler. Acquiring such a prestigious line launched Southland Plumbing into a new level.

Dad John's keen eye for new development led the company to open a branch on the Northshore in 1977. Son John took over running that operation in 1978. The next major move for Southland Plumbing was in 1979 when it moved into its thirty-thousand-square-foot custom-built facility on North Arnoult Road in Metairie, including a unique showroom.

Over the years, the founding Vinturella had been gifting shares of stock to each of the brothers and when all of the shares had been given to the "boys," Vinturella gave his two weeks notice. Two Fridays later, he told everyone goodbye and left the building. He never set foot in the building again. Alan kept him up to date on the business and Vinturella encouraged him to "make a decision, wrong or right and learn from it." But he believed that the decisions were no longer his to make and trusted his sons to continue running the company. The business that he had begun as a three man operation and nurtured into a multimillion dollar industry leader was now in someone else's hands. Fortunately, it was his own children whom he had raised and he had shared with them his belief that indecision was worse than a wrong decision. Because of that belief, he had seen his small business grow and provide needed services to the metropolitan New Orleans area and the Gulf Coast as well as provide his own children with an opportunity to carry on a legacy of quality.

In 2003, Alan was looking at a picture of his dad on the wall in his office when an interesting coincidence struck him. He was the same age his dad had been when Vinturella first started Southland Plumbing. This led Alan to thinking it was time for he himself to do something bold. So he placed a call to his oldest son, Chad, who lived in Memphis and made him a proposition. Alan asked if Chad would be interested in heading up a Kohler premier showroom on the Northshore. Chad obviously inherited the family's intelligence genes; he called his dad back after only two days to say yes. He moved back to New Orleans and went to work in the Metairie store in September 2003. Three months later he opened the first "premier" Kohler showroom in the Mandeville area.

A second "premier" Kohler showroom was opened in the Southland Plumbing Metairie Kitchen and Bath Design Center across from the Metairie office in 2005. Then came Hurricane Katrina. Eight inches of water in the showroom was enough to mildew everything. Realizing the importance of plumbing supplies at this time, Southland Plumbing opened for business only two weeks after the storm by operating out of its Mandeville location. They had only 16 of their 52 employees but those 16 worked from sunup to sundown to help our region recover from the nations worst-ever natural disaster. Some of the customers that Southland Plumbing was involved with in recovering from Katrina included the Superdome, Beau Rivage, the Ritz-Carlton, the Fairmont Hotel, UNO (the arena and other buildings), University Hospital, Holy Cross High School, Holiday Inn Airport, and numerous others.

It is incredible that all of this started with one man and an idea. Now, a third generation of the Vinturella family is cultivating that dream and providing much needed quality service to not just Jefferson Parish but the Gulf Coast region, especially in times of great need.

Southland Plumbing Supply, Inc., is located at 2321 North Arnoult Road in Metairie and at www.southlandplumbingsupply.

TERMINIX

The mission statement of Terminix explains their purpose clearly. "Insects play an important role in our world's ecosystem; however it is our job to intervene when those insects invade homes and businesses." While everyone understands the objective of Terminix, the mission statement expresses conscientiousness toward all living creatures and the environment.

Terminix began in 1925 in Memphis, Tennessee. E. L. Bruce, owner of a floor company, researched, and then offered a way to eliminate "nix" termites. In 1932, Terminix employee Frank Lyons patented the first U.S. termite chemical. The first Terminix franchise in Louisiana was in Baton Rouge around 1941. Bill Brothers bought the franchise for Southern Louisiana and opened the New Orleans office in 1947. The year 1960 proved to be a pivotal year for the company. Ed Martin, Jr., was hired to develop both commercial and residential pest control. Martin expanded Terminix's repertoire to include treatment for mice, ants, and the perennial New Orleans favorite, the cockroach. In 1962, LSU graduate Martin bought the franchise from Brothers. Apparently Martin's degree in Entomology is paying off since the success of Terminix since 1962 is the result of his leadership.

Clients of Terminix can be assured that Terminix has a customer-oriented attitude. As far back as Hurricane Betsy, Terminix employees answered the call of the community and became roof shingle nailers and debris removers. After Hurricane Katrina,

the Terminix employees once again adapted to the needs of their customers and community. This time they went so far as to gut and sanitize flooded houses.

Growth of Terminix has occurred through acquiring new territories and through mergers and acquisitions. In 1965 the Houma office opened, and then in 1970 Slidell came aboard. Laplace joined the family in 1985 and Gretna became part of the group. In addition to adding new areas, new companies were being merged into Terminix. One of the most notable mergers happened in 1969 when B&B Exterminating was bought by Terminix. Another remarkable acquisition was that of Very Professional Exterminating in 1995. This brought Vincent Palumbo into the company. In 2001, Ed and Vincent purchased Sears Pest Control along with several smaller companies. As the result of this latest venture, Terminix became the largest pest control operation in southeast Louisiana.

Interestingly enough, Terminix was the company to discover that the notorious Formosan termite was capable of establishing secondary colonies that allowed them to continue eating after traditional treatments. Of course, Terminix found a way to exterminate the problem.

The business plan for the future of Terminix? "To continue to provide our current and future customers with the most effective pest control possible using the latest technologically advanced products and techniques available to our industry."

Terminix is located on the Internet at www.terminixno.com where you will find answers to your questions and if not, just call 504-834-7330.

ALARIO BROS MARINE SUPPLIES, INC.

Walking through the door of Alario Bros Marine Supply, Inc., is like walking back in time. It is one of the oldest stores in Westwego and one of the largest commercial fishing supply stores in Louisiana. Alario Bros has supplied commercial fisherman for over fifty years. They carry one of the largest inventories of commercial shrimping and fishing supplies in Louisiana. Not only is the selection of merchandise vast but business is done the old fashioned way. Alario Bros is family owned and operated with family members on the premises doing the work everyday. Customer service is not just a phrase, it is an actual mission. Do not be fooled by the old-fashioned charm. The business tools used are very modern. Internet research and flat screen monitors are part of the business as well as handshakes. Not only do they manufacture and sell custom-made trawls and crab traps; they also sell supplies for those experienced or brave enough to attempt to make the traps or trawls themselves.

The business started when Antoine Alario sold the shrimp boat *Alert* in 1948, took on his brother Tom, and went into business with the blessing of their father and brothers who were also commercial fishermen. The company started in the seafood business on Sala Avenue selling fish, shrimp, crabs, crawfish, and live chickens. Then they added webbing (netting), trawls for catching shrimp and gill net for catching fish. Years later, a young Daniel Alario bought stock in the business and worked there. When times got tough, Daniel took a second job at Avondale Shipyard. He worked at the shipyard for many years and in 1976, he returned to Alario Bros.

After his father passed away, Daniel became the sole owner of the company. Today, Daniel's two daughters, Eva Alario Corcoran and Kathy Alario Choquette, run the business with Daniel's sister, Barbara Alario Ballas, a long-time employee who now works on a part-time basis.

The business has certainly grown since its humble beginnings. It now spans two warehouses on one side of the street plus the main business on Avenue A with an attached workshop for making crab traps.

Alario Bros maintains a large stock of fishing and marine supplies. You will find a wide selection of hydraulic and electric winches, motors and pumps, fish and shrimp netting, plastic shrimp baskets, rope, chain, cast nets, life saving equipment, rainwear, long line supplies, crabbing supplies, and all your commercial fishing needs. They also have a large selection of stainless steel rings, shackles, thimbles, swivels, turnbuckles, snap hooks, eye bolts, cable and chain.

The company is expanding in new items such as Croc shoes, pirogues, boiling pots, burners, and live animal traps. For more information, please visit Alario Bros Marine Supplies at www.alariobros.com.

Quality Inn Hotel and Conference Center

Soaring above Interstate 10 in the heart of Metairie is the Quality Hotel and Conference Center operated by Ambridge Hospitality.

The distinguished building is one of the oldest in the area; built in 1968 as an office building. As the need for hotel space in the booming New Orleans suburb of Metairie grew, in 1972, it was renovated into a Best Western hotel, then a Howard Johnson's, and finally its current incarnation, Quality Inn.

In 2005, Hurricane Katrina was no match for the spirit of those serving guests at the Quality Hotel. It never closed after the storm and immediately housed the National Guard, police, and various humanitarian workers. They also offered shelter to those forced to evacuate their homes with some evacuees living in the hotel for over a year. Regular hotel operations resumed in December 2006.

When the facility reopened to welcome regular guests, there were newly refurbished rooms and other wonderful amenities including free Internet access throughout the property. Quick and easy access to I-10, Lakeside Shopping Center, the airport, and downtown New Orleans continue to make the location appealing.

The Louis Armstrong New Orleans International Airport and the historic French Quarter are both just a short drive from the centrally located Quality Hotel. An added benefit of the hotel is the Conference Center, which boasts 16,000 square feet of meeting space, one of the largest in Metairie. And the ballroom can accommodate as many as 300 guests for a sit-down event.

Visitors can enjoy browsing the wide variety of specialty shops and dining options all nearby. The hotel's restaurant, Cromwell's, is a long time favorite of locals who work in the area and cocktails are available in Benson's Lounge, located right on the property.

The Quality Hotel and Conference Center offers ample free parking and features a seasonal outdoor pool. Business travelers will appreciate access to copy and fax services, free Internet access, data ports, voice mail, secretarial services, and competitive corporate rates. Banquet and meeting facilities are available to accommodate most events and business functions.

All lovely, spacious guest rooms come with microwaves, refrigerators, coffee makers, clock radios, irons, ironing boards, and cable television with pay-per-view movies. The hotel is also pleased to offer non-smoking floors and handicap accessible rooms. To round out the guest amenities available, a coin-operated laundry facility and valet cleaning service are available for guest convenience.

Guest service is the highest priority. At the Quality Hotel and Conference Center, guests experience Southern hospitality at its finest.

Quality Inn Hotel and Conference Center is located at 2261 North Causeway Boulevard in Metairie. For more information, please visit www.qualityhotelmetairie.com.

PATIO DRUGS

Patio Drugs is nestled among several independently owned shops in central Metairie. This gem of Jefferson is the oldest operating pharmacy in Jefferson Parish. The pharmacy started in 1958, when Jefferson Parish was still a new and developing community. Patio Drugs filled a great need in the fledgling community. Great service, great products, and an excellent reputation have made Patio Drugs the problem-solving pharmacy for New Orleans, Metairie, Kenner and surrounding areas. Current owners, John F. and Daisy DiMaggio, took the helm of Patio Drugs in 1992. The DiMaggios have over sixty years of healthcare experience between them. Between great experience and the personal service offered, Patio Drugs is the favorite for many local citizens. A great example of how Patio Drugs keeps the service personal is that during one of the many heavy rains, the dedicated employees of Patio braved the elements to deliver needed medication via an army duck to a baby that was sick with meningitis. What a shining example of going beyond the duty of the job!

The little pharmacy in the suburbs of the big city has grown to offer an impressive array of services. Patio's clinical services and home medical equipment services are accredited by the Joint Commission on Accreditation of Healthcare Organizations (JCAHO). Services offered at Patio Drugs include clinical respiratory, professional compounding, pharmacy consulting, diabetic supplies, enteral therapy, immunosuppressive drugs, infusion therapy, pain management, medical equipment, oral anticancer drugs, pharmacy services, respiratory therapy, and specialty pharmacy. Another wonderful service which Patio Drugs has offered from the very beginning is free delivery. Amazingly, this service is still available!

The company has grown from a staff of five in the early days to now over 100. The staff includes professionals from customer service representatives to pharmacists. Patio's caring employees are specially trained to provide Hospice pharmacy and other End-of-Life Care services. The original store serves as the primary location and there are nine other facilities for home medical equipment and immunization clinics.

In addition to their business of providing medical supplies and services to the community, the company and staff of Patio Drugs also participates in several charitable activities. They underwrite outreach programs that assist families and individuals in need. Participation in three different international outreach programs in Central America is another effort that this generous company helps.

Together, John and Daisy, along with their capable staff, have steered the company to the success it is today, fifty years after opening its doors.

Patio Drugs is located at 5208 Veterans Boulevard in Metairie and on the Internet at www.patiodrugs.com.

LOOP LINEN AND UNIFORM SERVICE

Loop Linen and Uniform Service has been keeping the New Orleans area looking good for close to eighty years. The ambition of this local company is to provide the best quality, on time, at the best price. Their mission statement describes it perfectly: "Loop Linen and Uniform Service is committed to our customers by delivering products and services which meet or exceed their expectations. Through mutual respect and integrity, innovation, sharing of information, and organizational accountability, we shall provide those products and services on time and at competitive prices." The name Loop comes from the Loop Hotel where the business was first located.

The Loop Linen staff is well trained, professional, and courteous. Immediate replacement of any worn linens or garments is provided as well as adjustment to your inventory to meet your changing needs. Clients range from medical facilities to oil fields and small restaurants to major corporations.

Linen services provide long-term performance and esthetic beauty woven into beautiful presentations. The wide variety of styles, colors, and textures complement and enhance the atmosphere you are creating, whether for every day or a special occasion.

There is no initial investment, so your enhanced image is cost effective. Plus, the products are not disposable, so the service is environmentally friendly. Another economical reason for utilizing Loop Linen Service is the man-hours saved by no longer having to purchase, reconcile, stock, reorder, and dispose of or wash so many things.

The floor mats are available in several sizes and are anti-fatigue thus adding to employee comfort which leads to improved morale and productivity. Plus they are fully washable but we can take care of that for you. They provide superior grease and oil resistance and the slip resistant surface reduces accidents resulting in fewer workers compensation cases. Add to all of this the anti-microbial treatment that each mat undergoes, which results in less sick days for employees, and the conclusion is that using Loop Linen Service just makes good business sense.

Today, Loop Linen and Uniform Service is a full-service textile rental company, offering a complete range of textile rental and related services, including cook clothes and chef uniforms, kitchen apparel, linen service, industrial uniforms, hospital service, wiping cloths, entry mats, dust mops, safety products, paper products, and other specialized products.

Loop has grown from a 120-square-foot room to a 35,000-square-foot plant. Their goal is "to provide the finest quality and most dependable service possible, specifically tailored to the requirements of each individual customer".

Locally owned and operated since 1929, Loop Linen and Uniform Service is located at 463 Avenue A in Westwego, Louisiana and at www.looplinen.com.

"We love food. We want to meet or exceed expectations on every shopping trip. We know that by doing so we turn customers into advocates for whole foods. We guarantee our customers one hundred percent product satisfaction or their money will be refunded." With such a great philosophy, is it any wonder that Whole Foods Market is such a success? Their mission statement says a lot as well... "We are dedicated to providing vitality and well-being for all individuals by supplying the highest quality, most wholesome foods available. Since the purity of our food and the health of our bodies are directly related to the purity and health of our environment, our core mission is devoted to the promotion of organically grown foods, food safety concerns, and sustainability of our entire ecosystem."

Whole Foods Market was started by four guys in Austin, Texas, in 1980. The concept of making natural food available supermarket-style was unique and greatly desired. The idea caught on and now there are almost three hundred stores between the United States, Canada, and United Kingdom.

The company motto is "Whole Foods, Whole People, Whole Planet"™, which the company takes seriously. Focused on value, they seek out the highest quality and freshest products from around the world. With the team members having such passion for the company and its core values, Whole Foods Market has been ranked for eleven consecutive years as one of the "100 Best Companies to Work For" in America by *Fortune* magazine. From complete lines of skin care, makeup, vitamins, bath products, and special supplements to essential oils and household products, the stores offer just about anything you can think of for your home. In addition, the company supports local producers and thus features the freshest seasonal items, cuts down on transportation, stimulates local economies, and reduces fuel consumption and packaging materials. The motto "Whole Foods, Whole People, Whole Planet"™ is not just a motto for this company, it is words they put into action every day.

Another thing that makes Whole Foods Market stand apart from other supermarkets is their extremely high quality standards. Every

WHOLE FOODS
MARKET

▲

Whole Foods Market has two locations in the area including the Veterans store at 3420 Veterans Boulevard and Arabella Station at 5600 Magazine Street.

product is evaluated. They look for competitive prices and feature foods free of artificial sweeteners, preservatives, colors, flavors, and hydrogenated fats. Whole Foods Market also honors their commitment to ethical trade. Their Whole Trade program regulates products purchased from foreign countries that must meet the criteria of high quality, ensuring better wages and working conditions for employees, and environmental care.

Whole Foods Market also has a growing private label brand with over two thousand products that meet or exceed the same quality standards as everything else in the stores and at a great value! Information on products, community outreach, special diets, green practices, recipes, and more is available at www.wholefoodsmarket.com.

AccuTrans, Inc.

Gary Osorno built his career from the ground up and has worked in all aspects on the tankerman business. His experience encompasses not only the technical side of the industry, dealing with various chemicals and fluids, but also the administrative and managerial aspects as well. Gary has grown the company into a multimillion dollar profitable business and is the key to its future growth. Marketing, financials, client relations, employee relations, quality control, and continuous improvement are among his primary responsibilities. His hands-on experience includes being an operations manager, vice president of operations, field inspector, and surveyor. He truly believes that his people are his greatest asset and makes a constant effort to see that they are well trained and have at their disposal the tools necessary to make his company a world ranked business.

Founded in the mid-1980s, AccuTrans began as an inspection service, but evolved into a full service company. Laboratory services were added, then in the 1990s customers began to request that AccuTrans provide tankerman services as well.

The company decided that in order to truly fill this need it would form a team of individuals who would could meet the highest standards of experience, professionalism and treat the equipment of the customers as their own. Over the next few years, AccuTrans hired tankermen who met these standards of service and established a reputation for excellence in the field.

As the company grew, Gary continued to refine and strive for constant improvement, hiring a team of experienced managers with backgrounds in compliance, regulatory preparation, root cause investigation, analysis, and teaching and mentoring tankermen. AccuTrans has since expanded further, completing a updated dispatch center complete with barge tracking and constant monitoring.

AccuTrans tankermen are proud to service and inspect barges and cargo along the waterway and its interconnected waters and tributary rivers.

In this spirit, AccuTrans has always placed the customer first, knowing that it takes years to build a bond with a client; but only moments to break one.

AccuTrans' mission statement is simple: "We serve the customers—our primary concern is to provide qualified, safe, and experienced tankerman in a timely manner and a professional support staff to ensure the best possible service. We produce quality—our service is constantly being modified for the fulfillment of our customer's expectations and it's optimization as input into their system. We adopt the continuous improvement philosophy—we constantly evaluate our system and compare it to what is possible. There is always room for improvement and innovation in everything that we do. We make every effort to find it."

Couhig Partners, LLC is not a typical law firm. The guiding principle at this unique firm is to "use our expertise, time, and resources to help a business maximize its success, not to maximize our billable hours." This honest approach to law is supported by many years experience in many areas of corporate law with large firms. Some of the practice areas are corporate, regulatory, construction, employment, environmental, and insurance law, civil and appellate litigation, and governmental relations.

Couhig Partners was founded in 2003 by Rob Couhig. Couhig practiced law at one of the largest firms in the South for thirty years before deciding that a smaller, more specialized firm could better serve businesses. He assembled a group of like-minded lawyers from top firms who were similarly frustrated with the constraints of their practices. Each lawyer at Couhig Partners shares Couhig's vision and passion for helping businesses realize their full potential and achieve success. The lawyers at Couhig Partners are not bound by the rigid formalities that have traditionally defined the relationships between lawyers and their clients. This flexibility allows Couhig Partners to better serve its clients by providing them with personal service tailored to their specific business objectives.

Additionally, the lawyers at Couhig Partners are business owners, investors, and entrepreneurs themselves. As both lawyers and businesspeople, the attorneys at Couhig Partners are in a unique position to give clients practical advice, as they have personally dealt with many of the same issues faced by clients. Among their many business ventures, Couhig Partners attorneys have owned and operated car dealerships, pest control companies, multifamily properties, retail centers, self storage facilities, construction companies, oil fields, and even a professional baseball team. Couhig Partners understands business because they have experienced it.

Another unique aspect of Couhig Partners is the availability of an alternative billing structure. While traditional hourly billing is available, Couhig Partners also offers its clients a value-driven fee structure. Unlike hourly billing, alternative billing offers clients a value-based billing structure that offers clients a fixed rate and shared risk.

Couhig Partners participates in a number of civic activities in Jefferson Parish and across the metro area, including the YMCA, Peace Corps, Jefferson Parish Intensive Probation Drug Court, Jefferson Parish Chamber of Commerce, and Celebration in the Oaks.

Collectively, the attorneys of Couhig Partners have the knowledge, experience, intelligence, and integrity to handle any legal business matter that arises.

Couhig Partners is located at 1100 Poydras Street, Suite 1150 in New Orleans and at www.couhigpartners.com.

✧
David C. Loeb and former Jefferson Parish Councilman Lloyd Giardina.

JEFFERSON PARISH
162

BUILDING A GREATER JEFFERSON PARISH

Jefferson Parish's utilities, construction companies, and manufacturing industries shape the parish's future and provide fuel for the state

EPIC DIVERS & MARINE

▲

Above: EPIC Chief Operations Officer Roger Rodriguez (second from right) with the crew of the EPIC Seahorse (from left to right): Captain Gary Ross, Rob Valdine, and Gene Lo Conte.

Below: EPIC's fleet of dive support vessels include (left to right) EPIC Seahorse, EPIC Diver, and EPIC Explorer. With these vessels, EPIC can support divers at depths to one thousand feet.

Julie Rivet Rodriguez is president and CEO of EPIC Divers & Marine, in Harvey, Louisiana. She is the second of four siblings—Dale, Julie, Larry and Ty—of two Jefferson Parish entrepreneurs, Marion Soniat Rivet King and Lawrence J. "Pie" Rivet, all of whom were raised as Jefferson Parish residents. Besides starting and owning EPIC Divers Inc., Marion and Lawrence also owned and operated a local White's Home & Auto Store and Tastee Donut franchise.

In 1972, Rivet found himself at a crossroad when the owner of the commercial diving company he worked for was killed in a plane crash. Rivet looked out over the Gulf of Mexico and saw an opportunity. The oil industry was booming. With his experience and reputation, he knew he could do what needed to be done in the Gulf. That year, Rivet sold the stock he owned in the diving company he had worked for, mortgaged his home and used the money to establish EPIC Divers, Inc. He founded the company with two silent partners, whom he bought out six months later. In those days, Rivet and a small crew operated out of a trailer on Breaux Avenue, Harvey. Today, he remains with the company which, under the leadership of his daughter, has grown into a global operation with some 400 employees, divers who can work 1,000 feet underwater and a fleet of Dive Support vessels which exceeds $100 million in business annually. EPIC has offices in Houston and Lafayette, but its

headquarters remain in Harvey, and the company remains rooted in Jefferson Parish.

Julie Rivet did not grow up planning to follow in her father's footsteps. She is not a diver herself. In fact, she has never donned the life support gear that enables EPIC's divers to do their jobs. When she first came to work at the EPIC office in 1976, shortly after graduating from L.W. Higgins High School, she did not plan to stay. She was just filling in as the receptionist. She told her father, "two weeks." After all, she did not know the business. She did not know a lot about what EPIC's divers did on and around—and under—the oil platforms in the Gulf. When she fielded phone calls about prospective projects, she had to call one of the divers to find out whether EPIC could take on the type of work the customer wanted. Day by day, her understanding grew. A quick study, she eventually knew enough to take responsibility for the company's finances, insurance, sales and operations. The business had grown on her—not just the projects themselves, but the people around her—the divers and tenders, the project managers and the office staff. They had become a big, extended family.

She was not going anywhere. In 1978 she married another West Banker, Roger Rodriguez of Marrero, and started taking accounting courses at Delgado Community College, while working full-time at the family business. If she had thought about leaving

EPIC, the company's strength in the face of the oil bust in the 1980s persuaded her to stay—and helped show her that she could make a difference in the industry. The decade started off strong—1982 was the company's best year to date—but then the tides turned. There were tough times in the Gulf region. Skeptical of the service sector, banks were calling in notes. With a couple dozen employees, the company did what it had to in order to survive. Diver Dan Bean, from Pennsylvania came to the area, looking for work and joined the company in 1986. When EPIC had a hard time making ends meet, he and a few others let the company float their paychecks. Single at the time, Bean could afford to do so. Today, he is married to a local woman and they have three children. He still lives in Jefferson Parish, and he still works for EPIC as a dive superintendent. The dive business does not attract many locals, but it does draw many men and women from around the country who come to work and call Jefferson Parish home.

By the end of the decade, Rivet was ready to get out of the industry. He had a prospective buyer lined up, but the buyer did not have a place for Julie in the company. By

then, she had invested too much of herself in EPIC and its people to walk away. Over the years, the divers in the field had pointed out opportunities for growing the business, and Julie Rodriguez had listened. She trusted their expertise and saw the potential. In 1991, with her father's approval and her husband's support, she bought EPIC Divers. At the time, the company employed about forty people, and annual revenues had reached just a little over $1 million. Six years later, she purchased three Offshore Supply Vessels and launched EPIC Marine L.L.C., which provided dive support vessels to complement the company's dive services. Today, the company has a fleet of six dive support and field support/utility vessels, including two boats that will support saturation divers working at depths down to one thousand feet.

EPIC's defining moment came not long after Rodriguez took over the company's helm. Patrick Walker, from Bridge City, joined EPIC as a tender and then trained as a diver under Dan Bean. In August 1992, Hurricane Andrew tore through the region; it stressed much of the Gulf's infrastructure. In March 1994, Walker was on a dive, repairing a leaking pipeline. Suddenly, a high-pressure

▲

Above: L. J. "Pie" Rivet, founder of EPIC Divers, and his daughter, Julie Rivet Rodriguez, president and CEO of EPIC Divers & Marine.

Below: The crew aboard the EPIC Explorer sending Happy Mothers Day wishes.

▲

*Above: EPIC's divers work on oil rig
pipelines in the Gulf and elsewhere. Here,
a diver uses special underwater
cutting equipment.*

*Below: Patrick Walker, of Bridge City,
Louisiana, was killed in 1994 when a high-
pressure line exploded underwater. His loss
inspired EPIC's industry-leading
commitment to safety on and off the job.*

line exploded, killing Walker instantly. For Rodriguez, the loss drove home the harsh realities of one of the world's most dangerous occupations. She made a commitment to her divers and to making a culture of safety the company's core value. It is her mission to invoke every safety precaution into each person and project, to ensure Patrick's death was not in vain.

Rodriguez credits her husband, Roger, and the dive team with helping her achieve her safety goals. A quality engineer who worked in the nuclear power industry before joining EPIC, Roger played a key role in developing the company's industry-leading DIVE 5™ continuous improvement safety and quality program. The program encourages employees to think outside the box to reduce the risk of injury. The company continues to focus on practices that safeguard its employees, the public and the environment. Today, Roger serves as EPIC's chief operations officer.

Still haunted by Walker's death, Rodriguez takes comfort in the fact that, as a result of his legacy, safety is the core value and the heart of EPIC. Her mission is to share Walker's life and what he meant to the company to all who will listen when she tours and talks to other companies about workplace safety. She

honors his memory so that others may not suffer the same fate. In addition, EPIC keeps Walker's spirit alive and honors his name each year by giving the Patrick Walker Memorial Award to the rising stars within the company. In order to recognize everyone who contributes to the company's various safety programs, EPIC gives out many awards dedicated to safety, quality and performance in and around the worksite, home and the community.

Perhaps a part of the reason why the company can put safety first is the sense of caring and commitment among the employees. EPIC has a strong sense of family. Some of them are family—like Rodriguez's brother Dale Rivet, who has worked for the company in various capacities since 1978. Her oldest daughter, Leigh Ann, a graduate of Louisiana State University, joined the company in 2003 as a safety assistant and is now project manager for companies like BP. Middle daughter, Julie Ann, also an LSU graduate, worked summers for the company and now works in marketing. Both girls are in the Houston office. Son Ryan, who attended Southeastern University, works in the Harvey office, learning the business from the ground up. Other employees just feel like family—like New Orleans native Joe Cieutat, who started as a diver under Rivet and who remains there today as a project manager for companies like Chevron. Sharon Estopinal, now director of business services, and Eva

Cancienne, now director of health, safety and environment, have been with the company since the early 1990s. They are trusted and loyal friends and advisors who always work in EPIC's best interests. Rodriguez credits much of her success to the people of EPIC. Many other long-time employees remain at Rodriguez's side today; Mike Brown, John Herren, Rob Sanchez, Mike Roehl, Jason Duke, Gene Lo Conte, Dane Stearns, Rob Valdine, Charlie Andre, Ann McGuire, Phil Crosby, Nichole Breaux, Captain Gary Ross, Captain Mike Boutwell, and Captain Brian O'Neill to name a few. It takes a team with various backgrounds and skills to provide the services that EPIC does, and Rodriguez recognizes the valuable role that each team member plays in the company's overall success. In 1999, Rodriguez and her team proudly accepted the "Entrepreneur of the Year" Award for the Gulf Coast Region from Ernst & Young.

EPIC also has close ties to the community. Rodriguez was instrumental in founding Women's Business Council Gulf Coast and the National Women's Business Council. She has been a strong supporter of the Restoration and Beautify the Westbank Program, the Junior Achievement Program and others. She is not alone in her civic-mindedness. More than thirty EPIC employees participated in Junior Achievement mentoring programs at Estelle Elementary School in Marrero. Company employees also turn out in large numbers for blood drives and fundraising events for cancer research and other worthy causes. They have participated in the Second Harvest Food Bank and House of Ruth for more than a decade, and they give back to the EPIC family with several annual events.

When disaster strikes, EPIC is there to help. At least twenty hurricanes have hit the region since Rivet founded the company and EPIC has weathered all of them. After Katrina, the company temporarily moved operations from Harvey to the Houston office. After ensuring its employees' safety, EPIC's priority was to help its customers get their oil and gas flowing again. EPIC's divers went to work in hundreds of feet of dark water, not knowing what they would encounter when they got to the bottom. Their work was not just critical for the region, but for the whole country. Back onshore, Rodriguez maintained her staff, even if they were unable to work, as she sorted through the rubble. The storm had made a mess of the Harvey office. Ultimately, the company decided to rebuild in the town where it had its roots.

Today, as a division of TETRA Technologies, EPIC Divers & Marine continues to grow and thrive, focusing on keeping its people safe and serving customers in the Gulf and around the world from its headquarters in Jefferson Parish. As Rodriguez says, "It's all about the people."

▲

Top, left: Captain Brian O'Neill onboard the EPIC Mariner 110-foot Dive Support/Utility Vessel.

Top, right: A crew from EPIC Divers & Marine is hoisted up to an oil platform.

Below: Leigh Ann, Ryan, Julie Ann, Julie, and Roger Rodriguez supporting their LSU team at the 2007 Sugar Bowl National Championship Game.

DynMcDermott Petroleum Operations Company

DynMcDermott Petroleum Operations Company is the sole Management and Operating Contractor for the Department of Energy (DOE) Strategic Petroleum Reserve (SPR). The contract is a performance-based contract, which means the company is paid based on achieving goals set by the DOE and per their contract. The DOE is DynMcDermott's only customer. The headquarters for DynMcDermott are located in the Elmwood Business District of Jefferson Parish.

The SPR stores 700 million barrels of crude oil in 62 underground salt caverns at sites along the U.S. Gulf Coast. Developed in the early 1900s, the SPR utilizes solution mining in order to develop storage within a salt dome. This method of storage is safe and environmentally friendly.

DynMcDermott is most proud of the accomplishment that no other Louisiana company has ever achieved. DynMcDermott is the only Louisiana company to ever be awarded the Malcolm Baldrige National Quality Award. The award was received in recognition for management performance excellence and continuous improvement for customers. Not only did they accomplish this impressive feat but they managed to receive the award against national competitors for that year so infamous in Louisiana history, 2005, the year of Hurricanes Katrina and Rita.

▲

Above: DynMcDermott Maintenance Technicians work on a pump on one of the site's pipelines.

Below: DynMcDermott personnel celebrated receiving the Malcolm Baldrige National Quality Award in April 2006 in Washington DC. The crystal award is in the center of the photo.

The Malcolm Baldridge examiners saw first-hand the effectiveness of the DynMcDermott Emergency Preparedness Plan. Due to hurricanes Katrina and Rita, President Bush ordered the release of oil from the SPR for only the second time in history. The site visit had been planned long in advance but due to the unusual circumstances the examiners offered to delay their examination until things calmed down. And although many of the DynMcDermott employees had been severely affected by the storms, they rose to the challenge before them. CEO Robert McGough did the same and invited the examiners to "come on down" anyway. The examiners took McGough up on his offer and apparently they were impressed with their findings!

"This honor will come as no surprise to those who are familiar with DynMcDermott and their work to support our nation's energy security," Secretary of Energy Samuel Bodman said. "Their heroic performance to move crude oil to the market in response to the devastation of Hurricanes Katrina and Rita—even while their own employees faced losses and displacement from their homes—was truly inspiring." Jefferson Parish is truly proud to be the home of a company of such amazing distinction. The Baldridge organization is not the only group impressed

with DynMcDermott. A few years earlier, another prestigious recognition was granted to the company by the International Organization of Standards (ISO) 9001 registration in 2001. ISO registration is granted only to organizations that adhere to strict and very high quality standards. The process for becoming ISO not only includes revising quality documentation and procedures to meet the exacting standards set forth by ISO but maintaining them. Several very thorough audits are performed, especially in the area of Quality Assurance, before ISO registration is granted.

Yet another recent award received by DynMcDermott is the 2006 Robert Campbell Award. "This international award for business excellence recognizes companies that successfully integrate health, safety and environmental management into their overall business operations. The award, cofounded by the National Safety Council and Exxon Mobil Corporation, is supported by a network of twenty global partner organizations."

All of these awards are made possible through the numerous methods used to build relationships that meet and exceed DynMcDermott customer expectations as well as increase loyalty and contract continuity. Apparently high ethics and hard work is a good basic strategy since DynMcDermott has

held the SPR contract longer than any other contractor in the Strategic Petroleum Reserve's thirty year history. The company has also incorporated Six Sigma practices into its most critical processes. Not only has DynMcDermott held the contract the longest but employee turnover averages an astonishingly low one percent per year, verifying that in addition to taking excellent care of its customer, DynMcDermott also takes excellent care of its employees.

For DynMcDermott, priority number one is operational readiness. In the event of oil supply interruption, and following an order from the President of the United States, the SPR is ALWAYS poised to distribute crude oil to refineries. When this happens, it is called a "Drawdown." Drawdown is DynMcDermott's primary mission. Another key process, "Fill," consists of ensuring that the SPR is filled to specified capacities at all times. DynMcDermott conducts oil storage, oil movement, and field-operating functions at the SPR sites in Louisiana and Texas, all to ensure that the SPR is ready for anything at anytime.

DynMcDermott uses a variety of exercises and drills to identify the many needs and challenges that may arise in their operating environment plus assess the ability to rapidly respond when those needs and conditions

▲

Representatives from the Japanese National Oil Company toured the Bayou Choctaw site near Baton Rouge. Groups from many countries have toured SPR sites to learn how the Department of Energy and DynMcDermott efficiently manage the reserve.

change. An EAGLE exercise is conducted every other year. This exercise examines operational readiness by testing various scenarios. The Drawdown Readiness Review is conducted quarterly. As the name implies, this exercise evaluates the organization's preparedness for a drawdown order from the President of the United States. Then, throughout the year, numerous security and fire drills are conducted to ascertain the readiness of these operations for other types of threats or incidents.

One way that DynMcDermott ensures a high-performing organization and empowers the employees is by having implemented the practice of authorizing employees at storage sites to stop any practice they deem unsafe. Additionally, employees are encouraged and rewarded for identifying improvement ideas. Reciprocal skill sharing and knowledge of best practices between storage sites and within job categories is encouraged through standardization of equipment, procedures, work instructions, and regularly scheduled meetings grouped by job title. A constant exchange of lessons learned both on the job and through continued professional development is another part of what make DynMcDermott the company that set the quality standard that so many other companies aspire to achieve.

DynMcDermott plans for potential adverse impacts on society and anticipates public and environmental concerns with current and future operations through its strategic planning process, environmental management system, and annual site environmental report. One of the most effective tools is a voluntary

West Hackberry, Louisiana, Maintenance Technicians prepare to remove piping from a wellhead so testing can be conducted.

Environmental Advisory Committee (EAC), which is composed of external scientists, technical experts, and community representatives who meet quarterly to discuss these issues then provide assessments and advice.

Environmental Safety and Health (ES&H) is also a high priority for DynMcDermott. Since 2004, DynMcDermott has amassed over forty awards in the area of ES&H. In 2007 alone the company received the National Safety Council's "Industry Leader Award" in the NSC Occupational Excellence Achievement Award Program—Bayou Choctaw and New Orleans; the EPA National Environmental Achievement Track Charter Membership Recertification—Big Hill, Bayou Choctaw, Bryan Mound, New Orleans, and West Hackberry; the National Safety Council's "Occupational Excellence Achievement Award" for Recognition of Outstanding Efforts in Occupational Safety Performance—New Orleans; the National Pollution Prevention Roundtable "Honorable Mention Award" for Greening the Janitorial Contracts; the Louisiana Environmental Management Award, Excellence Category—Bayou Choctaw, New Orleans, and West Hackberry; and the National Safety Council, South Louisiana Chapter, Award of Honor—Bayou Choctaw, New Orleans, and West Hackberry. And that is not even all of the ES&H awards they received that year!

One reason DynMcDermott has received so many awards for quality is that even subcontractors are held to the highest standards of both quality and ethics. The website for subcontractor inquiries states "DM (DynMcDermott) Procurement places significant emphasis on maximizing subcontracting opportunities with small, small disadvantaged, small woman owned, HUBZone, and service disabled veteran owned small business concerns in both the local and national marketplace." This clearly shows concern for helping small businesses realize their dreams. At the same time, those businesses will be held to the same standards of excellence as DynMcDermott itself. The same website also states "All DM Procurement personnel are required to comply with a stringent code of professional ethics and conduct, and all current and potential suppliers are expected to do the same." Obviously high quality and ethics are expected of everyone involved within the company in any way.

The unique storage method employed by DynMcDermott has played a big part in their ability to stay true to their philosophy of environmental awareness, which is described so well on their website for potential subcontractors: "Primary emphasis is placed on conducting all operations in an environmentally safe and responsible manner. This insures that the diverse populations of fish and wildlife living in the environmentally sensitive swamps, estuaries, harbors and other wetlands adjacent to the SPR sites are unaffected by the activities undertaken by DM in managing the SPR."

Philanthropic efforts of DynMcDermott have gone a long way towards improving the lives of the people in our community. A small sampling of the recipients of DynMcDermott's participation in giving back to the community includes such organizations as LSU Health Sciences Center Foundation, the printing of Hazardous Material brochures for Jefferson Parish, Keep Louisiana Beautiful, Inc., Voluntary Protection Programs Participants' Association, America's Wetlands, Junior Achievement, a variety of schools, and the Louisiana National Guard Youth Challenge Program.

DynMcDermott has proven to be innovative, trustworthy, and quality-minded. The company has shown its dedication to its customer, our nation, our environment, and its employees. Their contract was renewed in 2003 for a period through 2008 with options to renew until 2013. The option extending the contract to 2013 was granted in 2008 and DynMcDermott fully expects to participate in a rebid of the contract at that time. This distinguished company certainly showcases Jefferson Parish in a most positive and favorable light. DynMcDermott is an exemplary company that has proven to be the company most likely to succeed.

DynMcDermott President Robert McGough said that the company has faced many challenges since assuming the role of

Management and Operations Contractor for the SPR in 1993; one of the most difficult being Hurricanes Katrina and Rita.

"Shortly after the storms, we were fortunate enough to be recognized by receiving the Malcolm Baldrige National Quality Award," McGough said. "I was asked in press interviews how I would best characterize the performance of the company during and after these terrible catastrophes. I told them that extraordinary people do extraordinary things in extraordinary times. I can think of no other words than these to underline the accomplishments of the employees of DynMcDermott who even today as they work and live in Jefferson Parish continue to perform exceptional service to their parish, state and federal governments."

▲

Above: An operator monitors the opening of a forty-eight inch value controlling a crude oil movement.

Below: A site operator takes a sample of crude oil for testing to monitor characteristics like specific gravity or sulfur content.

NORTHROP GRUMMAN SHIPBUILDING'S AVONDALE SHIPYARD

Northrop Grumman's Avondale Shipyard in Avondale, Louisiana, has a rich and colorful seventy year history in Jefferson Parish and remains a legendary and prodigious presence in the world of shipbuilding today.

The company was founded as Avondale Marine Ways in 1938 at the site of an abandoned railroad ferry crossing no longer in use as a result of the construction of the Huey P. Long Railroad Bridge across the Mississippi River. This original location on the west bank of Jefferson Parish remains the present site of the 268-acre shipyard, about nine miles upriver from downtown New Orleans. Today, Avondale is the largest private manufacturing employer in Louisiana with about 5,500 employees and represents more than $500 million of economic impact to the state.

This humble barge repair operation has grown into what is today a part of the Northrop Grumman Corporation (NYSE:NOC), headquartered in Los Angeles, California. Avondale is aligned within the Northrop Grumman Shipbuilding (NGSB) sector, which consists of Avondale shipyard and the Tallulah facility in Louisiana, the former Ingalls shipyard in Pascagoula, and the Gulfport Composite Center, both in Mississippi, and Newport News Shipbuilding, in Virginia.

NGSB designs, builds, overhauls and repairs a wide variety of ships for the U.S. Navy, U.S. Coast Guard and world navies. Today, it is building more ships, in more ship classes, including nuclear-powered aircraft carriers and submarines, than any other U.S. naval shipbuilder. The NGSB sector has annual revenues of approximately $6 billion and it employs approximately 40,000 people, making Northrop Grumman the largest industrial employer in Louisiana, Mississippi and Virginia.

By the advent of World War II, Avondale Marine Ways received its first government contract for eight oceangoing tug boats. After the war, Avondale continued to build barges, fishing vessels and tugs, but also took advantage of the postwar offshore oil business and began building offshore oil rigs and vessels for the young Oil Patch, continuing this work at its Offshore Division in Bayou Black, Louisiana into the 1980s.

During the Korean War years, Avondale was busy building 63 LCUs, 196 LCMs, 29 oceangoing tugs, 22 barges, and 3 Patrol Craft Escorts, all for the U.S. Navy. In 1957, it built three cargo vessels for the U.S. Maritime Commission, and in 1959, began building four Destroyer Escorts for the Navy.

In 1959, Avondale was purchased by the Ogden Corporation, renamed Avondale Shipyards, Inc., and remained under the Ogden umbrella until 1985. The following year, it became an employee-owned (ESOP) company known as Avondale Industries, Inc.

During the 1960s, Avondale built two Navy Adams Class guided missile destroyers,

▲

Above: Avondale built thirty-one Destroyer Escorts for the U.S. Navy during the 1960s and early 1970s, delivering a DE about every six weeks, a phenomenal rate of production.

Below: Northrop Grumman Shipbuilding's Avondale shipyard occupies approximately 268 acres on the west bank of the Mississippi River about nine miles upriver from downtown New Orleans.

followed by twelve High Endurance Cutters for the Coast Guard, cutters still in use today. During this peak period it simultaneously constructed Navy Destroyer Escorts and LASH ships for the commercial industry. It delivered a DE every six weeks and a LASH ship every eight weeks, a phenomenal rate of production. Avondale delivered 31 DEs, and as the only U.S. builder of LASH ships, delivered 22 of these in a 13-year period.

During this same peak production period, Avondale also built several cargo ships for Lykes Bros. Steamship Company as well as other large commercial product carriers, tankers, self-propelled drill rigs and LNG ships for several other companies.

Beginning in the late 1970s, Avondale built five Navy AO 177 fleet oilers, which eventually led to a Navy contract for sixteen T-AO fleet oilers in the 1980s. At this time, Avondale also began construction on another big Navy contract—nine LSD amphibious assault ships.

In 1987, Avondale created the Composites Division in Gulfport, where it built Landing Craft Air Cushion vessels for the Navy, along with a series of Coastal Minehunters.

In 1990s, Avondale built three paddlewheel casino gaming boats at its Westwego Boat Division. Additional military work followed at the main shipyard with the construction of a Navy TAGS 45 research ship and a USCG Polar Icebreaker.

During that same decade, Avondale built a 192-MW floating hydroelectric power plant, as well as an 800-bed Floating Detention Center for the City of New York. It also landed a Navy contract to build seven Bob Hope Class Strategic Sealift ships, as well as a contract to build five double-hulled oil tankers for ConocoPhillips.

In 1996, Avondale was awarded a significant Navy contract for the revolutionary new San Antonio (LPD 17) Class of amphibious assault ships. The first four ships have been delivered to the Navy with five presently under construction across the Gulf Coast.

In 1997, Avondale formed a partnership with the State of Louisiana to establish the Tallulah Facility for the fabrication of ship modules. In 1998, Avondale entered into a similar partnership with the University of New Orleans to form the UNO-Avondale Maritime Technology Center in the shipyard for advancing marine engineering and ship design.

In 1999, Avondale became part of Litton Industries, Inc., which already owned Ingalls Shipbuilding. In 2001, Litton was acquired by Northrop Grumman, and Avondale and Ingalls were collectively known as Northrop Grumman Ship Systems. In 2008, Avondale, Ingalls and the other Gulf Coast operations were realigned with Newport News as Northrup Grumman Shipbuilding.

Today, as part of Northrop Grumman Shipbuilding, Avondale shares in a robust backlog of military work comprising several ship classes under construction across the Gulf Coast, including LPDs, DDG 51s, LHD 8, LHA 6, USCG Deepwater cutters, and the destroyer of the future, the DDG 1000.

Throughout its seven decades of continuous operation, Avondale has produced more than 300 ships and vessels and has amassed unmatched experience in designing, engineering, constructing and maintaining a diverse group of military and commercial vessels. Its future in Jefferson Parish continues to shine bright.

▲

Above: Avondale built and delivered to the U.S. Navy the second LPD 17-Class amphibious assault ship USS New Orleans (LPD 18), pictured here on sea trials in the Gulf of Mexico. Northrop Grumman Shipbuilding is building nine of these LPD-class ships across its Gulf Coast shipbuilding facilities.

Below: More than 5,000 people attended the christening ceremony for New York (LPD 21) in March 2008 at Avondale. Dedicated to the victims and heroes of the 9/11 terrorist attacks in New York City, LPD 21 has 7.5 tons of steel from the World Trade Center built into her bow.

ENTERGY LOUISIANA, LLC

Entergy and Jefferson Parish have a long history together dating back to the mid 1920s. As the main provider of electricity to parish residents, Entergy Louisiana, LLC—formerly Louisiana Power and Light Company—has had a significant impact on Jefferson, so much so that even the Westbank's Lapalco Boulevard was named after the company.

Entergy began in December 1913 as the idea of an Arkansas entrepreneur named Harvey Couch. Using sawdust from H.H. Foster's Arkansas Land and Lumber Company as fuel to generate electricity, Couch began electric service in his home state.

Couch, who also had invested in a phone company, radio station and railroad, decided his ultimate goal for this new power company was to have an integrated electric system with numerous sources of power at a reasonable price. Service reliability was foremost on his mind. He knew if he could provide a reliable product at a good price he would succeed.

Once Couch built Arkansas Light and Power Company, he set his sights on bringing the benefits of electricity to the rural South and began acquiring independent electric properties in Mississippi. His plan was to develop an interconnected system much like the one in Arkansas, but between states. On April 12, 1923, Mississippi Power and Light Company was incorporated.

The fuel and electricity for this new company, however, would come from Louisiana. The Louisiana Power Company was formed so Couch could take full advantage of the abundant supply of natural gas found in northern Louisiana. In November 1925, Couch's Sterlington generating station near Monroe was placed online. The largest power plant south of St. Louis, its 30,000 kilowatt capacity was owned by three companies: Arkansas Light and Power, Mississippi Power and Light, and Louisiana Power Company.

In 1927, Louisiana Power Company became Louisiana Power and Light Company and located its general offices in Algiers. By the end of that year, LP&L was providing electricity to some 15,000 customers in North and South Louisiana. It also provided manufactured gas, natural gas and water. The company also had 811 miles of electric lines, 41 miles of gas mains, 20 miles of water mains and its electric railway system included nine miles of track. LP&L built hundreds of miles of transmission and distribution lines and added several properties to its system in the late 1920s.

The Great Depression that began in 1929 brought hard times to all businesses and electric companies

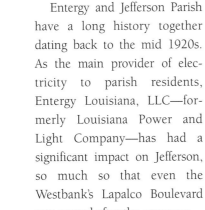

▲
Above: The Sterlington Plant near Monroe was placed online in November 1925.

Below: LP&L's early East Bank division was housed in a Metairie office building.

were no exception. Despite the hardships, however, Arkansas Light and Power, Mississippi Power and Light, Louisiana Power and Light and New Orleans Public Service—the company serving the New Orleans area—made it through intact. Some of the nation's largest utilities did not.

Things changed in 1935 when the Public Utility Holding Company Act was passed by Congress in a move to break up multilevel holding companies including the one directly competing with Couch's companies. In 1949, Middle South Utilities, Inc.—Entergy's former name—was formed as a holding company for AP&L, LP&L, MP&L and NOPSI. By special request of New Orleans officials, NOPSI was allowed to keep its gas and transit operations in the city.

During the 1950s, LP&L experienced steady growth as the area along the lower Mississippi River became more industrialized. To meet the growing demands for electric power, the company invested $11.3 million in property additions in 1950, the most expensive one-year construction program to that time. Included in the 1950 construction program was work on the Snake Farm substation to serve the growing requirements of the Metairie-Kenner area.

Continuing to exceed the national average in customer growth, LP&L connected its 200,000th electric customer in 1955 and, with the opening of the new Mississippi River Bridge from New Orleans to Algiers in mid-1958, further customer growth was on the horizon as

bridge travel was expected to have a major economic impact on the Westbank areas of Jefferson and Orleans Parishes.

Today, Entergy Louisiana, LLC serves more than 655,000 customers in north, middle and southeastern Louisiana. It employs nearly 800 people in Jefferson Parish alone with the two main offices in the parish located on Jefferson Highway and in Gretna. Together with its sister utility, Entergy Gulf States Louisiana, L.L.C.—formerly Gulf States Utilities—the companies serve a combined one million customers in fifty-eight parishes around the state. The two companies are part of Entergy Corporation's electric system serving 2.7 million customers in Louisiana, Arkansas, Mississippi and Texas.

Entergy Louisiana prides itself on providing quality service to its customers, whether in the aftermath of storms or on average days. Having weathered hurricanes Betsy and Camille in the 1960s, Andrew in 1992, Katrina and Rita in 2005 and numerous other storms, Entergy Louisiana has put the lessons learned from those storms into action.

Entergy Louisiana employees have proven their professionalism through their experience and incredible performance during the record-breaking storm season of 2005 and the company was recognized by the Edison Electric Institute as a result. Although recognition for restoration work is appreciated, Entergy Louisiana's priority is to provide safe, reliable service to power customers' lives.

▲

Above: An Entergy Louisiana lineman uses a bucket truck to safely assist with repairs.

Below: Entergy Louisiana linemen work to safely restore electric service.

ORLEANS SHORING

It is a familiar occurrence in the New Orleans area, your home has doors that stick, cracks in the wall, windows that will not open; it is probably due to shifting foundations. Left unrepaired, these problems can negatively impact the resale value of your property besides making life more complicated than necessary. Orleans Shoring can fix these problems, whether the problems are in your home or business.

Orleans Shoring founder Christian Cancienne has his roots in a family plumbing company that was established in 1994. When sewer lines broke and houses settled, the company would level the houses and adjust them so they would quit settling. More and more customers were pleased with the foundation work and after Hurricane Katrina requested that the company actually raise their houses so they would never flood again. So, in order to meet customer demand, Christian expanded his company, acquired equipment, sought out the best personnel from all across the nation, and joined the international association of structure movers. Joining the association introduced them to the best of the best in the industry. With just six employees, Orleans Shoring was born.

To do the job right Orleans Shoring invested in the Unified Jacking Systems to lift the whole house at once, "like an elevator" says Christian.

This method of raising houses eliminates the problems that were inherent in the old method, called "bottle-jacking", like the cracking and twisting of the house. We call it the Orleans Shoring "Gentle Lift Method", where all jacks are connected to one central control unit which is completely coordinated to lift a home slowly all at once, regardless of how the weight of the home is distributed. "It is a very costly system but well worth the investment," says Christian, "having the right tools and continued training insures a quality job and a satisfied customer." Orleans Shoring uses the "OS Level Pile" system which is engineer certified and the most widely accepted, proven pile system available today. To date Orleans Shoring has installed over 165 thousand piles without a settling problem or piling failure! Orleans Shorings quality of workmanship is held to such a high standard it is guaranteed with a transferable lifetime foundation warranty.

According to Christian, "Hurricane Katrina created tremendous growth. Any house that received fifty percent or more damage due to flooding had to be raised or no building permit would be issued. The demand for homeowners to avoid future flooding was there. One of Orleans Shoring's slogans is: "Never Flood Again." Christian recalled a memorable story of two brothers in their seventies. As we were

▲

Unified jacking machine.

raising their house after the storm, one brother began crying. When asked why he was crying the man explained that they had been stuck inside the house, in five feet of flood water for three days. One of the brothers had dropped the keys to the burglar bars in the water and had not been able to get out of the house. Knowing that this situation would never happen again now that the house was raised made the man cry with relief and joy. "That's what it's all about, changing lives, protecting our community, it's not just about the money" says Christian.

To ensure the job is done safely and properly, the firm has quality control specialists whose only function is to go from site to site and inspect the quality of work and safety standards. Quality control is a full time job at Orleans Shoring which holds itself to a higher standard than the parish codes.

While some companies might be content to think that improving lives through their jobs is enough, Orleans Shoring gives back to the community by sponsoring several kids' softball leagues, donating to police/firefighter, veterans, church activities, and the local Second Harvest Food Bank. "It's important to me to be involved in our community, the success of Orleans Shoring enables me to do that" says Christian.

Orleans Shoring was founded as a family business committed to doing five things:

- Ensure that the home Never Floods Again!

- Use state-of-the-art equipment with technicians properly trained to use it.
- Employ the best and brightest staff in all areas.
- Pay extreme close attention to every detail from start to finish.
- Treat every job as though it were a family member's job and help the customer through the process in the simplest manner possible.

Professional memberships of Orleans Shoring include the International Association of Structural Movers, the Better Business Bureau of Greater New Orleans, and the Home Builders Association of Greater New Orleans and it is licensed in the State of Louisiana for Foundations, House Moving and Wrecking, Structure Raising & Leveling. Orleans Shoring has always had a satisfactory record with the Better Business Bureau.

Orleans Shoring has grown from six employees to 140 employees in 2008. Along the way, they have repaired lives, assisted in the community, and stimulated the economy of Jefferson Parish. To top it off, they have been asked to be a Channel 6 community expert, quite an achievement for such a young organization. It will be exciting to see what the future brings for this innovative company.

Orleans Shoring is located at 25 Hickory Avenue in Harahan, Louisiana, and on the Internet at www.orleansshoring.com.

▲

Orleans Shoring's equipment yard.

F. H. MYERS CONSTRUCTION CORP.

F. H. Myers Construction Corp. is honored to be included in this historical book chronicling Jefferson Parish, where they work and live. You never get a second chance to make a first impression so F. H. Myers Construction works hard to ensure that each first impression is a positive and lasting one. The business philosophy of F. H. Myers is simple and straightforward: Always be professional, put quality first, and never sacrifice your business or personal integrity. It is a philosophy practiced by everyone in the organization and the basis of the company motto: "Quality and Integrity by Professionals."

In 1986, Founder Fred H. Myers was working for a local general contractor. After being promoted to president, opportunities seemed endless. The plan that created this opportunity was a reorganization of several companies into a single holding company to combat financial difficulties and a down turn in the construction market. They had a great organization, due to the efforts of the predecessor. However, within a year after the reorganization, it was evident that the economy and financial stresses at the time limited the potential for success. Myers considered a lot of possibilities. The one that made the most sense also carried the most risk. This marked the second time in Fred's career that despite the best efforts of the good hardworking employees, the company failed. Now it was decision time. He could start over with a new company and potentially face the same scenario at age 50 or 60 or take control of his own destiny. He was confident that his training and skills were sufficient to manage a business; therefore, it was time to control his and his family's future.

In June 1987, with the support of his wife and minor backing from an employee and a business associate, Myers formed F. H. Myers Construction Corp. They set out with five employees and a goal of reaching $5 million in annual revenue. The first public bid project won by the company was a GSA contract for renovating the interior of the Hebert Judicial Building in New Orleans. The company proved itself and completed a successful project. Word of the company quickly spread within three short years, and they reached their initial goal of $5 million in sales.

In 1996 the company moved into a renovated office facility that would allow for future expansion. The company maintained positive growth as word of their reputation for good, ethical work continued to spread. Myers was delighted when his two children graduated from college with degrees in civil

President and Founder of F. H. Myers Construction Corp., Fred H. Myers.

engineering and after working for other employers joined the company.

In 2005 company revenues passed $20 million, along with managing Hurricane Katrina. This would test the company's foundation and management skills and provide opportunity if they were properly prepared. On August 29, 2005, all employees searched for shelter for their families. Within a week, Myers organized a meeting of his management team in Baton Rouge. First order of business was to allow each person to reveal their personal experiences, find out about the safety of the area they were in, and the well being of their families. The time remaining was spent developing a "Smart Plan," a plan of action to get everyone refocused on positive accomplishments and moving forward. They created four simple goals: Access to the damaged area, regain contact with all employees/seek shelter for those in need, restore the computer system so that they could communicate with their business partners, and manage cash flow for their company and vendors who would be in immediate need. The established timeframe was one week. By September 15, they met their goals, reopened the office, and secured housing for employees in need. Within the first three months, ninety-six percent of the original workforce returned, and they were back in business. F. H. Myers Construction had passed the ultimate test and confirmed that the company was everything that Myers had worked to create.

As they move into their third decade, the company continues to depend on the people who are the foundation of its success.

In keeping with their core of integrity, F. H. Myers Construction believes in getting involved in the community where they work, live, and play. They are Corporate Contributors to the United Way and Key Supporters of St. Michael's Special School. The company participates in The Construction Specification Institute, is a charter member of the Associated Builders and Contractors-Bayou Chapter, and proudly participates in the Jefferson Parish Chamber of Commerce.

The company has forty-two full time employees and five different departments. Annual revenues are now $40 million. The business plan for the future is first and foremost to remain true to the company motto: "Quality and Integrity by Professionals." This motto and the way the employees embrace and practice it is why F. H. Myers remains "litigation-free" with all past clients. The management of this extraordinary company realizes that while the motto may be the cornerstone, the employees are the foundation of their success.

Additional information regarding current and past projects, company contacts, and much more is available at www.fhmyers.com.

▲

(From left to right) Ryan P. Myers, Rachelle M. Albright, and Fred H. Myers.

J. P. & Sons

J. P. & Sons is the parent company with J. P. & Sons Dredging, LLC; Waggaman Crane Service; Inc.; and J. P. & Sons Anchorage, LLC forming the rest of the family. The companies provide general contracting, land and water demolition, site work, clearing and grubbing, excavation, fill materials, equipment rental, barge fleeting, ship mooring, sand dredging, heavy hauling, and crane work. J. P. & Sons is a member of the Better Business Bureau (BBB) of Jefferson Parish with a satisfactory rating. According to the BBB, "Based on BBB files, this company has a satisfactory record with the BBB. The BBB has processed no customer complaints on this company in its three-year reporting period." Obviously J. P & Sons is a quality company. It is hard to believe that it all started with one dump truck and the vision of one man with "steely blue eyes and a quiet demeanor."

Joseph Phillips served his country during the Korean Conflict. Before he left, he married his sweetheart, Pauline. Upon returning home, Phillips went to work at Avondale Shipyard. After a while as a crane operator at the shipyard, Joseph realized that he had a dream. He wanted to be in business for himself. To make his dream come true he bought a dump truck and began hauling. Soon, Joseph's older brother, Victor, realized that baby brother Joe was doing pretty well. So Victor bought a dump truck, stopped working at Avondale, and went into business with Joe. After several years in business together, Joe decided to branch off by himself again. He wanted to build a business that his four sons could be part of if they wanted to. It was not

long before all four children were working with him. All four boys grew up in the business, learning it inside and out.

Safety is taken very seriously at J. P. & Sons. In fact, safety is taken so seriously that there is a safety meeting every morning to discuss lessons learned from the day before and issues that may arise during the planned activities for the upcoming day.

Throughout the years, two sons lost their lives. One son was lost due to an accident. The other drowned in relief efforts after Hurricane Isidore. A third brother David decided to leave the business and strike out on his own with his son, Colby, leaving brother, Marion to carry on the family business. Joe, Sr., retired due to illness. Marion married Sabrina who had seventeen

Above: Operating a 450 John Deere Dozer in the sand pit on July 14, 1970, is fifteen-year-old Joe Phillips, Jr. and thirteen-year-old Marion Phillips.

Below: Key employees of J.P. & Sons—without these individuals our company would not run so smoothly. Front row (from left to right): Carol Plaisance, Lisa Hamilton, and Lisa Calongne. Back row (from left to right): Norman Wolkart, Gerald Ford, Danny Cousin, Mark Williams, Danny Anderson, and David Bertucci.

years experience in the oil industry. Their son, Nicholas who is fourteen years old, is now working at J. P. & Sons as a third generation family member during the summers. This was Joseph Phillips' dream come to life.

J. P. & Sons, Inc. was founded on November 14, 1979. In the early days, Joseph and his wife, Pauline, were the key employees. In fact, a very pregnant Pauline could be seen running tickets out to the trucks at 4 o'clock in the morning. Over the years the little, one-man, then two-man business has grown quite a bit. Including the Phillips family members, there is a total of forty-five full time employees and five temporary employees. That number includes Joe's son, Marion; Sabrina, Marion's wife; Nicholas, Marion and Sabrina's son; and Pauline, Joe's wife. Pauline still comes into the office every day, goes to industry conventions in Las Vegas, and keeps up a pace to rival the younger generation. Sadly, Joe passed away in 2007.

The company has made quite an impact on the local community. They support the local playground by providing not just uniforms, but also the dirt, sand, and even the equipment necessary to maintain the fields. Most people realize that is quite an undertaking in an area below sea level. In addition to their philanthropic work with the playground, J. P. & Sons also provides assistance to the local church and the fire stations by contributing both equipment and money. Furthermore, the company helps out local children in the area when they find themselves in need of sponsors for sporting or academic events.

The company also takes on trainees. According to Sabrina, the trainees are "a little bit of a headache but worth it." Some of the trainees started in early summer and ended up being some of the most valued employees.

Future plans for J. P. & Sons include beginning more business ventures involving recycling products and earth products. One of the reasons behind this new venture is that there is a need for this particular service. The company takes scraped out barges and such and finds ways to recycle them. Not only does it help one company get rid of the product but it keeps the product out of the landfill. It is easy to see why J. P & Sons has succeeded. They keep an eye to the future and look for ways to serve the community in which they live.

J. P. & Sons can be reached at 504-431-9631 or e-mail mphillips@jpandsons.com or sphillips@jpandsons.com.

▲

Above: Fourteen year old Nicholas Phillips is the third generation to work at the sand pits stockpiling dirt and loading dump trucks.

Below: Joseph and Pauline Phillips, March 2007.

AQUA-AIR INDUSTRIES, INC.

Aqua-Air Industries, Inc., is an innovative leader in the supply and manufacture of commercial diving equipment. The company is currently celebrating its thirty-seventh anniversary in business and are a major distributor and dealer representing hundreds of products worldwide.

The company's founder, Rodney A. Cruze (1942-2005), worked as a commercial diver for nine years, which exposed him to the many deficiencies in diving equipment and lack of safety practices that were in use at the time. His uncanny mechanical ability, innovation, determination, and God-given talent drove him to open his own commercial diving supply business that he named Aqua-Air Industries, Inc., in 1972. His dream was to provide quality, innovative equipment for the commercial diving industry. After the supply business was established with the help of his wife, Dianne, Rod started Sta-Sea Offshore Rentals in 1976, named for their son Stacy Ayres Cruze, to further serve his customers needs. Air compressors, deck decompression chambers, hydraulic power units, underwater video systems, and underwater burning and welding equipment, are a few of the items available for rent.

Today, Stacy is executive vice president, along with his mother; Dianne, current AAI president and CFO are at the helm of AAI keeping Rodney's vision alive and well. Together, the Cruze Team and staff pledge to follow the great footprint that Rodney left behind because they know that is exactly what "Rod" would have wanted and expected.

Aqua-Air Industries designs and builds over seventy-five products under its AAI product line and also supplies all major brands of diving equipment that covers depth ranges from zero to 1,000 feet. Some of the products available for shallow water diving are deck decompression chambers, diving helmets, divers' umbilicals, hydraulic tools, and diving command centers. Other more industry-specific products include air/helium control consoles, communication units, oxygen analyzers, carbon dioxide analyzers, and underwater video technology.

Aqua-Air Industries' newest division manufactures Saturation Diving Systems. These systems allow divers to go as deep as one thousand feet and stay at those depths for extended periods without having to resurface or decompress nearly as frequently as shallow diving. Systems are designed for 6, 10, 12, or 16 divers. Each system's deck complex is comprised of a series of deck decompression chambers, a diving bell with launch/recovery System (LARS) and a hyperbaric rescue chamber (HRC) linked together by manway tunnels. This set of chambers provides living accommodations and restroom facilities for the divers. Modular containers serve as control centers to monitor the diver's environment. The self-floating HRC can be

Above: Founder Rodney A. Cruze, 1942-2005.

Below: A 1,000-foot, 12-man saturation diving system.

launched with diving personnel under pressure in case of a major vessel emergency. The bell functions like an elevator for transporting the diver(s) between the water work site and living quarters on the vessel deck. Aqua-Air was the first company in over twelve years, in the United States, to build a new saturation diving system. Sadly, Rodney passed away before this first system came to fruition and was delivered in July 2005.

The company's two acre facility in Harvey, Louisiana, includes its diver's locker showroom, warehouse, the Shallow Water Diving Division, the Saturation Diving Division, the Electronics Division, and fabrication facility. Aqua-Air competes in a worldwide marketplace. Its customer base has benefited from decades of experience, as well as from in-house and field research and development which yields end products of the highest quality.

What continues to be the driving force of this specialized company are the devoted employees and management that promise to continue to dedicate themselves to supplying top quality diving equipment to better serve its customers worldwide. The future of this amazing company is in good hands. There is a mentoring/training program in place so the art of creating these greatly needed components and systems is not lost. There are constant updates to the knowledge and skills of the employees as technology changes which helps to keep the equipment on the cutting edge. Rodney created something needed, appreciated, lasting, and wonderful that benefits not only his family and his local community, but the entire global diving community. What better legacy can a man leave?

Please visit www.aquaairind.com for additional information on Aqua-Air Industries products and services.

▲

Below: President Dianne Cruze and Executive Vice President Stacy Cruze.

CYTEC INDUSTRIES INC.

Founded in 1952 and dedicated in 1954, the Cytec Industries Fortier Complex is a flourishing plant operating on over eight hundred acres along the west bank of the Mississippi River in Waggaman. Cytec has become a major industry player and important community participant, reflecting both the company's significance to the local economy as well as its commitment to its neighbors and the environment.

Cytec Industries Inc. is a global specialty chemicals and materials company focused on developing, manufacturing and selling value-added products that serve a diverse range of end markets including aerospace, adhesives, automotive and industrial coatings, chemical intermediates, inks, mining and plastics.

Attracted by the direct access to transportation on the Mississippi River, natural gas pipelines, and several major refineries operating above and below the complex, Cytec (then American Cyanamid) purchased the square mile of land it occupies today in 1952. The land's history goes back much further though, having been granted to Eugene Fortier in 1776 by the King of Spain. Today the site bears the name of the family which owned the land into the 1930s.

Cytec has since had a significant impact on the local economy—the Fortier site currently employs more than 440 employees with an annual payroll of nearly $50 million. Each year the site pays up to $5.5 million in state and local taxes and fees.

Fortier produces many chemicals that go into goods to make life safer, help improve and protect the environment, and improve the longevity of many articles we use. The various chemicals produced at the Fortier site are used in consumer products such as CD players, cell phones, computers, tires, plastics, tissue paper, furniture, dinnerware, spray paint, laminate flooring, marine coatings, golf balls, car headlights, medical devices, dentures, eyeglasses, and car batteries. That is quite a diverse list and it is not even comprehensive.

"We make safety our first priority—the core of all we do." Safety and environmental impact are Cytec's top concerns, and Fortier has an ambitious program for promoting safety awareness and training for all employees. In addition, the site utilizes deep well disposal for hazardous materials, an on-site sulfuric acid regeneration facility, and thermal oxidation units. Fortier achieved ISO14001 certification in 2007.

Cytec has a system in place for notifying residents in the nearby community in the event of an incident, and does not stop there with community contact. There is the Cytec Community Advisory Panel, also known as CYCAP, a group of Cytec representatives and fifteen to twenty community members. The group meets every other month to discuss plant operations and "address concerns relating to the plant's impact on the local environment."

The Fortier Complex has been recognized with multiple awards since 2006 for the start-up of the Jefferson Parish Landfill Gas Project, a partnership between the parish, Cytec, and Renovar Corporation. Fortier has also been recognized by numerous rail carriers including CSX, Union Pacific, Canadian National and Burlington National Sante Fe for its excel-

Below: Plant operators at the acrylonitrile control room.

lence in loading and preparing railcars for safe transport. Other past awards have included the Louisiana Chemical Association's SAFE Certificate of Achievement, the Governor's Environmental Leadership Award, and the Environmental Protection Agency Region 6 Environmental Excellence Award.

Philanthropy is another area that Cytec has not overlooked. One big success has been the annual Fun Science for Families Day. In partnership with the Jefferson Parish Public School System and Oakwood and Clearview Shopping Centers, Cytec continues to bring local scientists and teachers together with children and parents to explore science with a hands-on approach.

Another important effort that Cytec participates in locally is the national HOSTS program. HOSTS stands for Help One Student To Succeed. This program pairs local business people with local elementary and middle school students for mentoring. Cytec partners with R. K. Smith Middle School in Luling and Norbert Rillieux Elementary in Waggaman.

Cytec envisions clients that will benefit from the "state-of-the-art, highly integrated chemical site infrastructure" along with the shared services that create a steadfast foundation upon which long-term cost-effective operations have been built. The advantages of building on site at Cytec are numerous. There are state tax and job training incentives plus Cytec's own history of cooperating with partners. Cytec's experience in construction and company startups and joint utilization of services and existing

infrastructure, use and/or finishing of Cytec products, and availability of raw materials are other benefits of being onsite. Partnership opportunities are available for producers of specialty chemicals, suppliers of raw materials and utilities, consumers of utilities and by-products, producers needing special infrastructure for waste treatment or recycling, and service providers for the location.

For more than half a century, the Cytec Fortier facility has provided a decidedly positive influence on Jefferson Parish, not just economically, but socially and emotionally as well. Cytec provides jobs, interaction among neighbors and contributes to the quality of life in the communities in which it does business, and the company has every intention of continuing those efforts. Doing business with Cytec not only helps your business, but your entire community.

Additional information is available to you at www.cytec.com/building-block.

▲

Above: The Fortier site celebrated its fiftieth anniversary in 2004.

Below: An aerial view of Cytec Industries' Fortier site in 1996.

RUELCO, INC.

Ruelco was founded in July of 1980 by Ruel Gober, doing business out of his garage. Today, Ruelco's new 60,000 square foot, air conditioned facility is located in Elmwood Industrial Park.

Ruelco manufactures instrumentation controls. The versatility of their products is the greatest strength that they possess. One look at the Ruelco mission statement and it is easy to see how they became so successful—"Ruelco is committed to innovation, quality, and total satisfaction for each individual customer. This commitment is what drives us to succeed in today's business world and will direct us well into the future." Honoring this commitment has earned Ruelco a reputation throughout the world as one of the leading instrumentation manufacturers in the industry. As new applications develop in the controls industry, they will be there to provide the design and manufacturing services to meet the demand of their customers.

Ruelco products are designed, manufactured, and rigorously tested without leaving the premises thus ensuring customer satisfaction. Ruelco engineers are available to help customers choose the best solutions for their specific circumstances. And with Ruelco's design services, custom-made solutions are no problem. In fact, Ruelco has even been awarded a total of six patents for their unique product designs.

One of the methods that Ruelco uses to maintain their high level of customer satisfaction is computer numerical control (CNC) machines. CNC machines also allow the company to utilize manpower and machinery in the most efficient methods possible by implementing 'lights-out' machining. This process allows production operations to continue well after the employees have left for the day. As a result, Ruelco is able to satisfy customer demands, without the added expense of shift workers. It is an excellent, innovative, progressive solution to many situations.

The Quality Assurance and Quality Control programs at Ruelco are remarkable. The guidelines are as tough as those set by the International Organization for Standardization (ISO). That toughness plus the experience and knowledge of Ruelco's QA/QC team members is now being put to use for Ruelco's customers. Several globally well-known clients of Ruelco have compared the two quality systems and commented on Ruelco's ability to continuously meet the exacting policies and regulations that they set for themselves. From design to production to testing, including all of the associated documentation, quality is paramount at Ruelco.

Ruelco's range of products is vast. There are pressure switches, level switches, relays (manual, automatic, and remote), tattletale indicators, quick exhausts, sand probes, hydraulic controllers, ESDs, overrides, lockout caps, fuse plugs, vent screens, panel accessories, and filler tubes. And if that incredible array of products is not enough, there is a full catalog on their website at www.ruelco.com. It is also their intention to "design and bring to the market two to three new products each year" according to Gober.

A few of the industries currently being served by Ruelco are oil and gas, petrochemical, utility companies (public and private), beverage bottling companies, military, and marine/shipping companies. Their combination of an experienced team of expert machinists and engineers combined with superior quality assurance standards results in products and services of outstanding quality for Ruelco customers.

Employee satisfaction is another key to the success of Ruelco. One employee recently said "you are totally correct when you state that Ruelco is an incredible company. It is also an incredible company to work for." That kind of loyalty does not come from just being paid well. In fact, that is not just loyalty its respect. It is the respect of your employees earned by taking care of them over the course of many years.

Ruelco has long practiced working closely with universities, high schools, and trade schools. The company provides apprentice and mentor-type programs as a way to interest young people in career paths they may not have previously considered. Not only does this open up potential career paths for the students, but it also ensures that there are quality machinists for future years.

Since the company began, Ruelco has taken care of more than just its customers and employees. Over the years Ruelco has supported numerous groups in our community including charities, churches, schools and the protection of animals. The company also supports all of the area's major sports teams. Ruelco obviously takes pride not just in their products but in the place they live and work as well.

Even though Ruelco is known worldwide for its quality products, it is still a family business. Gober's wife, Virginia is the secretary/treasurer of the company and daughter Nicole is the vice-president. Perhaps that is part of the secret to the success of Ruelco. Pay attention to and take care of your customers, extremely high-quality products, and keep family close by. It has certainly been a winning combination for Ruelco and its customers.

ATMOS ENERGY CORPORATION

Atmos Energy Corporation's history dates back to 1906 in the Panhandle of Texas. Over the years, through various business combinations and mergers, the company became known as Pioneer Corporation, a large diversified West Texas energy company. In 1983, Energas, the natural gas distribution division of Pioneer, was spun off and became an independent, publicly held natural gas distribution company. In October 1988, Energas changed its corporate name to Atmos Energy Corporation and its stock began trading on the New York Stock Exchange under the ticker symbol ATO. Today, Atmos Energy Corporation is the largest all-natural-gas distributor in the United States.

Atmos Energy is committed to improving the quality of life in the communities it serves through a far-reaching program of "giving" and "doing." Employees across the enterprise give their time and energy while the corporation provides the financial resources to support their activities.

"Atmos Energy understands that the joy is not in just making money, but in achieving goals, being good at what we do and giving back to the community. Ours is a labor of love, both at work and in the community," said Atmos Energy Vice President of Operations Ricky Burke.

Our employees live, work and raise families in these communities. By being close to our customers, we know them both personally and professionally. Our employees give their time and leadership to many excellent programs, such as United Way, chambers of commerce, regional economic development groups, school boards, Habitat for Humanity, Scouting and hundreds of other worthy causes.

Atmos Energy provides financial assistance to selected organizations within these areas of focus. Atmos Energy also encourages employees to become personally involved with community organizations and often makes community service opportunities available to employees during regular working hours.

Beneficiaries of the community development and civic programs at Atmos include chambers of commerce, economic development boards, Lions Clubs and Rotary Clubs and other organizations supporting civic and economic growth in the community.

Atmos strives to ensure the health and well-being of the community by supporting the improvement of the well-being of those in need through United Way, American Red Cross, American Cancer Association, American Heart Association and other associations.

The company is working to improve the education system through programs like Adopt-A-School and various other mentoring programs.

Arts and culture are important to a community and Atmos is committed to those organizations whose goal is to improve the quality of life in the community like the symphony, theater and museums.

For more information about Atmos Energy, please visit www.atmosenergy.com.

▲
Amarillo gas wagon.

Rault Resources Group, a family entity headed by Joseph M. Rault of Metairie has had business activities in oil and gas and real estate going back fifty years. At this time, its Jefferson Parish activities are concentrated in the Metairie-Veterans-Kenner corridor with the- ownership and operation of commercial office buildings including the 110 Veterans Building (formerly Stewart Building) a five story 120,000-square-foot office complex at Veterans and the Seventeenth Street Canal; further out Veterans is the 2400 Veterans Building, formerly Xerox, also a five-story 130,000-square-foot office complex. To fill out its half-million feet of space is the Park Tower Building, the largest office building in Lafayette.

Early on, the commercial real estate development was completed in downtown New Orleans with the original sixteen story Rault Centre Building. In 1972 the top floors of the building caught fire and was front page news covering a dramatic aftermath.

Early in the company's history, domestic and international petroleum activities included fabrication of rigs and boat construction for offshore operation; drilling operations for Petroleos Mexicanos in the Republic of Mexico and production and crude oil marketing in Venezuela; and the development and marketing of natural gas from New Mexico and Canada to the California markets. The company also owned and operated gas processing plants and pipelines in many New Mexico gas fields. It also cofounded the Offshore Transportation Company (OTC) in South Louisiana, which merged with and became Tidewater Marine.

Joseph M. Rault graduated from Jesuit High in New Orleans in 1943. Upon graduation, he entered naval officers training then served as an officer in the U.S. Naval Reserve including participation in the atomic bomb test at Bikini Atoll at the Eniwetok Islands in the South Pacific following World War II.

He is a graduate of the Massachusetts Institute of Technology with a degree in marine transportation from the School of Naval Architecture and Marine Engineering. He is also a graduate of Tulane University School of Law and initially practiced maritime and oil and gas law in New Orleans.

Rault and his wife, Bonnie, are natives of the city and have lived in Jefferson Parish for the past forty years. Their family includes eight children and twenty grandchildren. He is a member of a number of social, civic and community organizations, including the Jefferson Chamber, Metairie Country Club, Sugar Bowl Committee, Mystick Krewe of Louisianians in Washington and other carnival organizations. Since Katrina, he is actively working with the Parishes of Jefferson and Orleans to seek flood protection to correct the problems of the Seventeenth Street Canal flooding and helped established "PUMP TO THE RIVER," which has received initial Congressional approval and is pending funding. Rault is a member of the Jefferson Business Council and a member of the Jefferson Parish Hoey's Basin Pump to the River Joint Task Force.

WALTON
CONSTRUCTION

▲

Above: Ninth Ward Katrina Memorial in New Orleans, Louisiana.

Below: Harrah's New Orleans.

Walton Construction opened its New Orleans division in Harahan in 2003 offering all of the advantages of a national company right here in Jefferson Parish. Bill Petty started the division with only five people in a small office space in the Elmwood.

Walton has the capability to perform many of the project tasks that would normally require several different companies, including managing multiple subcontractors. The company's technology and resources, coupled with local knowledge and resources give Walton the cutting edge when it comes to construction in Jefferson Parish and the surrounding areas.

From estimating to value engineering, scheduling, budget management, site evaluation and development, design management, and code reviews all of the way through accounting, project documentation and reporting, to subcontractor closeout and project closeout, Walton has the experience and know-how, both nationally and locally, to get the job done well, safely, easily, and to the customer's satisfaction. They even provide electronic project site and web cams that allow clients and design professionals to have up-to-the minute images during meetings.

Safety is paramount for Walton Construction. Due to their superior Safety Management program, Walton New Orleans was presented with the Fourth Quarter Outstanding Contractor Award for maintaining the safest and cleanest site at the Keesler Air Force Base project. Randy Pierce, Walton-New Orleans project safety manager at the Sixty-first Jackson Barracks project, was awarded the distinguished Louisiana National Guard Safety Award for processes he proactively started.

Following Hurricane Katrina, the company has been a strong presence and put forth tremendous effort towards the recovery, helping families and local businesses all rebuild not just buildings, but lives. Through their selection of jobs such as Wilson Elementary in the Recovery School District to their philanthropic focus, the company has a strong dedication to the rebuilding of New Orleans. Walton takes great pride in building the Ninth Ward Memorial for residents of the area and also is heavily involved in the memorial for the late Sheriff Harry Lee, a good friend of Walton Construction.

Now, after recently celebrating its fifth year anniversary, Walton Construction employs over 200 people and has completed projects up to $150 million. Its projects are in just about every conceivable industry spanning from Texas to Florida. The company has received numerous awards, including the City Business Best Places to Work in 2007. Some of their more notable clients include Jefferson Parish, West Jefferson Hospital, Department of the Navy and numerous other facilities around the country.

Walton Construction is located at 2 Commerce Court in Harahan, Louisiana and on the Internet at www.waltonbuilt.com.

SPONSORS

ABOUT THE AUTHOR

PAUL F. STAHLS JR.

Paul F. Stahls Jr. is a former publicity director of the Louisiana Office of Tourism and a founding editor and current contributing editor of Louisiana Life magazine. He is the author of *Plantation Homes of the Lafourche Country*, *Plantation Homes of the Teche Country*, *A Century of World's Fairs in Old New Orleans* and a World's Fair children's book *A Wish Upon the Wonderwall*.

He and his wife Peggy Coleman Stahls are parents of Paul F. Stahls III, M.D., and Matthew C. Stahls, Esq.